OTHER TITLES OF INTEREST FROM ST. LUCIE PRESS

The 90-Day ISO 9000 Manual and Implementation Guide

The Executive Guide to Implementing Quality Systems

Focused Quality: Managing for Results

Improving Service Quality: Achieving High Performance in the Public and Private Sectors

Introduction to Modern Statistical Quality Control and Management

ISO 9000: Implementation Guide for Small to Mid-Sized Businesses

Organization Teams: Continuous Quality Improvement

Organization Teams: Facilitator's Guide

Principles of Total Quality

Quality Improvement Handbook: Team Guide to Tools and Techniques

The Textbook of Total Quality in Healthcare

Total Quality in Higher Education

Total Quality in Managing Human Resources

Total Quality in Marketing

Total Quality in Purchasing and Supplier Management

Total Quality in Radiology: A Guide to Implementation

Total Quality in Research and Development

Total Quality Management for Custodial Operations

Total Quality Management: Text, Cases, and Readings, 2nd Edition

Total Quality Service

For more information about these titles call, fax or write:

St. Lucie Press
100 E. Linton Blvd., Suite 403B
Delray Beach, FL 33483
TEL (407) 274-9906 • FAX (407) 274-9927

S^{t}L

SUSTAINING
High Performance

The Strategic Transformation to
A Customer-Focused Learning Organization

BY
Stephen G. Haines
President and Founder
Centre for Strategic Management
San Diego, California

WITH
Katie McCoy

S^t_L

St. Lucie Press
Delray Beach, Florida

Printed and bound in the U.S.A. Printed on acid-free paper.
10 9 8 7 6 5 4 3 2 1

Library of Congress Cataloging-in-Publication Data

Haines, Stephen.
   Sustaining high performance: the strategic transformation to a
customer-focused learning organization / by Stephen Haines with
Katie McCoy.
      p.   cm.
   Includes bibliographical references and index.
   ISBN 1-884015-55-7
   1. Strategic planning. I. McCoy, Katie. II. Title.
HD30.28.H3337   1995
658.4'012—dc20   94-46633
                                                               CIP

Phone: (407) 274-9906
Fax: (407) 274-9927

S_L^t

Published by
St. Lucie Press
100 E. Linton Blvd., Suite 403B
Delray Beach, FL 33483

CONTENTS

PART III. Mastering Strategic Change: "Where the Rubber Meets the Road"

PART IV. Getting Started: Different Options and Customized Applications

PREFACE

Sustaining High Performance: The Strategic Transformation to a Customer-Focused Learning Organization presents a revolutionary approach to reinventing strategic planning and change for the 21st century.

In 1994, I attended the Annual Conference of the International Planning Forum in New York City. The Planning Forum is the premiere association in Western society focused on improving the practice of strategic management (strategic planning and strategic change management). While this book claims to have "reinvented" strategic planning, I wondered if that claim was just so much hype. However, after attending that conference, I am more convinced than ever that we have actually created a new paradigm for managing strategically (planning cannot be separated from management because it is the first function of management).

This "state-of-the-art" conference featured numerous prestigious speakers, each armed with 35-mm color slides, big screens, darkened rooms, and the latest jargon in strategic management. Typically, when the lights were raised at the end of an hour of one-way passive communication and questions finally were invited, it was too late. People rarely had much to ask or comment on. Instead, many left the sessions early in the midst of this late attempt by the speakers to be "participative" and meet their customers' needs.

The message at these sessions seemed to be that finding the one "holy grail" to planning was the key—without regard for (1) customers, (2) participative dialogue, or (3) debate. Yet in our extensive research and successful practice of strategic management, these three points that were missed are precisely the keys to success in strategic planning and implementation.

Our main premise is that there is no "holy grail" to be found in strategic management; only a true "systems thinking" approach and framework can be used to achieve the two goals of strategic management:

Goal #1.   Develop a strategic plan and document

Goal #2.   Ensure and sustain its successful implementation

Instead, we found this planning conference similar in many ways to what we found in 1990 in our extensive literature search of fourteen different and popular strategic planning models; namely, that every one of the popular planning models in use was an analytic solution to a systems problem. Organizations are systems, no matter how well or how poorly they function. Peter Senge was right in *The Fifth Discipline*. His fifth discipline is systems thinking—and as a Western business society we have yet to understand, embrace, and develop skills in systems thinking. This is not surprising, since most of us were brought up and educated in scientific (read analytic) disciplines such as engineering (myself), law, accounting, computers, medicine, etc.

Out of the fourteen models we researched to develop our Ten-Step Reinvented Strategic Planning Model, none included three of our key steps: Parallel Process, Plan-to-Implement, and Strategic Change Management details. In addition, only four models had an initial "educating and organizing" step, which we call Plan-to-Plan, and only two out of fourteen had a measurement step (our Step #3: Key Success Factors). Worse yet, only four of fourteen tied strategic planning to business unit planning, and only seven of fourteen further tied it to annual planning and budgets.

Is it any wonder that Henry Minzberg, one of the most respected professors in the field of strategic management, just published a book entitled *The Rise and Fall of Strategic Planning*. We couldn't agree more with his views.

My experiences and observations at this 1994 international strategic planning conference clearly showed the reasons why analytic planners are an endangered species, yet the amount of strategic planning is increasing.

So read on and learn about our "systems thinking" approach to strategic management (planning and change), its ten unique concepts, and how they compare to today's dominant, yet obsolete, paradigm of planning. Further, this is a book about carefully researched "best practices" in:

1. A successful process for strategic planning and sustaining strategic change

2. The selection of successful strategies that give a company a competitive advantage over the long term

Yes, there are some right answers, just not singular analytic ones, in today's global, ever-changing world, where systems thinking should become the norm.

Stephen G. Haines
San Diego, California

THE AUTHOR

Stephen G. Haines is president and founder of the Centre for Strategic Management. He is an internationally recognized leader in strategic change with 25 years of diverse international executive experience in the private and public sectors.

Mr. Haines was formerly president and part owner of University Associates Consulting and Training Services. Prior to that, he was executive vice president of Imperial Corporation of America, a $13 billion nationwide financial services firm. He has been on eight top management teams with organization leadership for planning, human resources, training, organization development, marketing, communications, public relations, and facilities.

A U.S. Naval Academy engineering graduate with a foreign affairs minor, Mr. Haines has an Ed.D. (ABD) in management and educational psychology and a Master's in organization development with a minor in finance.

Mr. Haines has written two books and taught over sixty different seminars. He has served on a number of boards, currently serving as chairman of the board of Central Credit Union, and is in demand as a keynote speaker on CEO and board of directors issues.

ACKNOWLEDGMENTS

Any time a book is written, there are many people involved in its production. In this case, there are some unusual people to acknowledge who have had no involvement in the actual writing of this book but who have been instrumental in its formulation.

D. Patrick Miller, a writer of some note in his own field, taught me how to write a book, namely, that you don't "write one" but "let it emerge" from the relationship an author has with his writer/editor. Patrick sure was right in this instance.

Ken Thygerson, a former CEO and my boss at two companies, gave me my first (and second) opportunity to be accountable for the strategic planning function in two major financial services corporations, Freddie Mac and the Imperial Corporation of America.

My strategic planning clients over these past six years have shown a tremendous willingness to experiment with infinite variations in planning—to go boldly where no man has gone before—thus teaching me far more than can possibly be measured. Their practical planning and implementing problems which we grappled with together were the genesis for the many, many linkages in our "systems thinking" approach to strategic management.

Katie McCoy, who wrote this book with me, has been incredibly patient as she exposed every place throughout this book where our logic and linkages were not clear. Due to Katie, this book, our consulting process, and our strategist skills are 100% improved. Her unfailing good nature through numerous drafts and rewrites has also been most unusual.

Lastly, my wife and love of my life, Jayne, has been so supportive and helpful in so many ways and in so many roles, it is hard to put it into words. Without her, this book would not have been written.

To all of you, thank you from the bottom of my heart!

INTRODUCTION

REVOLUTIONARY CHANGE

Business as usual just won't cut it anymore.

When we try to imagine what business will be like in the new millennium, it seems that the only constant we can count on is change. When we consider fluctuating, competitive global markets, recessionary cost-cutting, and shorter life cycles for products and services juxtaposed with higher consumer quality and service expectations, revolutionary change, in fact, *is* our new reality.

These revolutionary changes present us with business challenges that test our creativity and endurance. What business and organizational strategies can we come up with that will help us respond to these challenges? Will it be possible to manage our way through these turbulent times to future successes? Most importantly, can we determine what the "right answers" are and choose the best path to follow amidst this revolution?

PAST PRACTICES/FUTURE SUCCESSES

One thing is certain today. Business as usual really *won't* cut it anymore. In these tumultuous times, it is tempting to look for answers among solutions that worked in the past—tempting, but perhaps not wise.

Applying past practices to current problems will only confuse our search for a future direction or innovative strategies. Nor is it practical to expect any single trend from today's popular line-up (such as TQM, empowerment, service management, delayering, benchmarking, or business process reengineering) to act as a general cure-all. There is a continuous stream of

1

books available on every conceivable type of management topic, each focusing on a different fad or trend. Each trend can lead us to believe that we have found salvation, when in truth we are only adding to the confusion. Searching for a "holy grail" solution simply is not realistic.

During my 25 years of active participation in organizations, I have observed a growing dissatisfaction with the way organizations are managed and led. Playing a variety of roles in a diverse range of public and private institutions has convinced me that *there is no one best solution* to the issues that confront organizations today. I believe, however, that there are "right answers" available to us. If it truly is our desire to build and lead a customer-focused, high-performance organization, we must completely rethink, reinvent, and replan the way we run our businesses.

Throughout my years of work, I have often seen strategic plans fall victim to the dreaded SPOTS (Strategic Plan On The Top Shelf...gathering dust) syndrome. Even where de facto strategic plans already exist, they are generally based on a single premise, such as purely financial or TQM considerations, with no provision for other complementary and necessary strategies and activities.

Most organizations today give only lip service to the vision and values portion of strategic planning; the number of paper documents continues to flourish. However, the number of planners is diminishing at an alarming rate. In fact, they are on their way to becoming an endangered species. Planners are decreasing, yet planning is increasing.

DISCIPLINED THINKING OR EMPTY RHETORIC?

Given the current state of global, revolutionary change, planning is needed more than ever before. Unfortunately, it seems that we have abandoned disciplined thinking and planning for the empty rhetoric of vision or values statements alone. In short, while the number of planners has dwindled drastically, strategic planning is increasing. Without a multi-level, disciplined, "systems" approach, however, a plan is not worth much more than the paper on which it is printed.

MY REASONS FOR WRITING THIS BOOK

My reasons for writing this book grew out of my conviction that these observations are not just isolated events but rather are part of a continuing pattern. Prior to developing the Strategic Planning Model for the 21st Century, which serves as the basis for this book, I observed and participated in a wide variety of planning processes. In addition, I researched and analyzed 14 other planning models that were well known and in use throughout North America.

However, each model presented only a piecemeal solution to the multi-level need of focusing on the customer from a "systems" and an organization-wide strategic perspective.

Thus, this book is organized around a systems framework in four parts:

Part I: An overview of the model and the rationale for it

Part II: Developing a strategic plan on a step-by-step basis

Part III: Mastering strategic change through successful implementation and sustaining your strategic plan

Part IV: Options for getting started with this systems approach to sustaining high performance

system (sis'tem) **n.** *a set of components that work together for the overall objective of the whole.* [From the General Systems Theory developed during the study of biology in the 1920s.]

THE A,B,C'S OF THE SYSTEMS THINKING APPROACH

Problems that are created by our current level of thinking can't be solved by that same level of thinking.

Albert Einstein

At first glance, the idea of reinventing the way we plan and manage our organizations on a day-to-day basis seems to be formidable. Thus, it is critical to put the strategic planning and change management process into simple, memorable language. It was for this reason that concrete phases were developed to frame strategic planning into a systems thinking framework, called the A,B,C's (actually, A, B, C, *and* D) of strategic management. Using systems thinking, the four phases are as follows:

- **Phase A. Output:** *Creating Your Ideal Future*—The magnet that pulls you toward the future, focusing on your desired outcomes and envisioning the year 2000 as if it were today

- **Phase B. Feedback Loop:** *Measurements of Success*—Creating quantifiable outcome measures of success or how will you measure the success of Phase A on a year-to-year basis

- **Phase C. Input into Action:** *Converting Strategies into Operations*—Developing the strategies you need to "close the gap" between today's status and your desired future vision (with the specific actions necessary to support the strategies)

- **Phase D. Throughput/Actions:** *Successful Implementation*—Developing your change management systems; putting your plans into motion, as well as tracking, monitoring, and adjusting as necessary

These phases and crucial "A,B,C,D" landmarks come from General Systems Theory, an offshoot of biology started in the 1920s. While these four phases may *seem* obvious and simple, they are a fundamentally different paradigm and way of thinking and reinventing strategic management. By following these phases as initial points of departure for systems thinking and planning, you can create any number of applications, including:

1. A comprehensive strategic plan for a large organization

2. A quick but meaningful plan for smaller organizations

3. A definitive plan for a specific business unit, division, department, or project in a large organization

4. A strategic plan for an entrepreneurial or family-owned businesses

5. Individuals have also successfully applied these same A,B,C,D phases to build a Strategic Life Plan for their personal life goals.

Work within diverse public and private organizations all across North America has proven that you *can* navigate turbulent organizational waters successfully using this framework. With Step #10, Strategic Review (and Update), you can sustain a high-performance organization.

A WRITER'S ARROGANCE: THE A,B,C'S

It would be pure arrogance to presume that I—or any individual—could set down the one, complete, perfect method for reinventing present and future strategic planning and change management. Indeed, if there is anything in the Strategic Planning Model for the 21st Century that comes close to the holy grail, it is the common sense, logical, A,B,C,D systems framework of General Systems Theory as a new paradigm, a systems thinking approach to planning and leading. When I view the glut of management books on every trend or management fad conceivable, I believe that the only way to create a cohesive whole is by looking at everything we do within the framework of systems thinking.

This systems thinking framework is the key to planning and progress. The most important part of the Strategic Planning Model is not the details. The significant aspect is that it provides a simple yet comprehensive way to strategically plan, lead, manage, and sustain an entire organization as a high-performance system, using the A, B, C, and D phases as a guide.

PART I

REINVENTING STRATEGIC MANAGEMENT: AN OVERVIEW

CHAPTER 1

REVOLUTIONARY CHANGE: IMPLICATIONS FOR ORGANIZATIONS

The end of one century, and the beginning of another,
ushers in a fundamental period of transition,
a time in which we all
must reshape our mental maps of the world.

One thing is certain: as we usher out the 20th century and look forward to the third millennium, we are vulnerable to more multi-faceted, simultaneous changes than ever before. The revolutionary change we are experiencing in the last part of the 20th century presents some harsh realities against a backdrop of promising horizons.

This change seems to rush at us with mind-numbing speed, affecting our personal lives, our choice of careers, our workplace, our governing bodies, our natural environment, our entire world. To fully understand how it will affect us, and what will be required to deal with it, we must examine the nature and extent of this change.

ASTONISHING CHANGES IN THE LAST TEN YEARS

First, it is important to understand that literally everything which impacts our daily lives is in transition. Countries, governments, companies, technologies, industries, the workplace—it would be difficult to imagine a more revolutionary period of change in both the geopolitical and business environments. Over the last decade, this unprecedented change has caused deep structural uprootings on a global basis.

The 1993 Joint Economic Summit of the Group of Seven (G7) industrialized democracies and Russia's Boris Yeltsin is a perfect example of this phenomenon. The leaders of Japan, Great Britain, France, Italy, Canada, Germany, and the United States traveled to the summit from nations that, while considered the strongest in the world, were in tremendous turmoil.

Gone were Bush (U.S.), Gorbachev (U.S.S.R.), and Mulrooney (Canada), victims of political upheavals of epic proportion. Japan's Prime Minister Miyazawa came as a lame duck less than a week before his conservative Liberal Democratic Party was ousted in favor of a coalition consisting of younger, more independent political contenders. France's President Mitterrand had just been forced by voters to team up with a prime minister of the opposition power, while Italy's government was caught in an all-out war on the centuries-old Mafia infiltration into its political system.

Add to this the astonishing changes of the past several years, such as the fall of the Berlin Wall, the reunification of Germany, the formation of the European Economic Common Market, and the toppling of communism throughout Eastern Europe and the former Soviet Union. At the same time, the Asian "tiger countries" and China's Communist mandarins appear to be mounting a campaign toward free markets, and Japan's *keiretsus* (interlocking companies with cross-ownership and financial, social, directorate links) are gaining in global strength.

All of this, and more, has a direct impact on the world economy. Former Eastern bloc countries are selling more manufactured goods to nations that were previously considered enemies, foreign investments in emerging Third World countries are causing rapid expansion of their economies, and Latin American dictatorships are veering toward the free market mindset.

Major U.S. corporations—once considered the strongest in the world—are also undergoing fundamental changes. The list of unseated or seriously wounded leaders of Fortune 500 corporations—Akers (IBM), Wang (Wang Corp.), Olson (D.E.C.), Stempel (General Motors), Brennan (Sears), Robinson (American Express), Lego (Westinghouse), Canion (Compaq), Reed (CitiCorp), Whitmore (Kodak), and Allen (Delta)—is legendary testament to this phenomenon of change.

The fiber of global business and industry has also changed dramatically. The breakup of AT&T, once a monopoly that virtually owned the U.S.

communications business, gave rise to a number of smaller (but surprisingly tough) competitors that now appear to be in it for the long haul. The introduction of fax machines and cellular phones has greatly expanded the time and space range of our interpersonal communications and the communications industry. Fiber-optic cables positioned beneath the ocean floor and satellites in outer space have broken through previous limitations to provide instantaneous global communication.

During these past ten years, who would have predicted that innovations in the personal computer market would spawn desktop publishing, a self-propagating rival that threatens to turn the printing industry inside out. For all of these industrial and commercial innovations, however, there are just as many changes in the work force itself that must be acknowledged.

Corporations around the globe have had to address cultural diversity, communication, and training barriers as they manage a more diverse work force. Immigrants, racial minorities, women, and disabled workers, once a relatively small part of the work force, are now entering the workplace in burgeoning numbers. Another group that is being heard from more and more lately are the senior members of the workplace. Older workers who once chose early or mid-60s retirement have recently started to demand longer and more flexible work options or part-time re-entry into the workplace.

In addition to the changing demographics of the work force, organizations are also facing radical paradigm shifts in employee values and expectations. As the hierarchical structure of organizations gives way to a more democratized workplace, employees have become more empowered and are seeking more active participation in the outcomes of their organizations. Teamwork has become a standard part of organizational frameworks, which has led to an increase in individual creativity and autonomy.

Jobs themselves are changing as organizations downsize and right-size. More and more telecommuting jobs and consulting needs are being created to fill the gaps caused by permanent layoffs, even among middle-management jobs, which are now obsolete and have been eliminated. Further, the spiritual and religious profile of the United States is undergoing a massive facelift away from traditional or mainstream religion. Even nuns and agnostics are now on the board of the National Conference of Christians and Jews as the Hindus, Buddhists, and Muslims take their new place as mainstream.

The public sector has also been in a state of metamorphosis over the past few years. Public resources are maxed out as global economies decline or integrate, yet the demands of the welfare state steadily increase. Also, as more and more governing bodies once based on socialism turn toward privatization and free enterprise, the lines between public and private organizations are becoming blurred. As a result, the public sector—from the U.S. government in Washington, D.C., to California, Oregon, Alberta, and Saskatchewan—finds itself needing to reorganize its services for greater efficiency and accountability.

This environment is also requiring the public and not-for-profit sectors to employ more business and market approaches. In effect, these sectors are undergoing an entrepreneurial renaissance in which such tactics as user pay, competition, privatization, and site-based management are becoming the standard rather than the exception. It is truly a renaissance whose time has come, as witnessed by the growing trends of decentralized authority, market-based incentives, preventing problems (versus curing crises), customer focus, and empowering communities to be proactive in solving their own problems.

This is clearly a time in which both the workplace and those in it are realizing enormous, life-altering change. In addition to the influence of corporate mergers and acquisitions so prevalent in the 1980s, today's organizations now face enormous global competition in production and financing and must learn to function in a much more deregulated environment.

ANTICIPATED CHANGES IN THE NEXT TEN YEARS

It is unrelentingly clear that the last ten years have produced fundamental upheavals in global leadership, marketplaces, and individual values. What is also becoming alarmingly clear is that the next ten years will bring even more change than the past ten years. Not only is our environment experiencing tremendous change; the rate of that change has virtually doubled. The changes we are dealing with today are happening at such a high rate of speed that the changes of the past ten years are essentially the equivalent of the previous *twenty* years, a disquieting thought at best.

The rapid waning of socialism around the globe will continue to bring a steady stream of change to the world economy. As more and more borders open up, from Eastern Europe to Mexico to Indonesia, numerous free trading blocs are developing. The North American Free Trade Agreement (NAFTA) between Mexico and the United States will further integrate our economies. It will dramatically impact future trade and create social change within North and South America as well, despite initial peso devaluations.

Previously unheard of regional affiliations are also entering the global trade market, particularly in Latin America, where such groups as Mercosur (a common market in the works between Argentina, Brazil, Paraguay, and Uruguay), the Andean Group, the Central American Common Market, the Mexico–Chile Free Trade Agreement, and the G3 Agreement between Mexico, Colombia, and Venezuela are rapidly gaining strength. By the end of the 1990s, it is expected that the six-member Association of Southeast Asian Nations will formulate a common market. In all, the overriding trend in trade is from nationalism to globalization.

Nationalism and fragmentation are on the rise in countries all over the globe as well. In North America, Quebec is seriously pushing for a form of secession from Canada. Ex-Soviet countries, Yugoslavia, and Czech-Slovakia are experiencing ongoing chaos; with their combustible nationalism, Southeast Asia and the Middle East are not faring much better. Africa's turbulent politics of the past several decades shows no sign of resolution (consider Rwanda). Only in South Africa is real change toward equality occurring.

Most futurists agree that technology is often the driving force of change, and the next ten years of technological growth will do nothing to disprove that theory. Continuing changes in robotics, automation, mechatronics (microprocessing within products), computer-assisted design (CAD), computer-assisted manufacturing (CAM), computer-integrated manufacturing (CIM), and graphical user interface (GUI) are expected to redefine industrialized manufacturing.

In addition, massively parallel processing (MPP) machines, with their ability to receive and transmit data at practically unlimited speeds, represent a phenomenal new growth market for just about everything from oil and biotech companies to banks, retail chains, and automobile manufacturers. The seemingly unlimited uses of the CD-ROM, with its massive storage capabilities, particularly in retail and consumer interactive applications, will also go a long way toward this redefining. With all this new technology, mass customization is fast becoming a new reality.

The explosions in biotechnology and genetics promise changes in science, health, and manufacturing at which we can only guess. The mapping of the human gene with its 100,000 genetic codes will be completed within the next five to ten years. Also, the recently developed computer program *Inventon* can literally invent new molecules, proffering an unimaginable boon for chemical and pharmaceutical companies. This is in addition to the explosive issue of health care reform in both the United States and Canada.

Information technology, or "infotech," and telecommunications will also be big winners, with further applications in miniaturization, fiber-optics, expert systems imaging, improvements in digital cellular communications, supercomputer networks, personal communications systems (PCS), and computer bulletin-board networks such as pocket phones, cellular-projected electronic mail, the Internet (frequently referred to as cyberspace), wireless computer networks, and video conferencing, to name a few.

Satellites, such as NAVSTAR (a 24-satellite global positioning system), TIROS (for meteorology), SKYNET IV (for submarine communications), Motorola's planned IRIDIUM network of 66 satellites, and Teledesic's planned global network of 840 satellites, are almost too huge an undertaking to imagine their ultimate effects on us.

Another offshoot already making itself known in telecommunications is infotainment, a radical new mega-industry that brings together (1) telephone communications, (2) network and cable television, (3) the publishing and computer industries, (4) retail and video stores, and (5) the multi-billion dollar entertainment industry. The home shopping television networks, already over a $2 billion industry and growing at approximately 20% each year, are but one example of this merger. Virtual reality (stereoscopic visual effects that project a 3-D image, making it seem real) is another phenomenon already making waves and is expected to explode within the next five years. Even imaging technology, which will make information systems more user-friendly, and artificial intelligence continue to grow into real possibilities.

Space-age designer materials will also be on the rise. Graphite, a relatively recent discovery, is being tested as a conductor of electrical energy. Heat- and resistance-free graphite could eventually greatly reduce the cost of energy transmission. Wood ceramic (sawdust injected with phenol resin) efficiently absorbs electromagnetic radiation, creating a wealth of potential uses in heat and electrical elements, as well as an effective shield for computers and electronic devices.

Answers are still being sought to counteract the relentless global warming, and the next decade will spawn an entire industry dedicated to this and other environmental sciences. In its earlier days, organizations complied with the environmental protection movement's 3 R's—reduce, reuse, recycle—largely as a response to governmental mandates. In fact, the business community was often at odds with governmental regulations, viewing them as an obstruction to doing business. The Windy Craggy copper mine in British Columbia was a 1993 example of this friction. Geddes Resources, a privately held corporation, wanted to level the summit of Windy Craggy Mountain in order to create an open-pit mine that was expected to produce 140,000 tons of copper annually. The threat of acid rock drainage, along with a 100-plus-mile access road, to the wildlife and fishing economy moved the government to veto the mine.

Although this type of political intervention created an initially negative reaction on the part of manufacturing, there is currently a surprising about-face in the environmental versus manufacturing evolution. What is happening is that organizations are discovering significant, ongoing cost and time savings in their environmentally regulated operating and manufacturing activities. As a result, they are now realizing that environmental protection is just good business and are therefore exploiting more and more environmentally friendly methods of operation.

The next ten years will almost certainly see many new industries and several more expand, some of which are obvious while others are still emerging. A consensus list, derived from my own experiences, publications of the World Future Society, the Deutsche Bank (Germany), MITI (Japan), and others, indicates targeted new industries for the 1990s and the third millennium, among which will be:

- Micro-electronics

- Robotics/machine tools

- Telecommunications

- Environmental protection

- Space-age metallurgy/"designer" materials

- Biotechnology

- Computers/software

- Infotainment

- Civil aviation

- Cottage industries

The cottage industry boom promises to be an interesting one. The catchphrase "think global, act local" is definitely at work in the 1990s. Originally perceived as a 1980s expansion industry, cottage industries of every description are just now starting to realize substantial growth, with no sign of slowing any time soon. One only need look at the explosion of mailbox, fax, and secretarial service franchises, as well as the huge spurt of growth in ergonomic computer furniture for the home office, to recognize that this particular wave is just beginning.

Questions to Ponder

- What changes are happening in the environment of your particular industry?

- Do you believe your organization is in the midst of revolutionary change?

- What are your organization's global opportunities and threats?

- Do you know who your future competitors are and where they are located?

- Does your organization formally scan the environment and stay abreast of the ongoing changes in technology, social values, telecommunications, etc.?

IMPLICATIONS FOR ORGANIZATIONS OF ALL TYPES— PUBLIC AND PRIVATE

On the face of it, it would seem that there is no reason for optimism. In the 1993 G7 summit, every nation represented faced economic and political crises of historic proportion. The Canadian, British, and U.S. economies are facing the harsh realities of an intensely competitive global market; employment in the richest nations has declined in the last few years to such an extent that more than 25 million people are out of work. In addition to these countries, Japan is also experiencing its biggest economic and political upheavals since World War II.

There is no doubt about it—*everything* is undergoing fundamental change. Indeed, despite the organizational turnarounds we are starting to hear about, the jobless rate is still unacceptably high across North America. Companies simply are not hiring people back. They are concentrating on increasing productivity and lowering fixed costs, while making do with a streamlined work force.

Overall, the leading socio-economic indicators show a global cycle of decline. We have overconsumed and underinvested. Increased expenditures, climbing budget deficits, tax increases, reduced revenues, and escalating unemployment levels all combine to present us with many questions and few answers.

Nothing seems to be immune, not entire nations or corporations, or even their leaders. While it is important not to surrender to pessimism, it is necessary to understand that without thought and careful planning, *anyone* is subject to this type of crash landing. *If presidents, national leaders, and CEOs of the largest and strongest organizations can fail, so too can you and I, as well as the organizations we represent.*

Change, by its very nature, brings with it fear and uncertainty as well as opportunity. Rules and boundaries change with no clear rationale; our paradigms shift, change, and even disappear. In order to enter the third millennium with a sure step, we will need to reshape our mental maps of the world. Einstein's great quote bears repeating here: *"Problems that are created by our current level of thinking can't be solved by that same level of thinking."* We must find ways to reinvent ourselves in order to survive, grow, and move on to future growth cycles. In doing so, we must remember *not to let the limits of our mind shape the limits of our world.*

Paradigms = "Limits of our minds"

Paradigm: n. 1) sets rules; 2) establishes boundaries

Paradigm shift: phraseology. 1) adapting new or revised frameworks and ways of thinking; 2) establishing new rules and boundaries

By shifting our mindsets and our paradigms, it is possible to move on to a new cycle of growth, in our nations and in our organizations. In fact, there are many examples of these new cycles across the globe. The brave (and, at the time, unpopular) attempts at change by Margaret Thatcher while serving as England's Prime Minister are just now starting to show results.

Germany has had innumerable paradigm shifts in its reunification efforts, which are beginning to take hold. So too has South Africa, especially in 1994. Even Russia, and other former Eastern Europe Communist countries, are starting to take halting steps toward private enterprise within a free market economy. Doing nothing, remaining static, or merely shifting resources and programs, however, changes nothing, as witnessed by Japan, where the same political party and philosophy have been in place for the past 38 years, with almost no change.

The question, then, is—how? How do we objectively step outside our organizations, reshape our paradigms, and regain our focus? How can we possibly know how to plan for future successes when we don't completely understand the changes that are occurring in the present? Are there *any* organizations out there that are "doing it right?" Are there, in fact, *any* "right answers?"

YES...THERE *ARE* RIGHT ANSWERS

The best way to guarantee your future
is to create it yourself.

Fortunately, the answer to this crucial question is a resounding yes. There *are* "right answers"; in fact, there are three "right answers." The plain truth, however, is that no organization can survive to implement these right answers unless it persistently—and with focused discipline—addresses the harsh realities of today's social changes and competitive marketplace and is willing to shift its paradigms in response to change. To make these changes, every organization must have an honest and realistic picture of where it is now. (Honesty really *is* Job #1!)

My work as a CEO, strategic management consultant, corporate senior executive, and naval officer, with an extensive research background and advanced academic degrees, has taken me through many, many public and private organizations and a wide variety of large-scale change projects. It has given me the opportunity to see what works—and what does not. Over and over again, three "right answers" have presented themselves as a recurring pattern for organizational success.

For the most part, these right answers are simple, straightforward steps that follow common sense and logic. None of them alone is the holy grail. Together, however, *each one becomes absolutely critical to the long-term success and viability of any organization, public or private.*

Right Answer #1:
Institutionalize a Strategic Management System

Highly successful corporations continuously re*structure* their organizations into a systems framework. The function of this framework is for all parts of the organization to be *strategically aligned and managed as a system, in order to focus on its only purpose or outcome of satisfying the customer.*

Hence, the need to institutionalize a strategic management system. Designing, building, and sustaining a strategic management system as the new way to run your business day to day is essential for success. This flows directly from our Seemingly Simple Element #1 of strategic management: *Planning and change are a part of management and leadership.*

Right Answer #2:
Create Professional Management and
Leadership Practices Organization-Wide

This is the *process*—the part where "the rubber meets the road" and eventually separates the winners from the losers. Over the long term, the only difference—and the ultimate competitive advantage—in any organization is the leadership of its managers, which includes their mindsets, paradigms, and behaviors.

All of the talk about employees as your competitive advantage misses the point that *management's actions* are the competitive advantage that leads to creative and innovative employees, who are free to use their hearts and minds as well as their hands. This flows directly from our Seemingly Simple Element #2: *People support what they help create.*

Right Answer #3:
Focus on Outcomes—Serve the Customer

This should be the focus—or *content*—of every core strategy you create and every system you set in place. It is obvious but true that the key task of each organization is to determine the needs and wants of its customers/markets and to adapt its products and services to delivering the desired satisfactions more effectively and efficiently than its competitors (i.e., unsurpassed customer satisfaction). This flows directly from our Seemingly Simple Element #3: *Our systems thinking approach to strategic management.*

Without exception, experience and research have shown that successful organizations have leaders who commit to these right answers for addressing change and moving forward to achieve their vision. Also, success most often has much to do with common sense and persistence; there really is no magic solution. The closest we can come to defining a holy grail for success is *when each of these three right answers folds into the overall organization as a system—a system with fit, alignment, and integrity to focus on the customer's wants and needs.* Even if that blend exists, however, it won't progress without persistence—*disciplined persistence of management and leadership organization-wide.* In other words, when all else fails, use common sense (which is what this book is based on).

There are many examples of businesses that are moving forward in spite of daily struggles and apprehension about the future: General Electric, Giant Industries of Phoenix, Bell of Canada, Ford, Motorola, Chrysler, Walt Disney, Poway Unified School District, the San Diego Zoo, the Marriott Corporation, the state of Oregon, the U.S. Postal Service (finally!), the state of West Virginia, the province of Alberta, the Environmental Protection Division of British Columbia, the Department of Agriculture in Alberta, and the cities of Phoenix, Saskatoon, Sunnyvale (California), and Indianapolis. Tom Peters' works and presentations are filled with examples of these and more highly successful corporations, big and small alike. None of them are perfect, but they are surviving—and thriving—through these tough times.

"If nothing else works, this may be a perfect opportunity to use common sense."

CHAPTER 2

YES...THERE *ARE* RIGHT ANSWERS

It's simple common sense, but it's true...
without prompt, consistent action, no change can occur.

RIGHT ANSWER #1:
Institutionalize a Strategic Management System
(As a New Way to Run Your Business Day to Day)

From the very beginning of strategic planning, you are actually creating the *structure,* or framework, within which you will implement your strategic plan. Without a structure that is systematically developed and institutionalized, your vision of a customer-focused, high-performance organization will not be implemented, and all your careful planning will indeed fall victim to the SPOTS (Strategic Plan On The Top Shelf...gathering dust) syndrome.

In order to implement your strategic plan successfully, it is best to look at planning as one part of an overall, two-part/two-goal structure called the strategic management system (see Figure 2.1). This system is crucial to designing, building, and sustaining a customer-focused, high-performance organization for the 21st century. It has two primary goals:

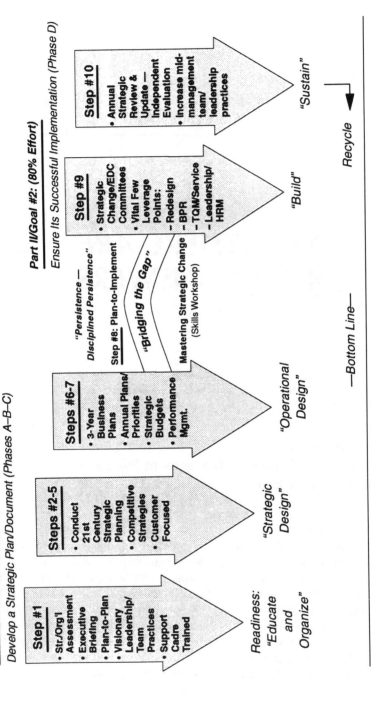

FIGURE 2.1 Designing, Building, and Sustaining a Customer-Focused High-Performance Organization for the 21st Century: A Two-Part Strategic Management Systems Solution to Create a Customer-Focused High-Performance Organization

Goal #1: Developing the actual strategic planning document

Goal #2: Ensuring and sustaining its successful implementation through a strategic change management system

It is critical to kick off the achievement of Goal #2, the Plan-to-Implement step, at the end of planning. It provides a way for your organization to bridge the gap from Goal #1 (the strategic plan document) to Goal #2 (successful implementation of the plan). What often happens is that when Goal #1 has been achieved, most planning processes end. Executives breathe a sigh of relief and move on to the next project, not realizing that we are talking about a new way to run the business day to day. Thus, they miss the point; the "persistence, disciplined persistence" that is so important in Goal #2 is just beginning.

Designing and building a Strategic Change Steering Committee made up of collective leadership is also vital to this process. It provides the organization with a structure for managing, leading, and guiding change and a resource of real people who are accountable for tracking the strategies from words on paper to successful results and outcomes.

Strategic Management Reality Check

If you're thinking that all this theory is fine, but how much of it makes a difference in the "real" world, consider the following. In an Oechsli Institute survey of over 500 small and mid-size companies published in *Inc.* magazine (March 1993), a whopping 97% of management and 77% of sales or frontline employees answered yes when asked if their company had a clear, written mission statement. Those statistics fell to 54% of management and 55% of sales/frontline employees when asked if that statement was supported by management's actions. It slipped again considerably, with only 46% of management and 38% of sales/frontline employees stating that each employee understood what was expected in terms of performance. Finally, a meager 21% of management and 22% of sales/frontline employees answered affirmatively when asked if all employees were held accountable for their daily performance.

What this says is that talk is cheap. We all want to sound good when asked the tough questions, but unless we find ways to back up our intentions with solid, disciplined, and persistent management systems, we simply won't survive. However, the ability to design, build, and sustain a customer-focused, high-performance organization requires incredible discipline and persistence over a period of years.

Setting a strategic management system in place, creating core strategies that will help you build toward your vision and desired customer-focused outcomes, implementing your strategic plan, and hanging in there when changes causes periodic upheavals is what makes an organization a long-term winner. This is what Seemingly Simple Element #1 means: *Planning and change are a part of management and leadership.* It is your job to create this strategic management system.

RIGHT ANSWER #2:
Organization-Wide Professional Management and Leadership Practices
(The Only True Competitive Business Advantage)

Like everything else facing us as we approach the 21st century, organizational management and leadership practices are undergoing fundamental change. Traditionally accepted managerial roles that developed out of the Industrial Age consisted of approximately (1) 5% strategizing; (2) 15% coaching, developing, supporting, and building; and (3) 80% directing and maintaining. The Information Age, however, is transforming the role of the manager into quite a different equation, which is roughly equal to (1) 20% strategy; (2) 60% coaching, developing, supporting, and building; and (3) 20% directing and maintaining.

This newer definition of the managerial role places a much greater emphasis on such interactive skills as coaching, facilitating, and developing staff and teams. In order for "people to support what they help create" (Seemingly Simple Element #2), these types of new leadership and management practices and skills are essential; hence Right Answer #2.

In order steer your organization through the revolutionary changes that will continue through the 1990s and into the 21st century, you must be willing to act as a visionary and leader of change, with the skills of a coach, trainer, and facilitator.

> *The routine manager tends to accept things the way they are.*
> *Leaders and leader/managers seek to revise processes,*
> *directions, cultures, and structures to reflect changing realities.*

Additionally, the best leaders know that *people support what they help create.* To implement strategies successfully, the best leaders recognize the wisdom of soliciting commitment at all levels of the organization. At the risk of being redundant, this will be repeated over and over again, because getting committed buy-in from all organizational members is the one element that can literally make or break successful implementation of any strategic plan.

Without this element, no organization can ever hope to gain a competitive business advantage. You only need to glance at a list of successful organizational leaders over the past twenty years—Ray Kroc (McDonald's), Sam Walton (Wal-Mart), J.W. Marriott, Sr. (Marriott Corp.), Jack Welch (General Electric), Walt Disney (Disney Corp.), Lee Iacocca (Chrysler), and John Watson, Sr. (IBM)—to recognize the underlying truth of this premise. Each of these organizational "winners" was a strong, proactive leader who valued his customers and introduced a philosophy of committed buy-in from all organizational members.

True leadership is the foundation for the four Vital Few Leverage Points for Strategic Change. Without these critical elements, it is virtually impossible to design, build, and sustain a customer focus and high performance in any organization. These four Vital Few Leverage Points, and the knowledge, attitudes, and skills associated with them, are reflected throughout the best practices of successful organizations today and into the 21st century. The Vital Few Leverage Points are:

- **Leverage Point #1. Operational tasks of total quality and customer service:** An organization-wide "close to the customer" focus on quality services and products (e.g., McDonald's, Disney)

- **Leverage Point #2. Organization redesign and restructuring:** Including delayering, empowering, and partnering, as well as designing jobs for service, innovation, and cost efficiencies (e.g., Chrysler's Platform teams)

- **Leverage Point #3. Customer-focused business process reengineering:** Reengineering business processes and systems to be more customer focused (e.g., General Electric's WorkOut)

And Right Answer #2:

- **Leverage Point #4. Sound professional management and leadership practices organization-wide:** Supported by strategic human resource management programs and policies that free your employees to become a full competitive business advantage, as evidenced by Marriott and others.

Again, the *only* true competitive business advantage that will help your organization thrive in the new millennium is strong, professional leadership and management at all levels. You will need to go beyond lip service and "walk the talk," starting with top management. How best to do this? Following the Ten Commandments of the Customer-Focused Organization is a good place to start, along with building good Customer Recovery Strategies and riding the "roller coaster of change" with both cutting *and* building strategies, as mentioned earlier.

In addition to these elements, you will need to acquire or enhance leadership skills that enable you to (1) listen and ask the right questions, (2) influence the right people, and (3) make the right decisions. You will need to develop sound interpersonal skills and supporting human resource programs, particularly in the areas of goal setting, performance appraisal, and career development.

A Leadership Effectiveness Triangle (Figure 2.2) has been developed based on field experience and literature searches. It outlines the building blocks that serve as the foundation for successful leaders and managers.

In today's organization, people want to be empowered within the context of the organizational mission and values; they want to contribute to the outcome of achieving the organization's vision. Based on my research, that of AMA and ASTD, and my experience in the public and private sectors, the leadership skills that will forge the organizational winners in the coming millennium boil down to the following three primary areas:

1. **Trainer:** Being a successful leader today is not about issuing orders. It is much more often about modifying or empowering individual and group behavior and teaching all organizational members to ask questions, to pay attention to quality issues, and to turn negatives into positives. In short, it is about teaching them to be fully competent in their jobs.

2. **Coach:** Fear-based management no longer works in today's organization. Instead, organizational members need leaders who are not afraid to confront and coach people toward high performance while maintaining or improving upon their relationships.

FIGURE 2.2 Needed 1990s Leadership Skills (at all levels of the organization, just applied in different ways) (Adapted from Stephen G. Haines, *First Step Training & Consulting,* 1991)

3. **Facilitator:** With the disappearance of organizational hierarchies, teamwork and cross-functional teams are becoming more popular and more effective. Today's leader must be able to encourage teams to lead themselves to high performance and guide or facilitate them toward taking the initiative.

The old Peter Principle of promoting the best salesperson into a management position, only to discover that he or she makes a lousy manager, isn't just an old cliche. It's an absolute truth. It is easy to lose sight of the reality that management and real leadership are a learned profession and set of skills. They require extensive vision, self-mastery, and persistence. In addition to creating a strong sense of employee involvement, you must also be open to the myriad of new concepts that will come out of the changing environments. Most important, you must reinvent your organization to do whatever it takes to satisfy the customer, first and foremost.

Questions to Ponder

- Have you shaped a strategic management structure and system that will help you bridge the gap from Goal #1 (the strategic plan document) to Goal #2 (successful implementation of the plan)?

- Does the leadership role in your organization generally follow the 20% strategy development, 60% coaching and development, 20% directing formula?

- Do the leaders in your organization actively seek commitment and buy-in from all their organizational members?

- Is the continuous development of your own management and leadership skills your top personal priority?

RIGHT ANSWER #3:
Focus on Outcomes: Serving the Customer
(As the Only Reason for Our Existence)

Almost every organization *says* it is customer driven, but the reality is that few are; they just talk a good game. What they really have is an analytic approach to an organization as a system, and they rarely use systems thinking throughout the organization (Seemingly Simple Element #3). In fact, most organizations today have become so distracted by more visible, immediate, or urgent issues (such as regulatory considerations, day-to-day operations, profits, product development, or employees) that they actually become enslaved to obsolete activities as ends to themselves. They only focus on finding one solution at a time and thereby lose any sense of an organization-wide *systems* focus, much less making the customer the focal point. The problem here is that no matter how much they concentrate on all these other issues, without a central, organization-wide focus on meeting the customer's needs and wants, no organization can stay in business over the long term. This is true for organizations in both the public and private sectors.

Figure 2.3 visually demonstrates the evolution of how organizations have been driven over a period of time. In earlier eras, when more business monopolies were prevalent, organizations were mainly driven by regulatory issues. In a marketplace with no competition, that worked fairly well. Earlier eras also saw organizations driven by the "better mousetrap theory." Organizations were able to keep their doors open as long as they came up with the best product or service.

Today's marketplace has enormous global competition and a more sophisticated customer. In such a marketplace, none of these answers to "how you are driven" alone will cause an organization to be successful. Of course,

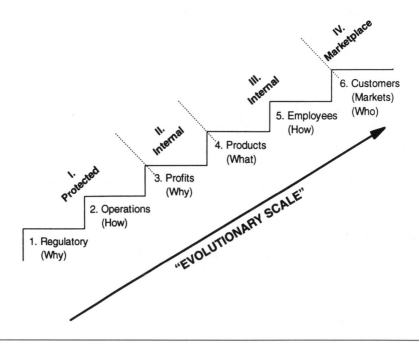

FIGURE 2.3 How Are We Driven? Who—What—Why—or How?

most of these issues are present and an ongoing concern in the day-to-day business of any organization.

However, every one of these methods for driving your organization must ultimately be evaluated in terms of how they fit into the overall focus of meeting the customer's needs and wants. A broad customer-driven orientation must be the outcome that sets the framework for all your core strategies and priorities.

This point cannot be overemphasized: any organization, whether public or private, that fails to focus on—or be driven by—the customer as its primary outcome and reason for existence will not survive the current decade, much less the coming millennium.

Following this basic fact of organizational life, I have researched all the literature of successful customer-focused organizations to develop the following Ten Commandments. They can help you quickly determine if your organization really is customer driven.

Ten Commandments of Customer-Focused Organizations

Commandment #1: Stay close to your customer, Especially senior executives (i.e., see, touch, feel, meet, and dialogue with them *face-to-face*—out of your office—on a regular basis).

Commandment #2: Know your customers' needs, wants, and desires. The driving force of your entire organization should be to surpass these customer needs.

Commandment #3: Survey your customers' satisfaction with your products and services on a regular basis. A constant flow of customer information is essential, whether it is positive, neutral, or negative. Don't resist it; welcome it!

Commandment #4: Focus on all your value-added benefits to the customer, such as quality and service, environmentally improved, cost effectiveness, responsiveness, and delivery speed, as well as performance, safety, and intangible aspects.

Commandment #5: Include your customers in your decisions, focus groups, meetings, planning, and even internal deliberations. Don't freeze them out.

Commandment #6: Require everyone in the organization to meet and serve your customers directly, at least one day or more each year. There is no substitute for everyone feeling the pulse of your business and its customers.

Commandment #7: Reengineer your business processes based on customer needs and perceptions. Do it horizontally across all functions within the
organization.

Commandment #8: Structure your organization to the marketplace.
Align the organization to fit your markets (i.e., 1 customer = 1 representative).

Commandment #9: Have a Customer Recovery Strategy (CRS). Reward
CRS behaviors, especially in cross-functional teams that work together to serve
the customer. Both the Marriott Corporation and Nordstrom's take seriously
the old adage, "If a customer is satisfied, he or she tells one to three others.
But each dissatisfied customer relates his or her story to eleven others." Both
organizations promptly respond to each complaint and correct and surpass
that customer's expectations immediately.

Commandment #10: Hire and promote only "customer-friendly" people.
Although this seem like a rather obvious, common-sense notion, the fact is
that most organizations (and this is particularly true in the public sector) have
gotten so buried under their own paperwork, activities, bureaucracies, and
hierarchies that they have lost sight of their raison d'être—the customer.

Once your organization has a clear vision of its ideal, customer-focused
vision, you will then need to develop a focused set of core strategies as the
main method for ensuring that your entire organization is focused on the
customer.

It is also essential that your core strategies be few in number and focused.
To successfully achieve the outcome of focusing on the customer, organizations should limit their core strategies to a maximum of three or four. Given
the present environment of changing paradigms, it will be difficult to resist the
temptation to develop six or even ten of these strategies. Trying to be all
things to all people is the single most common strategic planning failure.

STRATEGIES FOR THE 1990S AND BEYOND

As we move toward the 21st century, the organizational environment will
continue to experience radical change. Follow-the-leader will no longer work;
there are no easy solutions at hand. The revolutionary changes of the 1990s
have rendered the successful paradigms and strategies of the past obsolete.
Instead, these revolutionary changes have spawned newer or revised core
strategies that top successful organizations are employing to remain competitive and customer focused. The following is a list of typically successful core
strategies (with greater detail to follow in Chapter 9):

- Flexibility
- Speed
- Horizontally integrated products
- Networks and alliances
- "Value-added"
- Environmentally based products
- Commonization/simplification
- Mass customization
- Organizational learning
- "Family support" strategies
- Unsurpassed customer reputation
- High-quality products
- Growth through capital leverage
- Divestitures
- Retrenchments, turnarounds, cost reductions

Public Sector Strategies of the 1990s

Widespread disappointment in the general quality or lack of services in the public and not-for-profit sectors is creating the same need for new strategies that the private sector is experiencing. Confused means and ends and poorly defined visions and missions, along with a failure to know or care about the customer, have all contributed to a real lack of direction. Many organizations in this sector are now aggressively implementing strategies that are more like those used by the private sector (to be covered in more depth in Chapter 9). Osborne and Gaebler also discuss this in *Re-inventing Government: How the Entrepreneurial Spirit Is Transforming the Public Sector.*

Cost-Cutting Strategies: Necessary But Not Sufficient

Many organizations think that cost-cutting alone can produce long-term solutions. This is never true. Certainly, "cutting" strategies such as retrenchment, turnarounds, cost reductions, divestitures, reorganizing, business process reengineering, and layoffs are necessary, especially in today's recessionary climate. However, although they are necessary, they are not sufficient for long-term success.

In order for any strategy that involves "cutting" (i.e., "playing not to lose") to be successful, it must be conscientiously followed by a strategy of "building" toward your customer-focused vision ("playing to win"). One without the other will not work. Because results are not usually instantaneous, it is also important to recognize that you need to "hang in there" during the transition from "cutting" strategies to "building" strategies as you focus on systems thinking and outcomes of exceeding your customer expectations.

Board of Directors' Key Roles

There are also certain expectations regarding the board of directors' role in leading and managing the two goals of the strategic management system. In Goal #1 (developing a strategic plan/document), the board of directors should:

- Be actively involved in the development of *what* (your Ideal Future Vision step, i.e., your vision/mission/values) only and then allow management to figure out the *how to's* that are their responsibilities

- Formally approve the vision/mission/values as a guide for management in finalizing the rest of the strategic plan

- Formally approve the final strategic planning document after a full examination and debate, including approval of key success factors (outcome measures of success) as they are developed and tied to executive-level bonus programs

In Goal #2 (ensuring and sustaining the successful implementation of your strategic plan), the board will need to:

- Actively support the strategic plan and management's implementation of it

- Use the plan as a template for all items and actions that come before the board (i.e., the criteria for decision making) and have it present at all board meetings, especially as it pertains to yearly budgeting

- Use the plan as a guide for all board committees

- Use the plan actively in any public speaking roles within the company, with investors, or within the community (i.e., "stump speeches")

- Challenge parts of the plan that are unclear, confusing, or in need of adjustment over time (due to environmental changes)

- Have management formally report on the plan to the board each quarter

PERSISTENCE, DISCIPLINED PERSISTENCE

A final element of Right Answer #2 that must be a key ingredient of your organizational leadership is good old, *un-common*, everyday perseverance. It is probably the single most significant concept in each step of envisioning, planning, and implementation. Bringing persistence and discipline to your organization's vision seems like a simple enough thing to remember, yet without it, the chance of seeing your strategies acted upon and your vision take shape is less than none. As Bobby Ross, coach of the San Diego Chargers, put it in 1992 upon taking over his new job:

Persistence and Persevering

> I went through almost two years at Georgia Tech [before winning]. I hope it's not that long [before we win]. I'm not going to all of a sudden in midstream change the offense or change the defense. I'm going to persevere. I have a plan that I'm going to stick to, and I'm not going to back off it. *I'm going to be stubborn as hell.*

Regarding *discipline*, Ross went on to say:

> I'm going to be pretty demanding, but not in the sense of beating on guys. I'm going to be demanding in the sense of doing things right. I've [written] a philosophy on our football which is in our players' playbook, and one of the things is *discipline*. I made the statement that if discipline is doing things right, then that's what we're going to do. Discipline is not harassing someone or wearing your shoes a certain way; *it's just doing things right.*

In his first year as head coach, Ross's team went from a previous year's record of 6-10 to 11-5. In his third year, the Chargers won the American Football Conference and played (and lost) in the 1995 Super Bowl.

When you think about it, it makes perfect sense. After all, one of the main reasons so many of us are searching for "the right answers" is that we are not certain how to press on and persevere in the face of continuing and enormous change. Among all of the strategic planning efforts in which I have participated, without fail the ones that succeed and reach their goals are the organizations that persevere and patiently persist in being loyal to their plans. Yet they are flexible enough to adjust and to manage the "roller coaster of change" we're all on these days. This is what I call having *strategic consis-tency, yet operational flexibility.* This will be referred to often, as it is the key to *persistence, disciplined persistence* in good leaders.

As you persevere, keep in mind some additional common-sense findings from an extensive statistical survey (conducted by the American Quality Foundation, along with Ernst & Young) of over 580 organizations in the United States, Canada, and Germany in the automotive, banking, computer, and health care industries. According to this survey, *regardless of the starting position,* only the following three universal practices had a significant impact on organizational performance:

1. Strategic planning and implementation

2. Continually broadening the overall range of management practices

3. Business process improvement methods

The survey presupposed that the overall objective of the organizations studied was profit from serving the customer. In addition, the three practices that concluded the survey tie directly in with our three "right answers": strategic planning and implementation (#1 above) ties into Right Answer #1: *institu-tionalize an organization-wide strategic management system.* Business pro-cess improvement methods (#3) is linked to Right Answer #3: *focus on the customer.* After all, a fundamental aspect of focusing on the customer is the practice of business process reengineering, working backward to reengineer and refocus your processes. Finally, continually broadening the overall range of management practices (#2) ties directly to Right Answer #2: *professional management and leadership practices.* Together, these three right answers are absolutely essential for your organization to reinvent (i.e., design, build, and sustain) itself as a customer-focused, high-performance organization.

Questions to Ponder

- Is your organization's Ideal Future Vision customer focused?

- Have you defined your outcome measures of success (key success factors)?

- Have you established a focused set of core strategies so that your organization can achieve its desired outcomes?

- Do your organization's core strategies include customer-focused strategies—especially Customer Recovery Strategies?

- Does you follow the Ten Commandments of Customer-Focused Organizations?

- Does your board of directors take an active role in leading and managing the two goals of your strategic management system?

- Are you incorporating all three "right answers" into designing, building, and sustaining a customer-focused, high-performance organization?

IN SUMMARY: STARTING WITH THE "RIGHT ANSWERS"

To restate the basic premise of this book:

> The changes that have beset countries, organizations, and individuals in the past ten years have been staggering, to say the least. If you are to survive these changes, along with those that will surely come in the next ten years, you must now begin to plan for and apply the answers we know to be "right." It is not enough to wait for the perfect, simple, "holy grail" answer; it will never come. You need to take those elements that we have observed, researched, read, and heard about as being successful and put them into motion to the very best of your abilities.

Reinventing strategic planning for the 21st century is not simply a catchphrase; it is something we all must do in order to effectively integrate our organizations into the new "global village" that our instantaneous communication is creating. As telecommunications and technology continue to explode, so too does our political and socioeconomic world. It is a world in which a hierarchical, analytical approach is fast becoming extinct. It is being replaced by a systems approach, in which every action has a reaction, and each part must be considered in light of the whole organization, focusing on the customer.

In the early 1970s, as a part of my Master's of Science and Administration degree at George Washington University, I was required to take a comprehensive course on General Systems Theory (GST). GST was derived in the 1920s from biology. At the time, I felt it to be a somewhat arcane, even wasted, subject.

About five years later, however, it ultimately became the turning point of my professional life. I was working at Sunoco and had an opportunity to hear Russ Ackoff, a professor at the University of Pennsylvania and a renowned strategic planning expert, deliver a presentation. It was his belief that systems thinking, and GST, was the most practical approach to any life effort. A light went on in my mind. I went back to my old course papers and reevaluated my thinking from beginning to end. It dawned on me that this theory, this "systems thinking" approach, was one that could be applied to virtually *anything* in life.

My master's advisor at George Washington, Jerry Harvey, often told me, *"There is nothing so practical as a good theory."* At the time, I didn't believed it, but now I do.

What tipped the scale for me was the realization that systems thinking could not only be used in any application, but that it could be successfully applied to any time and any era of our lives. No matter what period of time we exist in, systems thinking will always work for us. As long as there exists a human society, there will be systems at every level that interlock and can potentially work together for mutual benefit. It is in identifying and analyzing those systems, and then working within them, that we can choose and achieve the outcome we desire.

Reinventing strategic planning for the 21st century, then, is all about becoming customer focused by incorporating the systems approach into everything that goes on inside our organizations. We must create a systems framework in which each process, action, and reaction is analyzed and fits our ultimate goal of sustaining a customer-focused, high-performance organization.

ACTION CHECKLIST

1. Be willing to face up to the harsh realities of today's revolutionary changes and make an honest commitment to an organization-wide planning and change effort. Honesty really *is* Job 1!

2. There *are* "right answers": (1) focus on the outcome (serving the customer), (2) institutionalize a strategic management system structure, and (3) create organization-wide professional management and leadership practices.

3. Be sure your organization is following the Ten Commandments of Customer-Focused Organizations.

4. Cost-"cutting" strategies are necessary, but not sufficient. Organizations need "building" strategies for the future as well.

5. The only true competitive advantage for organizations lies in strong, professional management and leadership practices.

6. In order to be successful, a strategic management system must have two goals: (1) create a strategic plan and (2) ensure and sustain its successful implementation.

7. Finally, remember what Bobby Ross said so well—persistence, *disciplined* persistence, is the key to all success.

CHAPTER 3

THE ORGANIZATION: A LIVING, BREATHING SYSTEM

*The great successful men (women) of the world
have used their imagination...They think ahead and create
their mental picture, and then go to work
materializing that picture in all its details, filling in here,
adding a little there, altering this a bit and that a bit,
but steadily building—steadily building.*

Robert Collier

"THINKING BACKWARDS" TO THE FUTURE

If you think about it, the whole reason behind reinventing the way you do business day to day is that you want to exercise control over achieving your organization's future. You want to be proactive in seeing that your organization realizes your desired vision and outcomes. To do this, you will need to practice "backwards (or systems) thinking." This calls for starting with your

Ideal Future Vision and then "thinking backwards" to where your organization is right now. From there, you have to determine how to bridge the gap between today's current state of operations and that vision you want to achieve.

If your organization is indeed customer focused, it is already performing the most crucial survival task—focusing on its outcomes. This is Right Answer #3, and it tells us *what* we must do to reinvent our organizations and withstand all the changes, present *and* future, that rock our global marketplace.

Right Answers #1 and #2, discussed earlier, provide the *how*—by "thinking backwards" to (1) build an organization-wide strategic management system and then (2) instill commitment throughout the organization by creating professional management and leadership practices.

Introducing these concepts, clarifying your terminology, and getting it all organized may seem like a lot of prework and not really related to the planning process. However, it is actually a part of the planning process; it is a way to fold each of the three "right answers" into the overall organization as a system, a system with the fit, alignment, and integrity necessary to focus on the customers' needs.

After all, the main reason you do strategic planning is because you want your organization to change and grow. This implies continuous progress. By maintaining a permanent mindset of strategic thinking, you get into the habit of thinking with clarity, meaning, focus, and direction. Skipping it is the surest way to create one more strategic plan that falls by the wayside. These concepts, and the system and structure in which they exist, are essential because they serve as tools for moving your plans into an integrated and successful implementation. This is especially true in the face of the revolutionary change that faces us now and will continue well into the 21st century.

STRATEGIC PLANNING DEFINED

Strategic planning is a dynamic, backwards thinking process by the collective leadership of an organization that:

- First defines the Ideal Future Vision and then the appropriate core directional statements (strategies) in order to...

- Establish consistent, meaningful annual operating plans and budgets that...

- Drive the measurement and achievement of this future vision.

Your organization's strategic plan should serve as a blueprint, with the annual plans and budgets that result from it providing the specific, necessary yearly details.

Once this plan has been put to paper, however, many organizations run into trouble. Committing a sleek, sophisticated plan to paper is one thing; getting it implemented can be quite another.

STRATEGIC *PLANNING* VS. STRATEGIC *MANAGEMENT*

To be successful, your strategic plan needs to be built into a structure that is designed to lead and manage your organization as it continues to grow, develop, and change. Thus, you will need a process, of which strategic *planning* is only one part, albeit in the lead position. The overall process— strategic *management*—is a new field of management that is rapidly gaining in popularity. It will be referred to here (and increasingly elsewhere in the field) often. It is an integral part of Seemingly Simple Element #1: *planning is a part of management.*

Most organizational planners make the mistake of looking at strategic planning as an event or a process that is an end in itself. Once the plan has been developed and implemented, that's the end of it. *Strategic management, on the other hand, is a new way to run your business day to day.* It incorporates strategic planning and thinking into the everyday, ongoing progress of the organization, making it the backbone and focus of every organizational activity.

Going beyond strategic planning into strategic management means making a commitment throughout your organization to ongoing strategic (backwards) thinking and continuous improvement. It means accepting that no one plan can possibly anticipate or resolve every need and that the organization must have in place a strategic management *system* for planning and dealing with all organizational change and growth, now and in the future and at all levels of management.

Whereas strategic *planning* once was mostly staff driven, strategic *management* is driven by line management leadership that aggressively pursues the commitment of all key stakeholders. As exhibited in the comparison in Table 3.1, strategic management also goes far beyond the "warm, fuzzies" that sound so nice in the organization's mission statement. It lays out clearly what specific actions and tasks must take place in order for the plan to be successful and then sets up concise, practical ways to lead, monitor, and measure its progress. It also incorporates a specific yearly update to keep the organization on track (much like a yearly independent financial audit).

TABLE 3.1   Strategic Management vs. Strategic Planning

Strategic Planning: *An Event*		*Strategic Management System:* *A New Way to Run the Business*
1. Project	vs.	Continuous/ongoing process
	vs.	With yearly strategic management system review to stay on track
2. Staff written	vs.	Line leadership driven
3. Analysis of today	vs.	Systems thinking/synthesis
4. "Motherhood/apple pie" words	vs.	Key success factor measures and action plans set/tracked
5. Strategic planning document as end	vs.	Execution/change management system
6. Leadership answers only	vs.	Key stakeholder commitment also
7. Weekend retreat	vs.	Strategic change in our roles
8. Strategic level only	vs.	Integrated into annual/daily decision making

The reason for reinventing the way we do business is the overwhelming change occurring within our environment and organizations today. Therefore, successful strategic management *must include mechanisms which address ongoing change*. Otherwise, change and good intentions always lose out to the day-to-day crises.

Strategic management system: (phraseology) A comprehensive, interactive, and participative system that leads, manages, and changes the total organization in a conscious, well-planned, and integrated fashion based on core strategies; using proven research that works, to develop and successfully achieve the ideal future vision.

SYSTEMS: AN OVERUSED, MISUNDERSTOOD TERM

In one way or another,
we are forced to deal with complexities,
with "wholes" or "systems" in all fields of knowledge.
This implies a basic re-orientation in scientific thinking.

Ludwig Van Bertalanffy

In spite of the fact that we are inundated with an infinite variety of business management trends these days, the idea of incorporating a systems framework into our organizations is *not* just another fad. It is far from it. In fact, it is a critical element that makes the difference between organizational success and organizational failure.

Because the term "system" is frequently applied to a veritable cornucopia of organizational concepts, however, the actual definitions of a "system" will be addressed first. Then, we will discuss how they can be used as a way to "think backwards" to your ideal future.

During the 1920s, the field of biology, with Ludwig Van Bertalanffy leading the way, brought forth a new way to look at the structure of all life— the system. In defining a system as *a set of components that work together for the overall objective of the whole*, scientists began to look at life and the elements that support it in a totally different perspective, ultimately ending up with a new theory called the General Systems Theory (GST). In describing this theory, author Geoffrey Vickers wrote:

> The words "general systems theory" imply that some things can usefully be said about systems in general, despite the immense diversity of their specific forms. One of these things should be a scheme of classification. Every science begins by classifying its subject matter, if only descriptively, and learns a lot about it in the process; and systems especially need this attention, because an adequate classification cuts across familiar boundaries and at the same time draws valid and important distinctions which have previously been sensed but not defined.
>
> In short, the task of GST is to find the most general conceptual framework in which a scientific theory or a technological problem can be placed without losing the essential features of the theory or the problem.

How is the systems concept best described? As depicted in the General Systems Theory chart illustrated in Figure 3.1, a system is described as an actual process with some key elements.* In the system process, there are a series of *inputs* to *throughputs* (or actions), resulting in *outputs* into the system's environment. A system also contains a *feedback loop*, for monitoring and evaluating the system's input, throughput, and output. Every living system also openly interacts with its own *environment.*

The ultimate outcome of this discovery was that theorists began to apply this reasoning to all forms of social structure, including socio-political and socio-economic focuses.

---

* Though this is not meant to be a treatise on General Systems Theory, the actual theory defined 12 elements in all. For further research and/or reading, see the Bibliography.

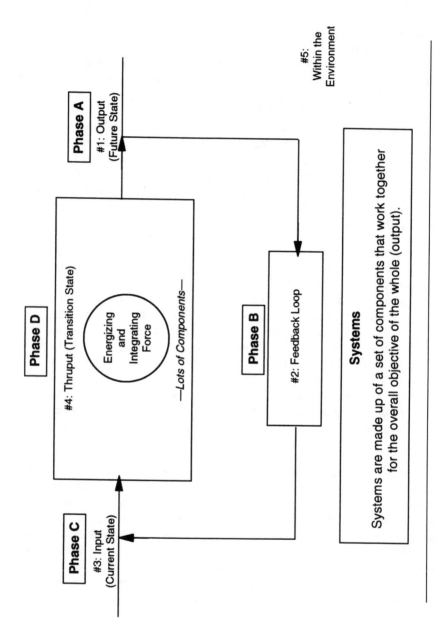

FIGURE 3.1 Systems Thinking: Five Key Elements

The point is that this systems thinking and structure has a permanence and a flexibility that permits it to readily adapt to all the variations and complexities of our revolutionary organizational environment as well, which is why it is called a *General* Systems Theory.

Conversely, in the traditional analytic approach to planning, organizations start with today's problems, breaking them out into separate parts, analyzing and resolving one area at a time, then moving on to the next. Systems thinking practices the exact opposite. It studies the organization as a whole in its interaction with its environment. Then, it works backwards to understand how each part of that whole works in relation to—and support of—the entire system's objectives. Only then can the core strategies be formulated.

SYSTEMS ("BACKWARDS") THINKING: AN ORIENTATION TO LIFE

*Everything everywhere
now truly affects everything else.*

Ian Mitroff

Systems thinking is referred to as an "orientation to life" because of its universal use in thinking about everything we do. It is about thinking backwards from your desired outcome, determining where you are now, and then finding the core strategies or actions that will take you from today to your desired outcome. Backwards—or true system—thinking employs four critical questions or phases that serve as locator points to clarify this thought process, the A,B,C,D guideposts:

Start at Phase A:

A. Where do we want to be?

B. How will we specifically know when we get there?

C. Where are we now?

D. How do we get from here to there?

Pretty simple, right? In a sense, it truly is a simple, common-sense approach, which is why it is incorporated as one of the three seemingly simple elements. Before deciding that it is *simplistic*, however, let's see how this changed orientation points to a new paradigm of how to lead and manage complex organizations.

These four questions relate directly to the guidepost phases of our systems model. They set up the sequential approach to strategic management starting with Phase A.

Systems thinking is fundamentally different from our standard analytical approach to problem solving, which starts with Phase C (where you are today). The analytical approach is the predominant paradigm in Western society today. It is taught to us in all of our disciplines, whether health and medicine, legal structures, finance and accounting, computer science, nuclear science, etc. It starts with today, breaks out each individual issue, and solves it before moving on to the next issue. Systems thinking, on the other hand, clarifies the overall objectives of the whole, starting at Phase A. It *simplifies the process* and makes sure all those pieces fit together in a continuous, growth-oriented system that focuses on outcomes. It is not simplistic, however, as it goes against the grain (or paradigm) of mainstream and popular Western society thought.

Questions to Ponder

- Do you understand the difference between systems and analytical thinking?

- Does your strategic plan incorporate the four elements of a true system: input, output, throughput, and feedback? Also, do you constantly scan the environment (the fifth element)?

- Do you understand the difference between strategic planning and strategic management?

- Does your organization view strategic planning as an isolated event or process, or has it created an ongoing, two-part strategic management system for achieving its ideal future vision?

EXACTLY WHAT *ARE* THE PROPERTIES OF A SYSTEM?

The most distinctive feature of any system is that each and every part influences and affects every other part of that same system. Ideally, all parts of a system fit and work together synergistically. By definition, no individual part can be independent. The following list identifies most of the properties of a true system:

- Systems, and organizations as systems, can only be understood holistically.

- Every system has properties that none of its parts can do.

- Parts/elements/subsystems are interdependent.

- Change in any element of a system affects the whole as well as the other elements or subsystems.

- A system cannot be subdivided into independent parts.

- Exclusive focus on one subsystem without simultaneous attention to other subsystems leads to suboptimal results and new disturbances.

- Organizations are open systems and, as such, are viable only in mutual interaction with and adaptation to the changing environment.

We have already discussed the difference between analytic and systems thinking. It is important at this point to mention that neither thought process is bad, nor do they automatically exclude one another. There will be times in our organizational environment when an analytical approach is called for. It is critical, however, that when we apply it to a problem, we apply it *within the context of an overall, integrated systems thinking framework.*

A good way to summarize the notion that every part of a system interacts with and depends upon every other part is to review some of the things that took place in the financial marketplace during one month in 1984. On March 4, 1984, E.S.M., a small Florida securities dealer, collapsed. Home State Savings Bank in Cincinnati, Ohio, having one-third of its loan portfolio in E.S.M. securities, then closed its doors.

Following this, there was a run on savings and loans throughout Ohio, which were then taken over by the Federal Home Loan Bank Board, the old Savings and Loan Insurance Corporation. Understandably, this caused some major jitters on the already deficit-ridden financial system and market of that time. From March 18th through the 20th, only two weeks later, the U.S. dollar fell 6% against the British pound, one of the largest drops in history. Finally, British oil assets took a severe beating due to the fact that they were measured and traded in U.S. dollars. This is a perfect example of systems theory in action.

ORGANIZATIONS AS SYSTEMS: BACKWARDS THINKING SYSTEMS

One of the primary reasons I began to research a systems approach to strategic management was due to the surfeit of organizational trends I kept running into throughout my years in senior management. Management by objective, quality circles, TQM, restructuring, downsizing, coaching, mentoring, benchmarking, business reengineering, etc. produce a lot of headaches—but resolve no real problems. It was becoming obvious to me that this analytical approach to problem solving was like trying to build the world's greatest car:

> **Example:** Picture yourself building the premiere car in the world. You have access to every automobile ever made. First, you examine them to determine which one has the undisputed best engine. Next, you select a distributor from a different car, one which you know has the very best distributor. Now it's time to select the best, most reliable carburetor, which of course comes from another, totally different car.
>
> One by one, you gather these "best parts" until you have every part necessary to make the world's best car. Once you've tried to put them all together, however, just what is it exactly that you have? You certainly don't have the world's greatest car. You don't even have a car, because the parts don't fit!
>
> Although you have in your possession all of the parts necessary to build a car, none of those individual parts were designed to fit with each other. They are all from different systems, and used independent of their systems, they are worth nothing.

After talking to hundreds of other business executives who were also trying to build "the world's greatest car" within their own organizations and felt the same sense of frustration and confusion that I did, I began to wonder: how in the world could any of us take all of the intricate components that exist (in infinite variations) within every organization, match them to whatever trend was the "flavor of the day," and make sense out of it all, much less come up with any answers that would truly serve our customers?

It was at this point that I realized that my earlier work on the General Systems Theory should serve as an overall framework that would accommodate all of the intricacies presented by a typical organization. In viewing the "organization as a system," we see it as an intricate puzzle, a network of inputs, processes, outputs, and feedback from suppliers, employees, customers, and other key stakeholders in the environment. Every part of this system depends on every other part working as it should. To successfully lead and manage this requires a specific and complex set of concepts, tools, and skills for wiring and aligning these components together for the overall objective of the whole (i.e., focusing on the outcome of serving the customer). The customer also has a complex set of expectations for quality products, high-level service, prompt delivery, and reasonable cost.

What I and my peers had been trying to do was to apply an issue-by-issue, analytical solution to a systems problem. No wonder it wasn't working! No wonder it is so difficult to lead and manage today's organizations.

Some of the attributes one could expect to find in a systems-oriented organization that might not exist in a more hierarchical one include:

- A shared vision of the overall organization's future

- Better horizontal, cross-functional communication, teamwork, and cooperation to serve the customer

- Cross-functional task forces and project teams

- Integrity of the various parts and departments of the organization fitting and working together for the good of the whole

- An alignment of work processes horizontally across the organization that meet the needs of the external customers

- Focus on system-wide core strategies rather than functional or departmental goals

- Fewer levels of hierarchy and management; greater operational flexibility and empowerment

The best place to begin establishing a true strategic management system in your organization is to set up the A,B,C,D guideposts referred to earlier. Then use them to set up your strategic plan/change process:

- **Phase A: Where do we want to be?** Focus on the outcomes you desire for your organization—envisioning the year 2000 as if it were today and then working backwards to the present.

- **Phase B: How will we know when we get there?** It is crucial to develop concrete feedback. You need to define your quantifiable outcome measures of success (key success factors). This is how you will be able to gauge whether the implementation of your core strategies is progressing successfully on a year-to-year basis.

- **Phase C: Where are we right now?** This is the step in which you design strategies and actions for "closing the gap" between your organization's current state and its desired future vision, with the specific action priorities necessary to support them.

- **Phase D: How do we get there from here?** It is at this point that you develop how to implement and manage change throughout your organization. Integrate your change management techniques into an organization-wide system and put your plans into motion, tracking, reporting, and adjusting as necessary.

While this systems thinking approach to strategic management seems to follow simple logic, it really is an "uncommon" common-sense approach. As noted earlier, during the development of the Reinvented Strategic Planning Model, I was surprised to find that not one of the fourteen other models I researched had systems thinking as its base foundation or assumption.

SIX USES OF THE A,B,C,D FRAMEWORK

As illustrated in Table 3.2, the A,B,C,D framework aligns directly with the four phases of a system: (1) output, (2) feedback loop, (3) input, and (4) through-put/actions. By addressing the four phases, starting with Phase A, and then following through with the implementation of the four phases of a systems framework, you lay the groundwork for a common-sense, practical strategic management system that focuses you on the changes you want to accomplish.

The real beauty of working within a systems framework is that you can be quite flexible in how you apply it. Remember, the General Systems Theory provides a generic, universal framework to which literally any set of requirements can be adapted. Depending upon your specific needs or situation, you can adapt this framework in numerous ways. You should always use the same A,B,C,D locator points or phases in sequence and in conjunction with backwards thinking. It is just applied more quickly or for different uses.

Different Uses

- **Use #1: A Comprehensive Strategic Plan.** For a large organization, this is a process in which your collective leadership develops a comprehensive plan that encompasses the entire organization. Your investment in time will depend on whether you are starting from scratch or tailoring and filling in the missing pieces of your organizational systems framework to achieve synergistic implementation. Expect to spend anywhere from 8 to 16 days off-site over a four- to six-month time frame.

- **Use #2: Strategic Planning Quick.** This allows you to conduct a less comprehensive version of strategic planning for a smaller to mid-size organization. It requires approximately five days off-site, over two to four months.

- **Use #3: Three-Year Business Planning.** If you need to create a strategic plan for a specific business unit or a major support function, section, or program of a larger organization, you can complete a shortened three-year business planning process in about four to six days off-site, over two to four months, as well.

TABLE 3.2 Strategic Planning Comparisons: Ten Unique Concepts

Other Models	*vs.*	*Reinvented Model*
1. Focus on plan content only		1. Team building and leadership skill building are an integral part of planning/change
2. Preset steps/actions		2. Plan-to-Plan phase determines flow, education, time needed
3. Current stage emphasis (starts with today's problems)		3. Future orientation (starts with ideal future vision—Phase A)
4. Total community participation (or none at all)		4. Corporate model (controlled stakeholder participation)
5. Written in platitudes (high-level only)		5. Gets specific focus (with measures—Phase B)
6. Smooth over conflict and disagreements with words		6. Making/forcing tough choices on strategies (priority setting at five levels—Phase C)
7. Discrete and separate *planning* process (business, annual budgets, strategic)		7. Systems approach (drives day-to-day decision making)
8. Set budgets; work within them		8. Focused plans and priorities drive budgets; budgets can grow
9. Focus on strategic planning document		9. Focus on strategy implementation and change (Phase D)
10. Plan on left, manage on the right—"structure" is not important		10. Systems approach—"new way/ structure" to run the business day to day; includes annual strategic review and update to recycle yearly

MACRO

11. Didactic (tell clients the answers; meaning outside client)		11. Experiential (help client find/own the answers/meaning internal to client)

- **Use #4: Micro Strategic Planning.** Even if your organization is very small, you still need to create a strategic plan for it. This "micro" process enables you to develop a strategic plan in only two days off-site, over two months, and complete the rest without off-site meetings. However, it does require immediate implementation through a Strategic Change Steering Committee to keep up the momentum started and to finish any planning pieces missed due to the short time frame.

- **Use #5: Project Planning and Strategic Changes.** With this A,B,C,D system, you can apply it to a major project or change effort, such as TQM, customer service, business process reengineering, empowerment, partnerships/teamwork, technology, etc. Even if you are going to go after change in this piecemeal fashion, use systems thinking to leverage your effectiveness and success in this project. Remember, always differentiate between analytical versus systems thinking; when you need to apply analytical thinking, do it within a systems framework and context.

- **Use #6: Strategic Life Plan.** Your personal life is even more important than your business life! This A,B,C,D systems framework can be used to conduct a personal (person, family, couple) life plan. My wife and I, along with numerous other personal and professional acquaintances, have developed life plans with very satisfying results.

Keep in mind that the systems or backwards framework can be applied to virtually any professional or personal situation. No matter what the particular requirement may be, as long as you stay focused on the four A,B,C,D phases in the proper sequence, they will work for you.

Remember, systems thinking is a way to think, as well as a new orientation to life!

Questions to Ponder

- Do you understand why it is crucial to start at Phase A (the future outcomes you desire) versus starting with the present?

- Are you clear on some of the key attributes of a systems-oriented organization versus a hierarchical one?

- Which of the six possible uses for the Reinvented Strategic Planning Model do you and/or your organization need?

  Use #1: A comprehensive strategic plan

  Use #2: Strategic planning "quick"

Use #3: Three-year business planning

Use #4: "Micro" strategic planning

Use #5: Project planning and strategic changes

Use #6: Strategic life plan

RECAP OF KEY POINTS

1. Focus on systems thinking in your strategic management.

2. Start with your Ideal Future Vision and then work backwards to determine the core strategies you will need to achieve it.

3. Goal #2, ensuring and sustaining successful implementation, is the key to strategic planning; the document is not.

4. Simply developing a strategic plan on paper will not work; you must incorporate a two-part strategic management system to ensure continuous improvement/change.

5. Whereas strategic planning is mostly staff driven, strategic management is driven by line management leadership and aggressively pursues the commitment of all key stakeholders.

6. Any system can be described as an actual process, with inputs, throughputs, outputs, and feedback within a dynamic and rapidly changing environment.

7. In traditional analytic thinking, issues are broken out and resolved one at a time. Systems thinking does the opposite; it studies the organization as a whole and the achievement of its objectives as it interacts with its environment.

8. A systems framework sets up an A,B,C,D, sequential, four-phase approach to strategic management: (A) concentrating on outcomes first, (B) establishing a quantifiable feedback system for measuring progress, (C) determining where you are now, and (D) identifying how you will reach your ultimate vision.

CHAPTER 4

REINVENTING STRATEGIC PLANNING FOR THE 21ST CENTURY

*Every moment spent planning
saves three or four in execution.*

Crawford Greenwalt
President, DuPont

Although most of the ideas presented in the previous chapters may seem like simple, old-fashioned common sense, your strategic plan will never see the light of day without a lot of elbow grease and commitment. The organizations that are successful are those that are willing to educate and organize themselves, create a clear plan, make the tough choices, and then get on with the process. The plans that fail are often just as good as those that succeed; *the difference lies in the organization's disciplined persistence and commitment to implementation* and its ability to keep the ball rolling over the long term.

Once you understand how to use a systems framework for planning and implementing your organization's core strategies, you are ready to begin shaping your plan.

REINVENTED STRATEGIC PLANNING MODEL FOR THE 21ST CENTURY

Following on the A,B,C,D phases is the Reinvented Strategic Planning Model, which provides a customer-focused systems solution for creating your own high-performance organization. It consists of the four phases just outlined, within which there are ten clear, practical steps (see Figure 4.1).

Phase A. Output: Ideal Future Vision

- **Step #1. Plan-to-Plan:**   This is the step that educates, organizes, and tailors the strategic planning process to your organization's specific needs. It includes setting up your core planning team and the concept of a parallel process that involves key stakeholders (back to "people support what they help create"). It also clarifies top management's role in leading, developing, and owning their strategic plan.

    Example: During the Plan-to-Plan step, the Apple Valley School District in California established a planning team of 15 people. However, because of the district's broad impact on the lives of thousands of families, its parallel process with key stakeholders included over 100 meetings involving more than 2000 people.

- **Step #2. Ideal Future Vision:**   This step concerns itself with formulating a vision and dreams that are worth believing in and fighting for. This is where you should focus on your desired outcomes (the customer). You also need to define your mission (reason for being) and core values (desired culture).

    Example: When you put it all together, you need, in eight words or less, an internally motivating "essence" of your ideal future, or a rallying cry. Ford's *Quality Is Job 1* is the most well-known rallying cry today and is even used liberally throughout its advertising.

Phase B. Feedback: Key Success Factors

- **Step #3. Key Success Factors (KSFs):**   It is at this point that you must begin developing ways in which to measure your organization's outcome measures of success toward its vision, mission, and values.

    Example: Some typical KSFs in the private sector include (1) customer satisfaction (quality, service, customer responsiveness), (2) employee satisfaction, (3) financial success (revenue, return on investment, profits, etc.), and (4) market share versus the competition.

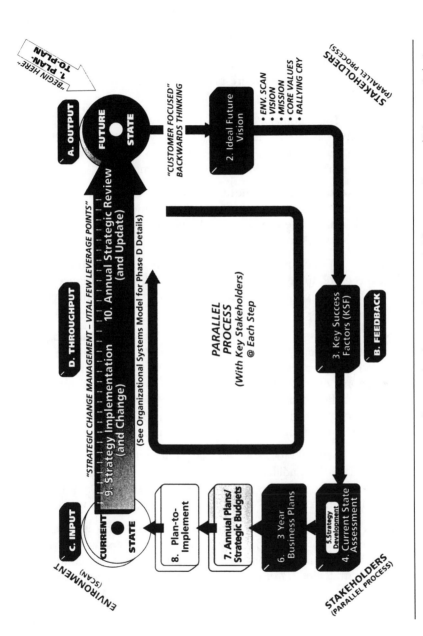

FIGURE 4.1 Reinventing Strategic Planning for the 21st Century: A "Customer-Focused" Systems Solution to Creating High Performance

Phase C. Input: Today's Assessment and Strategy Development

- **Step #4. Current State Assessment:** In this step, you analyze the organization's strengths, weaknesses, opportunities, and threats and contrast them against your vision. There are numerous sophisticated techniques to do this, which will be covered in Chapter 8 on Current State Assessment. This is where planners have historically spent their time—analyzing today only.

  Example: The Palomar Pomerado Health System in California did a thorough analysis of each major health care system in its marketplace. These analyses were crucial in deliberations on how to compete in an industry of shrinking margins and tougher competition.

- **Step #5. Strategy Development:** This step develops the core strategies, or major means and efforts, needed to bridge the gap between where you want to be in your Ideal Future Vision (Step #2) and your Current State Assessment (Step #4).

  Example: In developing your strategies, it is important to remember that less is more. In my doctoral research of 200 financial services firms, the top financial performers had 40% fewer core strategies than the poorer performers.

- **Step #6. Business Units and Three-Year Business Planning:** At this point, the strategic business units (SBUs) in the private sector or major project areas in the not-for-profit sector that comprise your organization's overall business portfolio are identified and prioritized according to their contribution to your future growth, profitability, and direction. Ideally, a three-year business plan for each of these needs to be developed along with overall proforma financial statements.

  Example: General Motors is generally criticized for having too many automobile SBUs: Cadillac, Buick, Pontiac, Chevy, Oldsmobile (frequently rumored to be closing), and their newest SBU, Saturn Corporation. They often overlap, duplicate, and compete with one another.

- **Step #7. Annual Plans and Strategic Budgets:** This is where the rubber meets the road—where you develop unit annual plans with prioritized tasks and then provide the resources to actually implement your core strategies. *Planning should lead budgeting, not vice versa.*

  Example: The Canadian city of Saskatoon, Saskatchewan now has all city departments with annual plans based on the corporate strategic plan (and organized by core strategies).

Phase D. Throughput: Actions, Implementation, and Change

- **Step #8. Plan-to-Implement:** This step serves as a crucial bridge between Goal #1 (developing a strategic plan) and Goal #2 (ensuring and sustaining the successful implementation of strategic change). Similar to the Plan-to-Plan step (#1), it also "educates and organizes" senior management for the change management process. It establishes a Strategic Change Steering Committee and a yearly comprehensive map (i.e., project plan) to guide the changes dictated by the strategic plan. It also develops a roll-out and communications plan for the newly developed strategic plan.

  Example: At a large suburban school district in California, the superintendent resigned at the end of strategic planning. However, because they had completed Step #8, Plan-to-Implement, a critical mass of both board and management who remained strongly committed to successful implementation was retained.

- **Step #9. Strategy Implementation (and Change):**   The goal of this step is to transform the strategic plan into all the hundreds of necessary individual plans, programs, and efforts and to tie a reward system to it.

  Example: The Environmental Protection Division in British Columbia, Canada regularly holds quarterly Strategic Change Steering Committee meetings, along with a highly successful implementation of its strategic plan, through strong leadership, even in a difficult government setting.

- **Step #10. Annual Strategic Review (and Update):**   A formal annual strategic review and update of the strategic management system process and results needs to be conducted, much like a yearly independent financial audit. In this way, you persistently keep your implementation up and running year after year as a strategic management system, even after the newness has worn off.

  Example: Giant Industries never misses this yearly update; hence its continuing financial, organizational, and human successes.

As would be expected, achieving the integrity of all the parts of your organization fitting together in support of your vision is extremely difficult. As illustrated below, each of the various steps in this planning model incorporates actions and accountability on the part of many different individuals throughout the organization. For example:

Strategic Management Step	Typical Accountability
Plan-to-Plan	Planning/CEO
Vision/mission/values	OD/training
Business plans	Business units or business development/planning
Current State Assessment	Planning/business development
Department plans	Department heads
Strategic budgets	Finance
Compensation/staffing	Human Resources
Individual MBO/goal setting	Human Resources
Pay/rewards systems	Compensation
Implementing change	CEO/all/no one
Annual strategic review	Finance

Looking at this, it's easy to see why the need for a systems framework is so great. Strategic management requires all of the various organizational strata to work together as efficiently as possible. After years of trying to "build the world's greatest car," only to fail, it has become obvious that the traditional paradigm of analytical thinking alone is not working—and will not work.

SOME PROGRESS: "PARTIAL" SYSTEMS SOLUTIONS

For a long time, organizations got away with approaching the future from an analytical perspective. Solving current issues was typically handled by analyzing problems, breaking down each part, solving the first separately, and then moving on to the next one. Analytical thinking also put the current state of affairs above all other considerations: handle today's issues, and deal with tomorrow when it gets here. Strategic planning mostly just extrapolated and projected today's issues into the future. This approach worked for organizations for quite a while, even into the 1980s. Some businesses are still working this way today and surviving, but not for long.

Today, when just about every existing organizational paradigm has flown out the window, organizations are beginning to respond with *partial systems thinking*. This seems to be a beginning stage in moving away from the traditional analytic approach and thinking. Organizations are attempting to find integrated answers for individual problems, rather than the earlier approach of applying a "one-time only" solution to a problem that had ongoing implications. It is due to this kind of "partial thinking approach" that we are seeing such an abundance of organizational change trends like TQM, business process reengineering, empowerment, and restructuring, to name a few. It is an attempt to begin combining parts of problems into more complete and integrated solutions.

STRATEGIC PLANNING LEADS THE WAY

The problem with this partial systems approach is that it creates a "what you see depends on where you sit" environment. As in the example of the "world's greatest car," some things get fixed or improved along the way. However, no provisions are made for questions that arise as a result of changing one area and leaving others as they were.

True systems thinking, on the other hand, studies each problem as it relates to the organization's objectives and interaction with its entire environment, looking at it as a whole within its universe. Taking your organization from a partial systems to a true systems state requires effective strategic management and backwards thinking.

As represented in Table 4.1, it is the most important tool you can use to create the necessary changes organization-wide while tying together all the other fads and concepts into one framework. Otherwise, how can you understand, much less keep track of, all the brilliant solutions being bandied about today?

Some of these popular solutions include TQM, customer service, business process reengineering, empowerment, leadership, visioning, teamwork, and self-directed work teams, among others. Each of these solutions is correct and effective in its own right. However, when viewed in a systems context, they are only partial solutions and therefore are only partially successful for the organizations that use them. On the other hand, if they are looked at as a part of the overall strategic plan, then the plan can "lead the way" to a fully successful implementation.

This is what systems thinking is all about. It is the idea of building an organization in which each piece, and partial solution, of the organization has the fit, alignment, and integrity with your overall organization as a system— and its outcome of serving the customer.

SEVEN LEVELS OF LIVING SYSTEMS

In addition to the previously stated definition of "systems," James G. Miller contributed a second key concept about systems that is often developed in organizations today. He identified seven levels of systems in his classic book *Living Systems.* These seven different levels of living systems include:

TABLE 4.1 Strategic Planning, Management, and Leadership Lead the Way

Strategic planning is *the* major A,B,C,D organizational intervention to develop a shared vision of your future and the values, culture, and business strategies/major changes needed to be implemented and managed to get you there.

Can you find all the current strategies/changes/fads in the following list?

OUTPUTS: A

Step #1: Vision and Mission

1. Who: customer focus

2. What: quality, service, response, environment, cost, profitability

3. Why: stockholders, stakeholders, customers, society

Step #2: Core Values

4. Self-directed work teams

5. Employee empowerment/creativity

6. Continuous improvement

7. GE's WorkOut (blowout bureaucracy); reinvent government

8. Communications effectiveness; drive out fear

FEEDBACK: B

Step #3: Key Success Factors

9. Benchmarking/measurement systems (world-class comparisons)

10. Employee and customer satisfaction surveys

11. Market research

12. Executive compensation and other rewards practices

INPUTS: C

Step #4: Core Strategies

13. TQM/TQL—some of Deming's 14 Points

14. Service management/quality service

15. Speed and response time

16. Business process improvement/re-engineering

17. Improved sales and market-driven culture

18. Cost efficiencies, reductions, and productivity improvements

19. Delayering

20. People as our competitive business advantage

21. Culture change

22. Organization structure/design

THROUGHPUTS: D

Steps #6–9: Operational Planning and Implementation

23. Annual/operations/tactical planning

24. Annual budgeting

25. Performance management/evaluation system

26. Strategic Change Leadership Steering Committee/Quality Management Boards

27. Annual strategic review and update

1. Cell (as in the cells that make up our physical bodies)

2. Organ (lungs, heart, kidneys, etc.)

3. Organism (humans, animals, fish, birds, etc.)

4. Group (teams, departments, strategic business units)

5. Organization (private, public, not-for-profit)

6. Society (German, French, American, Indonesian, etc.)

7. Supranational system (Western, Asian, Communist, global, etc.)

These seven levels of different living systems demonstrate that *each system impacts every other system and that there is a hierarchy of systems within systems.* What is a system or a department or category to you is only a piece of an organizational system. It also illustrates what is probably the single most important feature of any system: *its performance as a whole is affected by every one of its parts.* When viewed from an organizational perspective, the concept of a systems framework really does constitute a total reinvention of the ways in which we think and do business. It literally creates an environment in which all systems and subsystems are linked together to achieve the overall organizational system (or vision).

CASCADE OF PLANNING

Once your organization has a strategic plan in place, how do you keep it going successfully? How do you keep up the energy, momentum, and focus of your plan throughout all the multiple systems levels that make up your organization? In light of the General Systems Theory, this is a crucial question. One of its principles is that the minute a system is born (or set in place), it begins to die. This is the principle of *entropy,* and it is in direct opposition to the principle of continuous improvement. In entropy, there exists the natural phenomenon of incremental degradation which eventually causes every system to slowly run down. If this is not immediately clear, try not eating or sleeping for two to three days; you'll definitely experience entropy.

This is where the Cascade of Planning (Figure 4.2) comes in. By designing a framework for your strategic plan that automatically includes every level of your organization, you have a built-in protection against entropy. One way to view this is in terms of your organization having at least three levels of systems—individual, group, and organization—which requires you to "cascade" your planning and change down through each level. It is the only way your strategic management system can continue to move the plan forward and perpetuate its success.

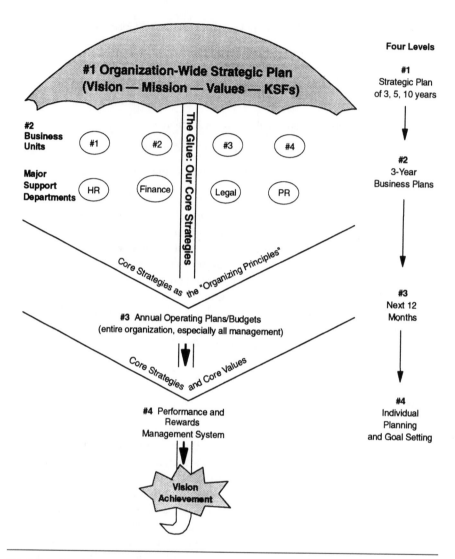

FIGURE 4.2   The Cascade of Planning: Strategic Consistency Yet Operational Flexibility

If you recognize that all the levels of your organization (departments, units, and people) must work together to align the system's output of serving the customer, you are well on your way to success. In addition, the Cascade of Planning ascertains that planning needs to be conducted for every part of the organization on two levels: (1) the strategic planning level and (2) the annual planning level.

Strategic Planning Levels

1. **Organization-wide strategic planning:** You need an organization-wide three-, five-, or ten-year strategic plan, defining the organization's vision, mission, core values, and key success factors, along with the core strategies for achieving them (the organizational level is Level #5 of living systems).

2. **Business unit strategic planning:** This is often called a business plan. You need a three-year business plan for each business unit, major program area, and major support department within the organization. (This is the fourth level of the seven levels of living systems.)

Annual Planning Levels

3. **Annual plans for all departments/functional units:** Annual operating plans are needed over the next 12 months (and budgets, too) for all parts of the entire organization. (This is also Level #4 of the seven levels of living systems.)

4. **Individual plans, goals, and objectives:** Individual plans are needed to show how each employee intends to accomplish the goals he or she must meet in order to carry out the organization-wide strategic plan. You also need to revise your performance appraisals, basing them on core strategies (results) and core values (behaviors). (This is the individual level or Level #3 of the seven levels of living systems.)

The Cascade of Planning also takes into account the fit that must exist between each of the interacting levels of the system that make up the organization. It does this by using the organization-wide core strategies as the "glue," or organizing principles, for the two levels of systems, group, and individual. This helps to establish the mindset of the organization around thinking about the core strategies needed to successfully carry out the plan. This, in turn, creates a critical mass for the desired change.

Questions to Ponder

1. Do you understand the specific steps in strategic planning, as well as how they relate to the systems model?

> **2.** Have you included the Cascade of Planning as a part of your strategic management process to ensure it is cascaded down from the organizational level to three-year plans for business units and major staff support units? Also, do you have 12-month annual departmental plans and individual goal setting?
>
> **3.** Do you understand what planning documents and performance appraisal format you need?

FIFTEEN COMMON MISTAKES IN STRATEGIC MANAGEMENT

Even the most dedicated, organized, or systems-oriented CEO is susceptible to mistakes. Even if your strategic plan is based on well-defined, common-sense systems or backwards thinking, the processes involved in planning and implementation are complex. Typical mistakes include the following.

Mistake #1: Failing to Integrate Planning at All Three Levels

Throughout my years in strategic management, I've lost count of the times I have gone into a situation where no previous plans included this type of integration. Whether or not an organization has a concise, well-thought-out strategic plan, it will almost always fails to cascade the plan down to the three levels (and four necessary documents) previously mentioned.

Mistake #2: Keeping Planning Separate from Day-to-Day Management

The most common mistake in public and private organizations is that people treat strategic planning as a process separate from management rather than as a way to reinvent the way we do business day to day. If done at all, strategic planning is probably treated as an exercise in planning, something to put behind you so you can get back to your "real work."

Mistake #3: Conducting Long-Range Forecasting Only

Another extremely common mistake that almost always results in strategic planning failure is long-range financial forecasting. This is where you begin with the present and project a straight line out into the future. Although some people view this as strategic planning, it is nothing more than budget projections. Oil companies suffered from this immensely in the 1970s, when everyone thought the price of a barrel of crude oil would go from $32 to $80. It never did (it is roughly $18 per barrel at the time of this writing).

Mistake #4: Taking a "Scattershot" Approach

This encompasses a failure to educate and organize yourself first, running off before you know how to successfully complete and implement the plan. Action-oriented firms often make this error.

Mistake #5: Developing Vision/Mission/Values Statements that Are Little More than "Fluff"

Many organizational development practitioners and planners have helped CEOs see the need for these documents. However, they do not know how to help you go any further and actually use the vision/values. If you, as an executive, really want to lose all your credibility with your employees, this is an excellent way to do so. Making up the statements and putting them out for all to see but failing to take them seriously is certain to make you look foolish in the eyes of your staff. Unsophisticated executives who merely follow the current fads are uniquely prone to this mistake.

Mistake #6: Having Only Yearly Weekend Retreats

In the past, the typical organizational approach to planning might have been to set aside a weekend for a yearly retreat for top management and/or board members at some luxury resort. During this time, which includes extensive and expensive social time, organizational leaders and planners more often than not develop a slick, sophisticated planning document. However, this is not a plan designed to be implemented. It just has to look good—all form and no substance. This approach was quite prevalent during the 1980s, especially with the Federal Home Loan Bank Board among organizations—and the result of the savings and loan debacle are apparent.

Mistake #7: Failing to Complete an Effective Implementation Process

One problem during the implementation stage arises after an organization develops an excellent strategic planning document. However, the organization may fail to set in place a Strategic Change Steering Committee responsible for initiating and maintaining implementation of the plan. Organizations in the not-for-profit sector, such as schools and governmental agencies, need to be especially aware of this potential pitfall.

Mistake #8: Violating the "People Support What They Help Create" Principle

Another problem arises when the planning process neglects the necessary involvement of key stakeholders (other than top management). This leaves the key stakeholders with a "not-invented-here" mentality, with no real understanding of the plan and, therefore, no comprehension of what is expected of them in implementating it. This is a mistake often found in private sector organizations that have control-oriented CEOs.

Mistake #9: Conducting Business as Usual

One of the most common failures in strategic planning is for the planning team to approach the job with a "business as usual" mentality, basing the entire plan strictly on how business is done today. This is often the result of starting strategic planning at Point C (the input side of the system) rather than Point A (the output side). Larger, established bureaucratic organizations often fall victim to this error. The result is the all-too-familiar SPOTS syndrome.

Mistake #10: Failing to "Make the Tough Choices"

This begins by taking a "tell 'em what they wanna hear" approach and often leads organizations straight into the failure to take a stand and make the tough choices. Some executives would rather be polite to each other than be effective through real dialogue and give-and-take. This is conflict avoidance at its worst. Some of our nicest, and largest, bureaucratic organizations and good corporate citizens are especially prone to this error in the form of being *too* polite. The key is *focus, focus, focus!*

Mistake #11: Lacking a Scoreboard

If the methods for measuring organizational success are not clearly defined up front, progress will be virtually impossible to determine. Unless key success factors (beyond financials) are established, the plan isn't worth the paper it was printed on. People are often tempted to measure what is easy (activities) instead of what is important (outcomes). For example, do you have regular, ongoing surveys of customer and employee satisfaction? If not, why? Companies that are not customer focused often fail to see the importance of a scoreboard that includes anything except financial numbers.

Mistake #12: Failing to Define Business Units or Major Program Areas in a Meaningful Way

Many organizations either fail to define their strategic business units in a meaningful way or initially gloss over this area, thinking they can always come back to it later. They never do; it is a losing proposition from the very beginning. Failure to differentiate between your business or reason for existence versus your staff support areas results in conflict and turf battles. Too many organizations are structured in such a hodgepodge way that the focus on the business (and the customer) is almost impossible to find.

Mistake #13: Neglecting to Benchmark Yourself vs. the Competition

One of the most common mistakes in strategic planning is in isolating your organization from its competitive environment. Without a specific sense of your competitors' best practices and market share, as well as strengths and weaknesses, it is impossible to know what to strive for or what your own competitive business advantage is. If you continually fail to be open and learn from others, your organization will soon fall victim to the "know-it-all" syndrome. The arrogance and ignorance some private sector executives show in disregarding this key area is astounding.

Mistake #14: Seeing the Planning Document as an End in Itself

Remember, the document is not the objective; it is only Goal #1. If this is a problem in your organization, you need to put Goal #2, implementation and sustaining high performance, back into your realm of thinking. Until recently, Goal #2 has not even been a part of the planning literature most executives read. Goal #2 must be viewed as the only true goal.

Mistake #15: Using Unclear or Confusing Terminology and Language

While this was mentioned in previous chapters, it bears repeating here: sometimes the English language tends to confuse rather than clarify. In strategic planning, it may be difficult to understand the difference between *means* and *ends*. As you attempt to establish a hierarchy of terms in your organization, the real meaning and level of importance of these concepts can be obscured by the use of similar descriptors such as "goals" or "objectives." (For example, just by looking at them, can you determine which of these descriptors is the higher order?)

Well-read private sector executives are especially prone to picking up the latest fads or terminology and using them independently, without regard to how they integrate or fit into the overall organizational system.

As illustrated in Figure 4.3, using the A,B,C,D framework is a much more effective way to clarify that the vision and mission will be the ultimate end or your desired outcomes. Your primary means to that end will be your core

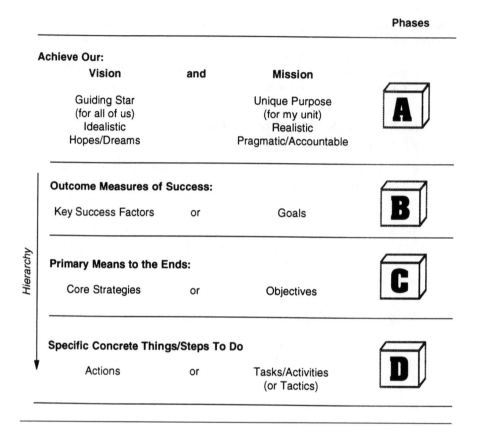

Achieve Our:

Vision	and	Mission
Guiding Star		Unique Purpose
(for all of us)		(for my unit)
Idealistic		Realistic
Hopes/Dreams		Pragmatic/Accountable

A

Outcome Measures of Success:

Key Success Factors   or   Goals

B

Primary Means to the Ends:

Core Strategies   or   Objectives

C

Specific Concrete Things/Steps To Do

Actions   or   Tasks/Activities (or Tactics)

D

Hierarchy

FIGURE 4.3 Ends–Outputs–Outcomes–Results

strategies, and your key success factors will be the quantifiers by which you measure success.

FIFTEEN KEY BENEFITS OF A STRATEGIC MANAGEMENT SYSTEM

Many organizations have overcome these mistakes and followed through by implementing their strategic planning successfully. Those that have fully implemented their strategic plan have uniformly seen vast improvement in the achievement of their primary outcomes.

Primary Bottom-Line Outcomes

1. Increased market share

2. Increase in stock price

3. Improved profitability and cash flow

4. Much more satisfied customers as a result of added value (quality, service, responsiveness, etc.)

5. Increased employee satisfaction

In addition to these primary bottom-line outcomes, other key benefits culled from the responses of these organizations over a period of time are as follows.

Benefit #1: Taking a Proactive Approach

This enables you to have a proactive adaptation to a changing global world, marketplace, and turbulent business environment, which increases the probability of both the healthy, long-term viability of the organization and job security for your executives and employees.

Benefit #2: Building an Executive Team

Strategic management enables your executive team to learn to function as a highly effective team in their own right. This modeling of cross-functional or horizontal teamwork is key to successful implementation.

Benefit #3: An Intensive Executive Development Experience

Strategic planning is also one of the most intense executive development and orientation processes a new or aspiring executive could ever experience.

Benefit #4: Quantifiable Outcome Measures of Success

Phase B, key success factors, enables your organization to develop a focused set of quantifiable outcome measures of success, including customer and employee satisfaction. These become the way to measure your success year after year.

Benefit #5: Intelligent Strategic Budgeting Decisions

Implementing your strategic plan in an organization-wide systems framework encourages organizational focus and priority setting to determine precision (i.e., strategic) budget cuts during tough economic times.

Benefit #6: Clarifying Your Competitive Advantage

It helps you clarify your competitive business advantage by providing a more thorough analysis of success factors, environmental influences, and core strategies.

Benefit #7: Reducing Conflict and Empowering People

It reduces or focuses conflict by providing a clear sense of direction with all parts of your organization as a system working together, focusing on the customer.

Benefit #8: Clear Guidelines for Daily Decisions

A constructive, visionary basis is provided for daily decisions throughout your organization, which makes it easier to set priorities for what to do and what not to do.

Benefit #9: Creating a Critical Mass for Change

Everyone involved as a key stakeholder has the opportunity to help create your organization's future, rather than being overwhelmed by the uncertainties of change. Remember, "people support what they help create."

Benefit #10: "Singing from the Same Hymnal"

Your leadership can clearly communicate organizational goals and core values to everyone. This enables everyone to "get on the same wavelength" and align their personal values and professional goals with the direction of your organization. This is essential for every firm, as today's employees have a great ability to provide or withhold their "discretionary effort."

Benefit #11: Clarifying and Simplifying Management Techniques

Strategic management enables you, other senior executives, and employees alike to make sense out of the confusion that results from the many different ideas and solutions coming from the proliferation of management books today. While many authors are convinced that they are providing the best answers, some of these answers are in conflict.

Benefit #12: Empowering Middle Managers

The A,B,C,D systems framework enables middle managers to conduct this process successfully within their own departments, even in organizations where no strategic planning is taking place.

Benefit #13: Focus, Focus, Focus

By having everything you do fit strategically within the same overall framework, employees are able to continually focus on the desired outcome and set their day-to-day priorities accordingly.

Benefit #14: Speeding Up Implementation

The ability to clarify and simplify strategic management within the systems framework will always speed up actual implementation. It becomes easier for you to identify problem areas and take action.

Benefit #15: Tools for Dealing with Stress

Your organization can provide your employees with the necessary direction to battle the stress of uncertainty in ongoing, revolutionary change. Everyone in your organization will feel better equipped to focus on, understand, and address issues within this overall context

In Summary

It is now abundantly clear to anyone still in business these days: what worked before will not work now. The traditional, time-consuming method of analyzing and solving one problem at a time has given way to the sweeping and sometimes obliterating winds of revolutionary change. A fresh new approach is called for, one that can set in place a framework sturdy enough to withstand the ongoing complexities of change.

Long-term success can only come from a systems approach. It alleviates most common mistakes and provides numerous benefits. In the coming chapters, a step-by-step guide through strategic management with a systems framework will be procided, beginning with Step #1, Plan-to-Plan.

RECAP OF KEY POINTS

- Viewing your organization as having at least three levels—individual, group, and organization—you will need to "cascade" your planning and change management down to all levels.

- Strategic planning should lead the way in integrating many of today's organizational change fads and concepts, such as TQM, business process reengineering, empowerment, and customer service.

- Which of the fifteen strategic management mistakes have you made?

1. Failing to integrate planning at all levels
2. Keeping planning separate from day-to-day management
3. Conducting long-range forecasting only
4. Having a scattershot approach to planning
5. Developing vision, mission, and value statements that are little more than fluff
6. Having yearly weekend retreats as your only planning activity
7. Failing to complete an effective implementation process
8. Violating the "people support what they help create" principle
9. Conducting business as usual after strategic planning
10. Failing to make the "tough choices"
11. Lacking a scoreboard; measuring what's easy instead of what's important
12. Failing to define strategic business units in a meaningful way
13. Neglecting to benchmark yourself against the competition
14. Seeing the planning document as an end in itself
15. Using confusing terminology and language

PART II

DEVELOPING A STRATEGIC PLAN: STEP-BY-STEP

CHAPTER 5

PLAN-TO-PLAN (STEP #1) (PHASE A: OUTPUT)

We never have time to do it right the first time,
*but we **always** have time to do it over.*

PLAN-TO-PLAN STEP #1:
ASSESSING, EDUCATING, AND ORGANIZING

The above quote is never more true than when applied to the art and science of strategic planning. Because the purpose of strategic planning is to develop and to implement a strategic plan through a strategic change management system that will cause your organization to grow and profit, it is something you definitely want to get right the first time. If you don't, you have polluted the organizational environment for good planning and management to the extent that it is usually years before it is ever attempted again.

In the Reinvented Strategic Planning Model for the 21st Century, getting it right the first time is what Step #1: Plan-to-Plan is all about. Another old maxim that perfectly describes this step is *"look before you leap."* As mentioned in the previous chapter, one of the most common mistakes planners make is running off to make the plan before "educating and organizing" themselves on precisely what needs and issues are critical to their organization and before properly organizing the effort. In failing to "engineer" the success of the planning and implementing up front (*before* you begin), you have set yourself up for failure before even starting.

ENGINEERING SUCCESS UP FRONT

Plan-to-Plan includes setting up your core planning team, along with the concept of a parallel process that involves key stakeholders. It also clarifies top management's role in leading, developing, and owning the strategic plan.

You often only get one shot at this type of planning. Done wrong, it can often result in long-term resentment, during which your plan will continue to weaken and ultimately go downhill.

Example

A good example of this was an initial meeting on strategic planning in 1989 to implement the strategic plan, called the Quality Network, for a $1 billion division of General Motors. (The Quality Network is a total quality process developed organization-wide at General Motors.)

In the middle of the meeting, the facilitator got so angry and frustrated with the various disagreements among joint union–management executives that he threw up his hands and quit, leaving the meeting. Needless to say, the meeting quickly deteriorated and was soon called to a halt. It was over four years before that same collective leadership got together to finally begin their Plan-to-Plan step and implement their strategic plan.

Avoiding this pitfall is what the Plan-to-Plan step is all about. There are a number of specific tasks (listed below) that you can follow in order to successfully complete this step.

SOME INITIAL STEPS IN PLAN-TO-PLAN

The Plan-to-Plan step is really pretty straightforward, once you know how and where to get started. The following are several steps that can be helpful in initiating this step.

#1. Conduct a Strategic/Organizational Assessment

Conduct an overall assessment of your entire organization and where it stands currently. What kind of strategies (if any) are you currently following? Are they still valid or do they need to be reassessed and worked into your new strategic plan? Try to get the most realistic overview possible of your organization.

#2. Establish Your Internal Support Cadre

This is where capacity building comes in. Keep in mind that no matter what your strategic plan entails, you will need to engineer your organization's capacity for support, persistence, and coordination by real people over a long period of time. Think this facet through, and select and assign those individuals who will be accountable for this process.

#3. Conduct an Executive Team-Building and Visionary Leadership Practices Workshop

Even before the capacity building just mentioned, you should conduct a leadership workshop to build motivation within your executives. The leadership skills issue is absolutely essential to the success of any organization in strategic management.

There has been a quantum change in the roles of executives in the 1990s. In addition, the list in Table 5.1 was compiled from extensive research by myself and a colleague in 1990. However, in order to boil all this down to a useful leadership skills program for the 1990s, it comes down to the three skills mentioned earlier: trainer, coach, and facilitator. The key here is not knowledge alone. The key is the skills and attitudes of today's leaders: their willingness to learn, to be open to feedback, to accept responsibility, and, above all, to change.

Many authors have written whole books on this area. The key, however, is to set up a structured leadership skills development and practices process right away, even before strategic planning. You must build the capacity of the organization's senior management to successfully implement the strategic plans they design.

#4. Plan-to-Plan Off-Site Day A.M.: Executive Briefing—The Educating Task

The Plan-to-Plan off-site day prepares your organization for Goal #1: developing your strategic plan. The first stage in the Plan-to-Plan off-site is an executive briefing for senior management and other key stakeholders. This is a crucial part of the process, because it is one in which your organization's CEO, executive directors, and senior management more fully understand strategic management and all its pitfalls, mistakes, and benefits. It is also where the systems model for Reinvented Strategic Planning for the 21st Century is explained, discussed, and bought into as a practical common-sense approach to success.

The executive briefing generally requires a half day. Depending on the complexities of your particular issues, however, you may feel that you need more or less time to devote to this preparatory planning step.

TABLE 5.1   The Changing Role of the Manager

1.* Process management skills
2.* Facilitator and coordinator skills
3.* Group process, dynamics skills
4.* Managing group performance skills
5.* Team-building skills
6.* Managing key stakeholders
7. Systemic orientation to work/strategic thinking
8.* Coaching skills (counseling, mentoring, tutoring, confronting)
9. Diagnostic skills
10.* Managing change skills
11.* Influence/persuasion vs. authoritarian skills
12.* Negotiation skills (win–win)
13. Computer literacy skills
14. Tools to enhance communication
15.* Self-knowledge and awareness/modeling
16.* Self-confidence/flexibility in dealing with uncertainty
17. Selection/promotional skills
18.* Leadership (and management) skills
19.* Innovative/resourceful/creative (with less) skills
20.* Participative and consensus management skills/open to involvement
21.* Skills in enabling, empowering, involving employees
22.* Managing/leading a diverse work force
23.* Developing employees/enhancing self-esteem

* = all these skills require some form of self-management/discipline in interpersonal relationships vs. positional authority.

Source: Barry Leskin and Steve Haines, 1990.

#5. Plan-to-Plan Off-Site Day P.M.: The Organizing Tasks

The Plan-to-Plan off-site also needs to include a half day or so devoted to completing a series of organizing tasks to properly set up the planning process. These tasks include:

- Identifying who your key stakeholders are
- Designing a parallel process for key stakeholder involvement/ commitment

- Organizing and committing the planning effort and team to its success

- Feeding back the strategic/organizational assessment to the leadership team

- Developing a "strategic issues" list to help guide the planning content

- Examining ongoing communication, leadership, and team-building skills

- Identifying potential barriers to the planning process

- Linking your strategic planning sequence to your annual planning/budget sequence and to your performance management system

- Defining the level of environmental scanning you will need to stimulate your strategic planning process properly

Finally, this Plan-to-Plan day should include a summary of the day. This is the time for senior management, key stakeholders, and the CEO to "get behind" the plan, educating, organizing, and committing themselves as the driving force behind the strategic plan and change management system and making sure they are all "singing from the same hymnal." Also, this is the point at which your executive team should have uniquely tailored the strategic plan to fit your particular organization.

Questions to Ponder

1. Have you conducted an executive briefing so that all top executives in your organization are in sync with the strategic management process?

2. Is your CEO committed to and actively leading the planning process or has it been delegated?

3. Are you willing to take the time to get organized before you begin, or are you tackling a planning activity without thinking it through first?

4. Have you begun your capacity building with executive team-building/leadership skills, including an internal support cadre?

The details of each organizing task are as follow.

Organizing Task #1: Determining the Entity to Plan For

Following the executive briefing, the first task in the Plan-to-Plan organizing time frame is to determine the precise entity for which you are planning. While this may seem simple or obvious to many in the private sector, failing to do so is an all-too-common mistake in strategic planning. In the public sector, for instance, people frequently try to create a strategic plan for curing health care for an entire geographic area or county. This is not realistic; instead, it would be better to plan for an entity such as the county department of health and define what its role should be in accounting for that particular area's health system. Do not take responsibility for what is far beyond what you can control. (Besides, the theory that Big Government should take care of society's ills doesn't make sense in the first place, because it is a dependency relationship.)

For some, the entity to plan for will be obvious; a large corporation, a city, or an entire school district are good examples of obvious entities. It is also possible, however, to conduct strategic planning for a strategic business unit (such as General Motors' North American operations or its Cadillac division) or a major support area (such as the finance department of a large corporation). Ideally, this corporation would have its overall strategic plan completed first, but there are many instances in which it is appropriate (though a bit more difficult) to plan for an entity that is a single piece of the larger whole. The key here is to make certain that any entity you select is specific, with well-defined boundaries.

Organizing Task #2: Identifying Strategic Issues

Plan-to-Plan is a critical step because it is the time you set aside for creative brainstorming *before the planning begins.* It is a time to identify the strategic issues that are pivotal to your organization, and it is important to get input from all your executive stakeholders. You will get many different opinions, and that is exactly what you want at this point. You want everyone who has a stake in your organization's strategic plan to bring his or her own list to the table. Use both (1) the strategic/organizational assessment and (2) the team-building/leadership training as input to this step.

After this has happened, it is not atypical to find that you have a pool of as many as 30 to 50 issues on the table. Keep in mind, however, that this is only a brainstorming list to be used as a checklist to keep your strategic plan practical throughout. However, because there are no limits on your executives' imaginations during this part of the process, the resulting lists are often quite enlightening.

Organizing Task #3: Examining Personal Readiness and Concerns

Throughout this chapter, the importance of enthusiasm and commitment on the part of your senior executives will continually be emphasized. This is a critical aspect; in fact, I have never seen a strategic planning and change management process succeed without it.

The top members of your collective leadership must be personally ready and committed to your strategic management process. This task requires them to focus on their personal readiness and to determine what exactly they want to see happen as a result of this process.

Start by asking each of your executives to list their three to five most important concerns about conducting a strategic management process. Then ask them to specifically describe what prework or other actions should be taken to cope with those concerns before beginning planning. It can also be helpful to start this task by requesting that your executives define what it is they might fear about setting this process in motion. In Plan-to-Plan, it is just as important to examine negative impact as it is to address the positive side of strategic management.

Tip: "Skeptics Are My Best Friends." At this point, don't shy away from resistance from any individual, even if he or she is negative or skeptical. At times during strategic management, skeptics can actually be your best friends. They are more willing to bring up the more unpopular areas that others are either too reserved or too conservative to broach.

Organizing Task #4: Addressing Potential Barriers/Mistakes in the Planning Process

This is where you get additional organizational problem areas in strategic planning out on the table, so that your executives and stakeholders can address them collectively. In this task, it is important to ask:

1. What problems have you had in past strategic planning efforts as an organization?

2. What potential barriers/mistakes do you think exist or will happen that will prevent us from doing future strategic planning in an effective way?

A list of the most common mistakes to effective strategic planning in organizations is provided in Chapter 4.

Once you have gathered a working list of potential mistakes/barriers, you can get to work on problem-solving them now, up front—*before* you begin the actual plan—so that they do not come back to haunt you and derail your plan at a later date.

It is also important to assess your organization's current level of effectiveness in strategic planning. In my research on and implementation of strategic planning over the years, I have observed ten levels of planning effectiveness, under three types of organizational cultures: (1) reactive, (2) traditional, and (3) proactive.

Determine where your organization fits into the ten-point scale on the chart illustrated in Figure 5.1. If you are too low, that may very well be one of your biggest potential barriers to strategic planning. Resolving this now will save you numerous headaches later.

Organizing Task #5: Environmental Scanning

To make sure you are not trying to create your strategic plan in a vacuum, you will need to conduct an environmental scanning process on a regular basis. For instance, if you are planning out to the year 2000, it will be helpful to scan the environment to see what is and what will potentially be happening over the next seven years.

It is useful to focus on the SKEPTIC factors when beginning environmental scanning. In general terms, "S" represents socio-demographic scanning, "K" stands for your (k)competitors, "E" stands for scanning the economic and employee environments, "P" is for political, "T" represents technology, "I" is for industry, and "C" represents the customers.

Whether they choose the SKEPTIC formula as a general guideline or create their own unique environmental scanning formula, the planning team should examine what the future might hold, especially in such a dynamic and revolutionary changing environment.

Remember that by trying to create a strategic plan in a vacuum, with no real facts and figures on the environmental changes you can expect, you will end up with just one more strategic plan that is worth nothing more than the paper on which it is printed.

Organizing Task #6: Tailoring Your Strategic Plan

It's probably a safe bet that you have done some form of strategic planning before, whether a vision/mission/values statement, analyses of your organization's current state, etc. You may have already put a lot of thought and effort into a vision statement, for example, but have not yet developed a measurement system to know whether or not you have factually achieved your vision.

If this is the case in your organization, it does not make sense for you to blindly adhere to each step of the Reinvented Strategic Planning Model. Rather, you should *always* tailor it to fit your own needs by assessing what you already have, and come to mutual consensus with your planning team on which steps will require greater time and effort.

At this point, the planning team should carefully review the list in Table

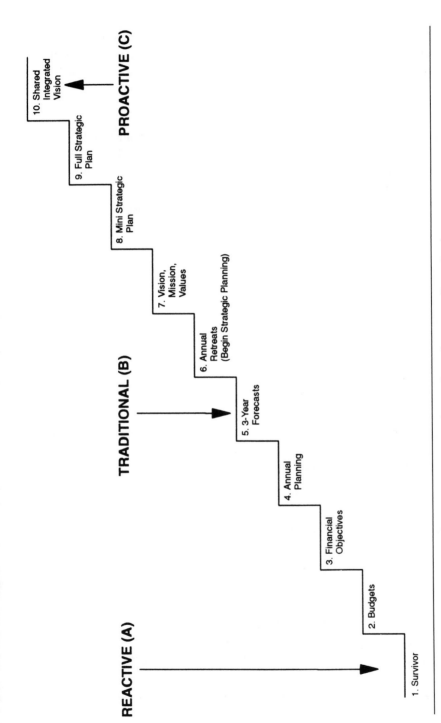

FIGURE 5.1 Levels of Planning Effectiveness Toward a High-Performance Organization

5.2 and prioritize each line item in terms of its level of importance for you to spend time on in your strategic planning process (based on a high/medium/low scale). See Table 5.2, along with an example of how it would appear filled out.

TABLE 5.2   Reinventing Strategic Planning Tailored to Your Needs

Based on your current understanding of strategic planning, list the importance of now developing each deliverable for your organization.

Importance (H-M-L) of Potential Deliverables

1. _____ Environmental scanning system
2. _____ Vision
3. _____ Mission
4. _____ Values
5. _____ Driving force(s)
6. _____ Rallying cry
7. _____ Key success factors
8. _____ Current stage assessment
9. _____ Core strategies
10. _____ SBUs/MPAs defined
11. _____ Business/key support plans (3-year mini strategic plans)
12. _____ Annual plans/priorities/department plans
13. _____ Resource allocation/budgeting (including guidelines)
14. _____ Individual performance management system
15. _____ Reward and recognition system
16. _____ Plan-to-Implement

Focus on the Four Vital Few:

17. _____ A. Quality products and services
18. _____ B. Organization structure/redesign
19. _____ C. Business process reengineering to create the desired organization (customer focused)
20. _____ D. Sound professional management and leadership practices
21. _____ Skills built through workshop on managing strategic change
22. _____ Annual strategic review and update

Organizing Task #7: Linking Strategic Planning to Your Budget

This should be simple, obvious logic. Your organization's vision and the strategic planning for that vision is what drives your budget, not vice versa. Right? You would be amazed at how few organizations really *get* this concept and how many actually let the budget set their planning boundaries. This is one of the ways that business as usual is perpetuated.

One of the key reasons for strategic planning is to create a tension and conflict between your future vision and the resources you need to complete key tasks to achieve it versus your current way of allocating your budget. This tension and "gap" in resources is what can motivate you to make the hard choices in terms of how you spend your budget—either on past, obsolete activities or future-oriented priorities.

Another critical mistake many organizations make at this point is not allowing an appropriate span of time for the integration of planning into budgeting.

Tip: Putting your strategic management system in place is a long-term effort. Looking at it realistically, it often will require as much as two annual budgeting cycles before it is fully coordinated and implemented.

The executive members of your planning team need to lay out a specific time line for when and how the strategic plan will be linked to the budget.

Organizing Task #8: Identifying Key Stakeholders

This is one of the key tasks in the Plan-to-Plan step. If purposely utilized, your key stakeholders will actually become the primary supporters and cheerleaders for the implementation of your strategic management system on an ongoing basis. A stakeholder is defined as "any group or individual who affects or is affected by the organization's strategic plan."

Most organizations make the mistake of assuming that only top management can perform as their strategic plans' stakeholders. Because organizations exist in a complex system, however, it is virtually impossible for senior executives to monitor what is happening at every level. In order to implement the organization's strategic plan at every level, therefore, you will need to involve stakeholders both inside and outside the organization that bring different vantage points to the table. Members of middle management absolutely need to be involved, but it is also crucial to involve the employee's point of view, as well as customers, union representatives, and even suppliers. In some instances, it may be important to include members of special interest groups as well. Once you have selected your list of stakeholders, then identify the top five to seven stakeholders in terms of importance to the success of your plan and fully involve them in the planning and change processes.

Organizing Task #9: Planning Team Membership

Once you have identified the key stakeholders for your strategic plan, you are ready to build the planning team. At this point, keep in mind that *people support what they help create.* The first, most obvious group of people who have to support implementation is the top management team; they will form the "core" of the planning team.

Next, you'll have to consider the size of the planning team. A typical top management team in a medium-sized organization may consist of six to eight executives. (Another thing to keep in mind is that in addition to their peer members, these executives must feel comfortable with every other member of the planning team as well.) Although research on effective group dynamics indicates that keeping the total group at 6 to 8 members is preferable, my experience has shown me that you can double that size to around 14 or 15 and still have a reasonably effective team. Beyond 15, however, you no longer have a planning team—you have a mob.

If you have eight people on the top management team, you could conceivably seed the rest of the team membership with an additional six or seven from your key stakeholder list. You may want to select an up-and-coming middle manager, and use this as an executive development experience. You could also select a key worker and informed leader who is strongly committed to the plan's implementation or someone more on the fringe who can act as a stimulating resource and bring a different perspective into the mix. You could also choose a union leader, a retired businessperson, a supplier or vendor, or even a customer.

Core Planning Team Composition

- Sense of clear direction
- Ownership and commitment—senior/middle-level management
- Data reality—key players
- Stakeholders—key to broad perspective
- Helps implementation—key players
- Staff support team
- Leader preference/comfort

In any case, composition and involvement of the planning team is the first place you will begin to make tough choices. It is important to be selective, not only in terms of the size of the team, but also in terms of conceptual and strategic abilities, as well as diversity and commitment to your organization's strategic management system.

For example: You might consider the eligibility of having a union executive on your team. However, unless he or she has full commitment to your organization's strategic plan, rather than an overriding loyalty to the union's mission alone, it might make better sense to include that individual as a key stakeholder rather than as a member of the planning team. If you are on the planning team, you are *not* there as a representative of a constituency, but as a member committed to the organization's overall vision and mission.

Organizing Task #10: Assigning Planning Staff Support Roles

Your planning team must also include individuals who can play a supportive (and process) role to the leadership, so they can concentrate on the content and strategies of the strategic plan. Generally speaking, these support persons do not count as members of the planning team, since they are expected to focus on the process instead of the content. There are instances, however, in which these individuals would also naturally be a part of the planning team anyway.

For many organizations, these support and process roles can make the difference between the success or failure of the strategic plan. You will still need individuals who are responsible for the myriad of details involved in the planning and change management process, mechanics, and logistics. These individuals are necessary to (1) ensure that the day-to-day planning and change process linkages occur and (2) develop the internal organizational capability for ongoing development and institutionalization of the strategic management system as the new way to run the business day to day.

To start, the planning team will need at least one person in the room (usually an administrative assistant) who takes care of the minutes and logistics of each meeting, lunches, and distributing the "to do" lists and strategic planning drafts that will be an ongoing result of all the meetings.

A second and critical role that needs to be assigned at this time is that of an internal coordinator/facilitator of the entire strategic management system process. This should be someone who is concerned mainly with the process of the plan rather than someone who is a member of the senior management team and has a high stake in the content of the plan. Therefore, those executives in planning, finance, human resources, etc. who are on the senior management team cannot be an objective or effective facilitator of the planning process. This overall role should include facilitating parallel process meetings, coordinating the Strategic Change Steering Committee, developing other internal consultants, and assisting with annual and three-year departmental and strategic business unit planning.

In addition, the planning team will probably need to call on other individual members for specific support resources. For example, one of the members of your planning team may be a vice-president of finance, so when you begin to develop the financial data and budgeting based on the strategic plan, you would look to that individual for supporting advice, input, and coordination. This person also often coordinates the overall key success factors.

Another need could be from your organization's vice-president of human resources, who is also a part of your core planning team. He or she would also serve as the team's support person in the area of staffing, personnel support, and rewards systems concerns. This person often handles communications as well.

Tip: Bear in mind that these support roles are not always meant to be full-time jobs. However, they do become permanent parts of regular jobs. They exist so that the planning team has resources that will help link them to the various parts of the organization.

Organizing Task #11: Selecting an External Strategic Planning Facilitator

In addition to the internal coordinator/facilitator, you will need an external professional strategic planning facilitator to conduct your strategic planning process. The fact is that no matter how skilled or experienced your internal facilitator may be, his or her ultimate loyalties lay within the confines of the organization; after all, this person's paycheck comes from you! His or her ability to be neutral, to challenge, and to play devil's advocate with senior management (including their own boss) is usually quite suspect. He or she also usually lacks the breadth and depth of a professional strategic planning facilitator.

Tip: In fact, most experienced organizational development practitioners can still only facilitate about 75% of the planning process effectively. In my personal experience, I have seen numerous instances where these professionals cannot navigate serious business and conflict issues to a consensus and closure among strong-willed and opinionated senior executives. While they can do an excellent job with the vision/mission/values step, they get lost beyond that point.

Particularly in the strategic planning phase, you will be dealing with sensitive issues and looking at some very tough choices. The professional strategic planning facilitator has no personal stake in any of these issues and is trained to keep the process moving, resolve conflict, and methodically work through each tough choice. He or she should be equipped to play devil's advocate and push for concrete decisions, directions, and priorities. An external facilitator is better able to challenge you and confront key issues if you back away from your desired outcomes.

In choosing an external strategic planning facilitator, look for someone who has the following seven qualifications:

1. A strong business, economic, and industry orientation

2. Expertise in strategic management and project management

3. An excellent sense of overall organization fit, functioning, and design

4. Understanding of group dynamics and human behavior

5. Knowledge of large-scale change and transition management

6. Consulting steps and facilitator/process/meeting management skills

7. Strong internal sense of self, ego, and self-esteem

Tip: In short, an external facilitator must have the maturity and wisdom to consciously act in a "loose–tight" fashion so as to guide (but not intrude).

One of the last key reasons for having an external professional strategic planning facilitator is to assist in developing your strong internal staff support team. A good facilitator should be capable of showing your internal team how to facilitate the planning process and actually develop the knowledge and skills to handle the change management process internally.

Organizing Task #12: Initiating a Parallel Process

Trust is a big part of successful change.
The way you build trust
is by practicing the politics of inclusion.

David Osborne

The key stakeholders you have identified are all a part of your planning community. They do not all play the same role, however. Some are part of the core planning team, while others play an adjunct or input role that lies within the parallel process (Figure 5.2). In this process, it becomes obvious why your community of key stakeholders is so essential to the success of the plan.

In the parallel process, the planning team sends each document they draft out for review by the larger key stakeholder community. Invariably, those stakeholders will have recommendations for the inclusion or exclusion of certain points. Once the planning team has incorporated this feedback into the document, they are ready to prepare a final draft. In this way, the key stakeholders act in a sort of "check-and-balance" input role to the planning team, reacting from a different perspective.

Parallel process meetings should have a twofold purpose: (1) key stakeholders give their input and feedback to the core planning team in order to improve the quality and direction of the document and (2) to ensure that each

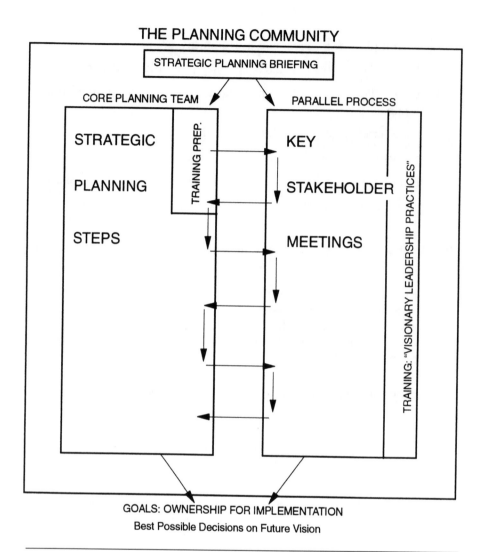

FIGURE 5.2   Parallel Process

document reads clearly and can be understood by everyone in the organization, thus increasing the ownership and commitment of the stakeholders to the successful implementation of the plan.

As these meetings progress, input will be gathered from many different individuals. Although it would be impossible to list every single opinion in each planning document, these meetings provide a built-in assurance that many different perspectives are sought and seriously considered in the planning process.

Tip: Each parallel process usually needs two planning team members: one to explain the documents and process and the other to facilitate and write up the feedback on a flip chart. If you do not use a flip chart or some other visual or written form of note-taking, people often become skeptical as to whether or not you have really heard them.

Another key point is that training needs to be conducted for the planning team members prior to their first parallel process, again to engineer success up front.

Following each core planning team meeting, it is also critical for one individual to be responsible for developing and sending out written communications, *from the CEO* to all key stakeholders. These communications should be simple memos in a question-and-answer format that highlight the status, what actions have been taken, what still needs to be done, etc. Most importantly, they should update each key stakeholder on his or her role in your strategic planning and change management (i.e., what specifically is expected of each person).

Organizing Task #13: Establishing Ground Rules and Documents

Setting up clear, mutually agreed-upon ground rules for the planning team is essential to the success of any planning and large-scale change activity. Considering the extent of change involved in implementing a strategic plan, you will greatly increase your chances of success if you establish some basic rules or norms of behavior right from the start around such topics as openness and honesty, handling conflict in a positive way, persistence, listening and explaining why (the logic or rationale behind a position) versus positioning yourself, consensus decision making, and making tough choices.

Adopting a "win–win" discussion framework is crucial here. The key to true win–win discussions is twofold:

1. To expand your base of information and develop an understanding of the logic, rationale, and criteria behind other points of view

2. To listen first and exhibit a clear understanding of others' perspectives and logic *before* trying to influence with your point of view

Keep in mind that a fair amount of negotiating and manipulating is going on in every discussion. Remember, you are either *claiming* value (defending your "piece of the pie") or *creating* value (expanding the information available and exploring alternative solutions). Obviously, it is more desirable to move toward creating value in win–win discussions. In truly listening to and incorporating all points of view in an overall solution, you begin the process of thinking laterally in new paradigm ways.

In addition, you need to clarify the final planning document in Goal #1 (see Table 5.3).

TABLE 5.3　Strategic Planning Final Document

KISS: 16–20 pages maximum; in overhead slide format

Sections/Documents	*# of Pages*
I.　Introduction	2–4
1.　Cover sheet with Rallying Cry	
2.　Executive Summary; History	
3.　Strategic Planning Model	
4.　Acknowledgments	
5.　Table of Contents	
6.　Environmental Scanning and Strategic Issues	1–2
II.　Ideal Future Vision and Strategies	
1.　Vision/Back-Up	1–2
2.　Mission/Driving Force(s)	1
3.　Values/Back-Up	1–3
4.　KSF Matrix/First-Year Action Plan	2–3
5.　SBUs/MPAs Clarified with Pro Formas	1–2
6.　Three-Year Business/Department Planning Process	1
(Mini Strategic Plans for SBUs/MPAs and Major Support Units)	
7.　Core Strategies	2–3
_____ With Strategic Action Items/priorities for each	
_____ "From–To" Changes of Core Strategies	
III.　Next Year	
1.　Annual Planning Top Three Priorities/Resource Allocation	1–2
2.　Implementation Plan, including:	2–3
_____ Strategic Change Steering Committee	
_____ Change and Transition Process/Yearly Comprehensive Map	
_____ Game Plan for focusing on the four Vital Few Leverage Points for Change—to create the desired organizational culture/results	
_____ Game Plan for Annual Strategic Management System Review and Update to assess implementation success and keep us "on track," plus redoing Annual Plans/Priorities	
TOTAL PLAN	**Maximum of 16–20**
IV.　Appendix	
1.　Current State Assessment	
2.　Key Working Papers	

In Summary

The Plan-to-Plan step can make all the difference in how smoothly and effectively your planning and change process proceeds. By assessing the organization, building your capacity (with leader and support staff), and educating and organizing via the executive briefing and each of the fourteen organizing tasks, you will have already completed much of the hard work that engineers success of the plan up front, before you even begin.

RECAP OF KEY POINTS

1. Before you begin the Plan-to-Plan step, make sure you understand what it is (i.e., an executive briefing and an opportunity to organize your approach to the strategic planning process—educate and organize).

2. Be specific and clear about the exact entity you are going to plan for (organization, geographic community sector, business unit, etc.).

3. Identify up front the key issues that are critical to your organization's success, as a guide to keeping planning practical. (Use the strategic/ organizational assessment to accomplish this.)

4. Make sure the top members of your collective leadership are personally ready for and committed to leading your strategic planning and change management process. (In other words, conduct capacity building through team-building/visionary leadership priorities and skills training, right away.)

5. Use Plan-to-Plan as an opportunity to problem-solve potential barriers/mistakes to strategic planning that your organization may encounter—before you begin.

6. Be sure to scan your organization's environment, both internal and external, to make certain you are not trying to create your plan in a vacuum.

7. Don't blindly follow the ten steps of the planning model. Tailor your strategic plan in a way that best fits your particular organization.

8. Make sure your strategic plan drives your budget (i.e., "strategic" budgeting) instead of vice versa. Be sure to set up a yearly cycle.

9. Don't let your planning team grow beyond 14 or 15 individuals.

10. Create a staff support cadre to support the planning team.

11. Have an experienced strategic planning facilitator who can play devil's advocate and facilitate strong egos, especially during the planning process.

12. Incorporate a parallel process to integrate the planning team's progress with other key stakeholders, inside and out of the organization. (*Communicate, communicate, communicate!*)

13. Set up clear, mutually agreed-upon ground rules that will be in effect for the entire planning and implementation process.

PLAN-TO-PLAN TASKS: ACTION CHECKLIST

1. Hold a kick off meeting to share with all key stakeholders the planning process and their role in it.

2. Select an external strategic planning facilitator to start the planning process, but also set up the staff support cadre right away, so you eventually develop the internal capacity to run this process yourself.

3. Complete all the Plan-to-Plan tasks either in a formal, half-day session following the executive briefing session or informally with the CEO and top management team. Use the following list of tasks as your checklist:

1. Executive briefing on strategic management

2. Personal readiness for strategic management

3. Strategic planning problems/barriers and readiness actions

4. Strategic issues list

5. Strategic planning staff support team/needed meetings

6. Planning team membership

7. Identification of key stakeholder/involvement

8. Initial environmental scanning/current state assessment required

9. Reinvented Strategic Planning Model tailored to your needs

10. Strategic planning link to budgets

11. Strategic implementation and change commitments

12. Strategic planning updates communicated to others

CHAPTER 6

IDEAL FUTURE VISION
(STEP #2)
(PHASE A: OUTPUT)

The only limits, as always, are those of vision.

WHY IS THE IDEAL FUTURE VISION STEP IMPORTANT?
WHERE SHOULD I START?

The Ideal Future Vision step (#2) is the first real action step in strategic planning. It is the step in which you formulate those dreams that are worth believing in and fighting for. Most importantly, this is where you set in motion the outcome of becoming a customer-focused, high-performance organization.

As in every facet of systems thinking, the Ideal Future Vision step must *begin with (and keep) the end in mind.* In this step, your collective leadership should begin the process of selecting those outcomes that you most want to achieve. Keep in mind that these outcomes directly influence the type of organization you will become. If the organization you see in your ideal future is high performance and customer focused, for instance, you need to select outcomes that will help you achieve this. Typical outcomes for this type of organization would involve the following six areas:

1. Customer satisfaction

2. Quality products/services

3. Profitability/retained earnings

4. Employee satisfaction

5. Contribution to society

6. Stockholder return

At this stage in beginning your actual strategic planning process, cries of "It can't be done!" are irrelevant and unacceptable. This exercise is not about limiting your organization's possibilities; it is about attempting to discover just what those possibilities can be.

Most organizations today have, at some point, hired a consultant to help them create their organizational mission and vision statements. Unfortunately, consultants often espouse the latest business trend or fad, essentially offering not much more than a piecemeal approach to a systems problem.

> *The last thing IBM needs right now is a vision.*
>
> Louis V. Gerstner
> IBM

As is apparent from the quote above, the last few years have seen vision and mission statements, along with other business trends, fall along the wayside. As a result, these statements often end up being superficial and meaningless. Your collective leadership must be completely committed to agreeing on the ends and working on the means of your Ideal Future Vision and then must work together to achieve them. This is the only way in which your organization's vision statement can truly make a difference in how you run your business and serve your customer day to day.

> *Goal-setting is **the #1 criteria for success***
> *in all the literature.*

Example

The well-known study of 100 Harvard Business School graduates supports this so well. A follow-up 20 years later found that the ten who had originally set a vision and clear goals owned 96% of the wealth. Despite ex-President George Bush's well-publicized problems with "this vision thing," the simple fact is that without a focused future vision and clear goals for carrying it out, you will not have any growth problems to worry about.

It is imperative that every organizational member understand and be committed to your Ideal Future Vision. Those who are not in agreement may go so far as to leave the organization if the vision is not the direction in which they personally or professionally want to go. This can actually be a healthy outcome, because an organization cannot successfully achieve its Ideal Future Vision if individual members of its collective leadership are not all pulling in the same direction. After all, if you can't all agree on your desired ends, your means will never be in sync.

HOW TO BEGIN

> *Whatever you can do, or dream you can, begin it.*
> *Boldness has genius, power, and magic in it.*
>
> Goethe

The Ideal Future Vision step generates direction and order. Although it does not replace the common-sense fundamentals of running your business day to day, your organization cannot have an adequate sense of purpose without it. It is important that all organizational leaders participate in this key step.

In effect, the Ideal Future Vision step is where you focus on the outcomes and direction that will become the context for determining what you have to do in order to successfully implement your strategic plan. It is the point at which your collective leadership should step outside of all preconceived boundaries or limitations, as well as your present business and habits, and begin to form a view of your organization's ideal future.

When your organization's collective leadership begins developing your Ideal Future Vision, don't be afraid to admit that you don't know all the answers. After all, you are seeking those answers that will define the best possible outcomes for your organization. Be willing to let go of what is not working and then develop and keep the detailed image of the future you desire in full view at all times.

> *Everything that can be invented has been invented.*
>
> Charles H. Duell
> Director of U.S. Patent Office, 1899

Being willing to go after what you really want is one thing; defining what that is, however, can be quite another. As the above quotes so clearly illustrate, it can sometimes be extremely challenging to step outside the boundaries of the world you have always known and reshape the possibilities of that world by exercising your imagination. Failure to look beyond "what is today" (our familiar paradigms) to the possibilities of tomorrow happens to all of us. The following quote eloquently express this point:

Heavier-than-air flying machines are impossible.

Lord Kelvin
President, Royal Society, 1895

CONFRONT YOUR PARADIGMS

Paradigms are a set of rules and regulations that:

1. Establish boundaries

2. Set rules for success

3. Show what is—and is not—important

The world-famous futurist Joel Barker brought the paradigm concept dramatically to our attention in the 1980s and 1990s. It was his observation that organizations (and people, too) establish a set of paradigms (i.e., a set of rules and regulations that establish boundaries as to what is important and what is not) which eventually become so entrenched that they are never challenged.

Barker maintained that while these paradigms are useful in focusing attention, they tend to blind people from seeking effective strategies for future success. He argued that in order to become high performance and customer focused, organizations need to undergo a "paradigm shift," which poses the question:

*What is impossible to do today...but if it could be done...
would fundamentally change the way you do business?*

Barker advised organizations to look outside their existing boundaries—in effect, learn to "shift" their paradigms. He believed that in order to be truly visionary, organizational leaders must become "paradigm pioneers" (i.e., they must be courageous and willing to take risks, even in the face of the unknown).

A typical example of a paradigm shift is man's progress in flight: from balloon to bi-planes, to single-wing propeller planes, to jets, to the Concorde, to satellites and rockets, and, finally, to the space shuttle.

The worlds of transportation and mass media electronics provide dramatic examples of paradigm shifts:

- In the field of transportation, humans first walked; then graduated to animals, carts, and wheels; then on to boats, trains, cars, and buses.

- Mass media electronics has shifted paradigms in the span of a few decades: first the tube, followed by the transistor, and then the chip.

Other key paradigm shifts include:

- In California, the Poway Unified School District is focusing its energies on the outcome of *learning* as opposed to the activity of teaching.

- Privatization of companies by the hundreds in Chile and Mexico, as well as city services in Philadelphia, Chicago, Dallas, etc., are substantial examples of paradigm shifts in today's world.

Perhaps the heart of the matter is that we can all choose our own paradigms, today *and* tomorrow. Completing the Ideal Future Vision step is a process that enables us to put aside reason *temporarily* and look beyond the present to the future as we would like it to be.

Above all, see the future as an empty slate at first; approach it as a new beginning. You will need to conduct an environmental scan of how the world is changing; then you'll be off and running in a proactive manner, thus creating your own Ideal Future Vision. In the words of Joel Barker, "You can and should shape your own future...if you don't, somebody else surely will!"

THE IDEAL FUTURE VISION STEP: FOUR CHALLENGES

Completing the Ideal Future Vision step successfully requires taking your collective leadership through four main challenges.

Challenge #1: Shaping your Organization's *Vision Statement,* or "Guiding Star"

- This should be idealistic, something you want your organization to aspire to—your vision of what the future looks like at time X.

- Even if they are not fully attainable, your vision should include dreamlike qualities and future hopes.

- Develop an energizing, positive, and inspiring statement of where and what you want to be in the future.

The first challenge is developing your Ideal Future Vision via a "visioning" process. This is probably one of the most complex components of the four because you are asking your collective leadership to consciously step outside their familiar boundaries that exist in your day-to-day operations and create new, previously unexplored scenarios. It can be an intimidating process. Done correctly, however, it can become immensely rewarding.

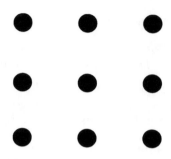

FIGURE 6.1 Nine Dots (Instructions: Connect the nine dots in any way you can, with the only instructions being to use four straight lines, connected end to end)

Tip: Introducing the "nine dots exercise" (see Figure 6.1) is an ideal, hands-on way to initiate group participation. It is an excellent example of the limits most of us place on our own abilities to imagine beyond that which we already know. Once you have been shown the answer (which is that there is no rule that says you cannot go outside of the dots to complete the puzzle), it seems ridiculously obvious. Yet all of us are usually so good at conforming to everyday rules and boundaries (i.e., paradigms) that we have almost forgotten how to "get outside the nine dots" to solve problems.

You will need to conduct an environmental scan to fully open up the unknown possibilities the future may present. By scanning the environment to see what is and will potentially be happening in your future, you will avoid working in a vacuum. Most importantly, you will have thought it through carefully enough to know whether you are actually creating an Ideal Future Vision or just a hallucination.

Creating your vision statement (Challenge #1) includes two activities.

Activity #1: List Ideas and Brainstorm for Your Ideal Future Vision

Get all participants started in private brainstorming sessions. Encourage brainstorming participants to be creative, innovative, and limitless and to go for their ideals. Come back into a group session, with each participant sharing his or her list for the group to address and compare.

At this point in the visioning process, you should begin developing consensus by getting a sense of the key areas in your visions. The following list is an example of part of an initial brainstorming document that Giant Industries developed during its visioning process.

Giant Industries
Future Vision Brainstorming List

Our Vision [Includes]:

1. Highest quality customer service

2. Using strategies to lead and guide our [organization]

3. [Creating] an integrated energy company that consistently leads our industry group relative to total stockholder return

4. Flexible and opportunistic in substantially increasing our supply and refinery capacity

5. Engage in related businesses

6. Good corporate citizen[ship]

7. Maintain a secure raw materials supply

Activity #2: Create a Visual Picture of Your New Paradigm at Year X

Participants should now create symbols or illustrations for the new vision. Have them draw a visual picture of your new paradigm for Year X. This will aid greatly in establishing a crystal-clear image in each participant's mind of exactly what your new Ideal Future Vision looks like.

Lastly, when you have reached final consensus and checked for pitfalls, another subgroup of two to four people maximum should then write a first-draft final vision statement based on this consensus. After this draft has been formally reported to the total group and refined, use the parallel process to check it and then redo it one last time.

For example: After completing these activities, Giant Industries came up with the following:

Giant Industries Vision

We are a multi-regional, vertically integrated energy company of innovative people. We are dedicated to excellence in providing the highest quality products and services to our customers.

We are positioned to take advantage of opportunities for growth through strategic acquisitions and expansion of our energy-related businesses. We constantly lead our industry group in total shareholder value.

Challenge #2: Developing a Realistic Future *Mission Statement* that States Your Organization's Desired, Unique Purpose

- The mission states what business you want to be in versus the activities you do today

- It also states why your organization should continue to exist—its reason for being

- Your mission statement concerns itself with the *content* of your business—what you produce, its benefits, and who you serve

This may sound simple, but in actual practice, a mission statement often proves to be an elusive concept. A 1987 survey, published in *Planning Review* magazine by Lloyd Byars and Thomas Neil, questioned 208 members of the Planning Forum (the world's largest organization on strategic planning and management) and found that an astonishing 33% of the organizations queried did not have a written philosophy or only had an informal philosophy.

Byars and Neil concluded that, first, most organizations need to define their philosophy more explicitly and clearly. The statements they did receive generally had no clear focus. Second, most statements were written in such vague language that they had little meaning.

Instead, you can begin developing a high-quality mission statement with the introduction of the Mission Development Triangle (Figure 6.2). Have each person begin the exercise by individually answering the first three questions:

1. *Why* do we exist?

2. *Who* do we serve?

3. *What* do we produce as outcomes?

Once this has been completed on an individual basis, form the participants into three subgroups and have each subgroup develop a visual answer to the same three questions on a flip chart. (Though at times the participants may feel that these questions are repetitive, it is important that they go through the process of answering them, both individually and as a group, in order to come up with a true, synthesized list.)

Next, select one person from each subgroup to work with the facilitator in synthesizing the three charts into one. Take care not to eliminate any answer; filtering and closure will come later. Following this, the entire group should analyze each question from the synthesized list. Tests to ensure clarity and closure should include:

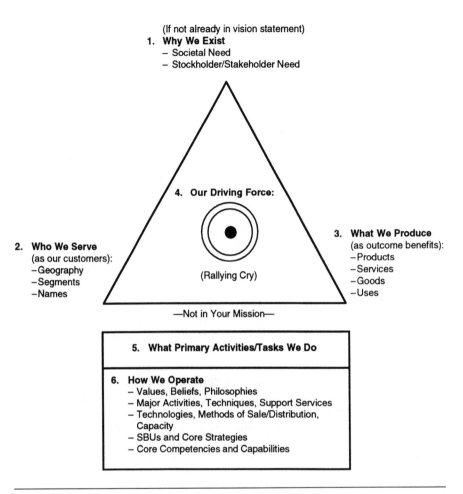

(If not already in vision statement)
1. **Why We Exist**
    – Societal Need
    – Stockholder/Stakeholder Need

4. **Our Driving Force:**

(Rallying Cry)

2. **Who We Serve**
    (as our customers):
    – Geography
    – Segments
    – Names

3. **What We Produce**
    (as outcome benefits):
    – Products
    – Services
    – Goods
    – Uses

—Not in Your Mission—

5. **What Primary Activities/Tasks We Do**

6. **How We Operate**
    – Values, Beliefs, Philosophies
    – Major Activities, Techniques, Support Services
    – Technologies, Methods of Sale/Distribution,
      Capacity
    – SBUs and Core Strategies
    – Core Competencies and Capabilities

FIGURE 6.2   Mission Development Triangle Exercise (Adapted from P. Below, G. Morrisey, and B. Acomb, "Executive Guide to Strategic Planning," 1978; S. Haines, "Internal Sun Co., Inc. Working Paper," 1979; J.W. Pfeiffer, L.D. Goodstein, and T.M. Nolan, *Applied Strategic Planning: A How to Do It Guide,* Pfeiffer & Co., San Diego, 1986)

1. Does each *who* relate to a *what* and vice versa?
2. Looking at the *why,* ask: What will be better as a result of your existence as an organization? Does it tie to the vision statement?
3. Are the *whats* the outputs of your activities, as opposed to being the activities themselves?
4. What risk is being taken by this future mission; is anything changing?

Gain agreement on the exact words for each *who, what,* and *why.* If you are following a parallel process, get general agreement on wording. Then assign a subgroup of three people to write a first-draft mission statement and bring it back to the group for final review, discussion, agreement, and closure. Considerations should include:

1. Is it brief, concise, and understandable?

2. Is it broad and continuing, but not so broad as to be meaningless?

3. Is it stated in results (output terms) vs. activities (inputs/through-puts)?

4. Is it future oriented?

5. Will it drive behavior in the organization?

6. What will be different in the future as a result of this mission?

For example: This mission statement created by the highly successful Poway (California) Unified School District reflects a forward-looking shift from the traditional educational paradigm of "teaching" to "learning":

We Believe All Students Can Learn

Our mission is to ensure that each student will master the knowledge and develop the skills and attitudes essential for success in school and society.

Another good example of a mission statement is that of BC Systems Corporation, in Victoria, British Columbia:

BC Systems Corporation
Mission Statement

BC Systems Corporation is a public sector enterprise
whose business mission is:
To provide information technology solutions which assist
public sector organizations in B.C. to maintain and
fundamentally improve the quality of service to the public.

By shaping a succinct, clear mission statement, it will be much easier for your organization to stay on its self-directed track, constantly checking, for example: *Is our mission teaching or learning?...railroads or transportation?...selling computers or information handling systems?*

Five Mistakes with Mission Statements

Regardless of whether an organization is large or small, privately or publicly owned, or public or private sector, the mistakes that recur fall into the following five areas.

Mistake #1: Mistaking the "How" as Being Part of the Mission

Most people mistake the "how to" as belonging with the mission. *How* your business operates—its values, techniques, technologies, capabilities, and strategies—is important enough to merit consideration in almost everything you do. In fact, it is included (#4) along with your organizational driving force (#5) in the earlier Mission Development Triangle (see Figure 6.2).

It is important not to confuse means and ends and processes and outputs. A current example of this problem is the Malcolm Baldrige Award, which has been criticized for focusing exclusively on process, causing some award winners to lose focus on their customer and their profits. Also, Deming's 14 Points, while significant, do not even mention the customer, resulting in further confusion.

Mistake #2: Failing to Specifically Identify Who Your Customer Is

Most mission statements fail to clearly define "who" the customer is. Instead, they merely refer, generically, to "the customer," without stating specifically who the customer is. Look closely at your mission statement. Nine out of ten mission statements fail to clearly identify the customer, in which case the organization is definitely *not* customer focused.

Mistake #3: The Control vs. Service Dilemma in Staff Departments

Staff departments usually find that they face serious issues when developing mission statements. The finance or human resources departments of an organization, for example, can find the contrast between control and service issues confusing. The staff department's primary job may be controlling the organization's finances for the CEO, but it still needs to fulfill the role of a service department to the rest of the organization.

Keep in mind that there is a difference between "serving" other departments in your organization and being "subservient" to them. *All* departments are important; each just has a different role. The single most important job of every organizational department is to serve the customer or to serve someone else who is serving the customer directly.

*Mistake #4: Failing to Properly Define
Your "Entity" in the Public Sector*

Because its own defined entity and purpose is part of a larger continuum, the public sector often experiences difficulty in developing mission statements. It is often confusing just where their organizational entity ends and the rest of the industry or public responsibility begins. As indicated in Figure 6.3, this confusion can often result in poor direction and focus.

Thus, some of the public sector's most common mistakes in clarifying their mission include:

1. Confusing means and ends, or activities vs. results, is very similar to the failure to eliminate the "how to" from the mission statement and concentrate only on outcomes.

2. Trying to "do it all" themselves, in a mission that is outside their roles and responsibilities (i.e., "do-gooders" vs. self-help missionaries). This assumes the public they serve is incapable of taking responsibility for itself and, instead, is dependent on the government.

3. Failing to clarify, focus on, or even care about the customer they are supposed to serve. This often translates into a government organization that sees its real mission day to day as serving politicians only.

4. Failing to distinguish between the business products and services that they provide and the staff support areas that will be necessary to support them. This is a result of not knowing "what business we are in" or denial that you are even in a "business" at all.

Example: It is perfectly acceptable, for instance, for the San Diego Department of Health to create a rather broad vision statement, such as having "a

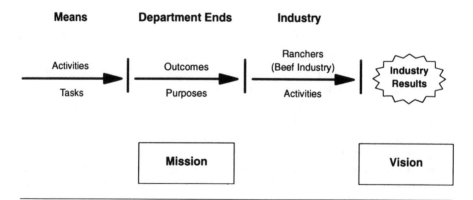

FIGURE 6.3　Public Sector Mission Problems

high standard of health throughout San Diego County." In their mission statement, however, they need to be much more specific and concern themselves with defining their particular role in achieving this county-wide health standard "vision" above.

Mistake #5: "Going Through the Motions" Only

A strong word of caution is appropriate here. As in the strategic planning process itself, it is all too easy to just "go through the motions" and end up with vision and mission statements that sound great but say little and mean even less. Many people see vision and mission statements as ends in and of themselves instead of the beginning of an ongoing strategic management (i.e., strategic planning and strategic change) process.

Also, vision and mission statements issued by top management all too frequently bear little relation to the day-to-day realities of an organization. As Intel's CEO once said, "You look at corporate vision/strategy statements, and a lot of them are such pap. You know how they go: 'We're going to be world-class this, and a leader in that, and we're going to keep all our customers smiling.'" Yet, nothing really changes.

The truth is that your vision and mission statements are crucial components of your strategic planning process; in fact, they literally become the fundamental destination that guides you through every step of the planning and implementation process.

Customer-Focused, High-Performance Organizations

When analyzing who your "real" customer is, pay careful attention to the question of internal versus external customers. There is a difference. When all is said and done, of course, your only real customer will always be the external customer who buys your product or service. However, you may exist to serve someone else internally in the organization but external to your department. In the final analysis, it should always come down to:

My job is to serve the customer or to serve someone who does.

Do not lose this customer focus, which is altogether too easy to do:

Our purpose...customer satisfaction...
the reason for being in business often gets lost
in the shuffle of corporate initiatives (i.e., TQM, BPR, etc.).

From a synergistic point of view, your customers will increase if their needs are met; conversely, they will decrease when their needs are not met. Therefore, all of your organizational operations, processes, and procedures must be geared toward accommodating customer needs. As those needs change, you must continually anticipate, introduce, and improve on new products, services, and systems.

Example: Imperial Corporation of America, a $1.3 billion financial services corporation, had an exceptional customer service creed during the late 1980s:

> ### *Imperial Service Corporation*
> ### *Customer Service Creed*
>
> *Service is our most valuable product. To increase the value of this product and secure a position of industry leadership for Imperial Corporation of America, we will implement and support superior customer service standards. We will make those standards a fundamental part of every employee's activities every business day.*
>
> *Always remember: our business success and profitability depend on serving our customers better than anyone else.*

It is rare to find a high-performance organization in existence over the long term that does not make customer satisfaction its number one priority. Therefore, if you want to be a high-performance organization, you will have to be clearly, emphatically, and totally customer focused throughout every level and aspect of your business.

Challenge #3: Developing Your *Core Values* that Collectively Make Up Your Organization's Culture: "What We Believe In"

> *A leader's role is to manage the values of the organization;*
> *a leader's role is to harness the social forces in the organization,*
> *to shape, and to guide values.*
> Chester Barnard
> Past President, New Jersey Bell Telephone

- Core values are the principles that guide your daily organizational behavior

- They specify *how* you should act while accomplishing your mission; they specify your way—or *process*—of doing business

- Your organization's core values must state not only how you will act at work, but what you believe in as well

In addition to customer focus, high-performance organizations invest heavily in defining and implementing their core values. The formation and observance of core organizational values has many productive outcomes. High-performance organizations use their core values as a stability factor for employees. When employees share organizational values, they feel more committed and loyal, identify more strongly with important organizational issues, and display a willingness to "get the job done."

Core values can contribute insight and direction when your organization is faced with unpleasant choices. In addition, they can serve as a rudder in tough times, helping your organization to pursue the high road of ethical conduct, respect, and dignity for the individual. Increased employee motivation, effort, and clarity of focus also serve to develop a competitive edge for your organization. Perhaps most significant, strong core values will be invaluable in guiding employees in the 10,000 or more small decisions they make daily.

As you develop your organization's core values, keep in mind that they must meet the following six criteria:

1. Is it a collective belief organization-wide—simple and clear?

2. Does it determine the standards of acceptable work behaviors?

3. Will people know and care if it is not followed?

4. Is it a value that will endure consistently over time?

5. Are there myths, rituals, or other well-known organizational stories to support its existence?

6. Is it crystallized and driven by the top management level?

Because core values by their very nature must be of key importance, they are usually few in number. Some typical core values consistently seen in today's high-performance organizations include:

- Quality/service/responsive/speed (customer focused)
- Creativity/innovation/flexibility
- Wise, focused use of resources
- Energizing, motivating, and positive leadership
- Teamwork and collaboration
- Empowerment/accountability
- Mutual respect/recognition/honesty/dignity

For example: A good example of core values that benefit today's high-performance organization is the following list from Wal-Mart, put out under founder's Sam Walton's mantra: "A bias for action":

Wal-Mart Principles

- Managers are servants
- The customer is the boss
- Employees and suppliers are partners
- Costs must be driven down to keep prices low

In developing your own core values, your core planning team should individually complete the exercise in Table 6.1. Once they have finished, they should then discuss, analyze, and evaluate each other's lists of values.

After this discussion, the team should develop a first draft of your core values statement, bulleting simple, clear phrases that have been arrived at by consensus. Keep in mind that you will be troubleshooting it, so the statement needn't be perfect yet. Also at this time, your key stakeholders should be involved in a parallel process to give you feedback on whether anything is fundamentally wrong with the core values draft, whether anything should be added or deleted, and what the gaps are between your ideal core values and today's reality.

Option: Some organizations opt to conduct a personal values exercise first, since, in reality, organizational values are just the result of the values of management.

Tip: Why do an analysis of core values now? Employees at this point are often impatient to witness instant behavior changes in management; they want to see them "walk the talk." However, it usually take 12 to 18 months to change behavior.

Therefore, once you have a completed values statement, there should be an assessment of the current status and uses of the values right away. (See Table 6.2 for this assessment.) While it should permeate all organizational activities, communicating the core values throughout the company without being prepared to put them visibly into practice immediately can be a sure way for senior executives to "shoot themselves in the foot."

With your core values firmly in place throughout your organization, there is one more element to consider: the implications of your organization's culture.

TABLE 6.1   Organizational Values Exercise

Complete Column #2 by selecting ten of the following values that have the most importance to your organization's future success. Complete Column #1 at a later time.

	#1 *The Way* *It Is Now*	#2 *The Way You* *Think It Should Be*
1. Long-term strategic perspective	❏	❏
2. Energizing leadership	❏	❏
3. Innovation/risk taking	❏	❏
4. Teamwork/collaboration	❏	❏
5. Recognition of achievements	❏	❏
6. Wise use of resources	❏	❏
7. Quality work/products/services	❏	❏
8. Contribution to society	❏	❏
9. Continuous improvement	❏	❏
10. Safe and orderly environment	❏	❏
11. Positive organizational management	❏	❏
12. High staff productivity/performance	❏	❏
13. Customer service/sensitivity	❏	❏
14. Ethical and legal behavior	❏	❏
15. Stability/security	❏	❏
16. Profitability/cost conscious	❏	❏
17. Employee development/growth	❏	❏
18. Growth/size of organization	❏	❏
19. Openness/trust/positive confrontation	❏	❏
20. Respect/caring for individuals	❏	❏
21. Quality of work life	❏	❏
22. High staff satisfaction/morale	❏	❏
23. Decision making at lowest level	❏	❏
24. Employees involved prior to decisions	❏	❏
25. Employee self-initiative/freedom	❏	❏
26. Diversity and equal opportunity	❏	❏

Adapted from S. Haines, "Internal Sun Co., Inc. Working Paper," 1979; J.W. Pfeiffer, L.D. Goodstein, and T.M. Nolan, *Applied Strategic Planning: A How to Do It Guide,* Pfeiffer & Co., San Diego, 1986; T. Rusk, "Ethical Persuasion Working Paper," 1989.

**TABLE 6.2   Core Values Assessment and Uses
Throughout All Seven Tracks to a High-Performing Organization**

The following are typical categories where core values should appear and be reinforced within an organization. Where else should they appear and be reinforced in your organization?

1. Flow of organization and assimilation vs. sign-up
2. Job aids/descriptions
3. Internal communication (vehicles/publications)
4. Press releases, external publications/brochures
5. Image nationwide (as seen by others)
6. Recruiting handbook; selection criteria
7. How applicants are treated (vs. values)
8. How "rewards for performance" operates (vs. values), especially non-financial rewards
9. Explicit corporate philosophy/values statement—visuals on walls/in rooms
10. Role of training/training programs (vs. values)
11. Corporate and product advertising
12. New customers and suppliers vs. current customer and supplier treatment and focus (vs. values)
13. Performance evaluation/appraisal forms (assess values adherence)/team rewards
14. New executive start-up
15. Policies and procedures (HR, Finance, Administrative, etc.)/day-to-day decisions
16. Cross-departmental events, flows, task forces
17. To whom and how promotions occur (values consequence assessed)/criteria
18. Executive leadership ("walk the talk"); ethical decisions; how we manage
19. Dealing with difficult times/issues (i.e., layoffs, reorganizations)
20. Strategy decisions—how to do something
21. Managing change
22. Organization and job design
23. Resource allocation
24. Operational tasks of quality and service
25. Stakeholder relationships

Where else in our organization?

Organizational Culture Implications

As companies move from hierarchical, top-down organizations,
a greater number of the decisions individuals make
are shaped by the firm's culture.

Personnel Journal
November 1989

While core values are guides to organization-wide behavior, the collective behaviors in your organization make up its culture. Although "the way we do business around here" seems a simplistic way to define culture, Figure 6.4 clearly shows how appropriate this definition really is.

THE WAY WE DO BUSINESS AROUND HERE

Organizational culture is a set of interrelated beliefs or norms shared by most of the employees of an organization about how one should behave at work and what activities are more important than others.

Assumptions/Philosophy =
Our World View
("Weltanschauung")

∨

Personal Values

∨

Organizational Values

∨

Norms of Behavior
(i.e., the standards for action)

∨

Individual Behavior

Collectively
Leads to Our
Culture

FIGURE 6.4   Organizational Culture Defined

It is an important element to pay attention to; a healthy organizational culture can go a long way toward supporting your organization's vision and mission statements. The old admonition, "Do as I say, not as I do," however, no longer works in today's high-performance organization; the ill will generated by this approach can seriously impede the achievement of your vision and mission.

Because today's revolutionary change is causing organizations to change the way they do business, organizational culture is not something you can afford to ignore or treat lightly. Thus, one of your key strategies will be to create one desired culture throughout your entire organization. You will probably need a specific project resulting from your strategic plan in order to accomplish this. Your option will be to either begin it now or wait until you have completed strategic planning and then begin. Decide which makes the best sense for your organization and then develop the appropriate strategies, with an action plan, to implement it.

Tip: It may be tempting to skirt around this issue, but avoid the temptation. While your organization's culture will definitely affect its core strategies, the reverse is equally true. Whenever strategy and culture collide, culture *always* wins out; therefore, ignoring it will undo a lot of hard work.

Whenever you decide to get started on your culture change strategies, you will need to begin by analyzing how many different subculture levels presently exist in your organization. Typically, organizations tend to have different subcultures at different levels throughout the organization, and they can frequently be at odds with each other. Common subculture levels could include (1) top executive, (2) upper management, (3) middle management, and (4) workers.

There are other kinds of subcultures which are often adversarial to one another, including field versus headquarters departments, line versus staff, and the manufacturing subculture and the marketing department subculture, among others.

In Summary

Establishing or changing an organizational culture takes persistence and patience over the long haul. It is difficult, but it can be done. You will need an organizational leader with an almost fanatical adherence to your core values, and one who never deviates during times of trouble.

Examples of entrepreneurs who have successfully created a strong culture that is resistant to change include Ray Kroc (McDonald's), J.W. Marriott, Sr., Bill McGowan (MCI), Izzy Cohen (Giant Food), and Walt Disney. All are leaders who were not afraid to change their own behavior first, thus lending credibility and believability to the importance of cultural change.

Remember, you can change your mission, you can change your strategies, and you can change your structure, but if you don't change your culture, it will only serve to defeat all the other changes you desire.

Challenge #4: Identifying Future Driving Forces and Your Rallying Cry, which States the Essence of Your Organization's Ideal Future Vision Step

- This should be a crisp, motivational slogan—eight words or less (such as Ford Corporation's *"Quality Is Job 1"*)—that can be easily remembered by all organizational members.

- Be sure it is a powerful, motivating force for your staff that is inspirational, believable, and repeatable on a daily basis across the organization.

To come up with a rallying cry, you will need to first define your organization's driving force. This is the key single thrust within your vision and mission statements that your organization uses to achieve its vision and mission:

1. All other functions, directions, decisions, and criteria are subordinate.

2. It is usually comprised of the *whos, whats,* or *hows* taken from your mission and values statements (*why* is a given).

3. It is your organization's core or distinctive competency which makes it unique from your competition.

4. It will sustain as your competitive edge over a period of years.

5. It cannot be readily duplicated.

6. It is either your current reality or can become your reality within the period of time for which you are planning.

Your rallying cry should not be treated as an advertising slogan. Instead, it should be consistently used throughout your day-to-day internal operations over the entire length of your strategic plan; you should not change it as you would, say, a slogan for your ad campaign. External use of your rallying cry is optional and can be used to promote an added-value concept.

Your rallying cry will act as a motivational force to continually remind internal staff of your vision statement. It is meant to be used over the long term; therefore, it should be memorable, believable, and able to be repeated on a daily basis.

For example: Some of the particularly effective rallying cries of other high-performance organizations include:

- Disney: *We Create Happiness*
- Canadian Standards Association: *Making Our Mark on the World*
- McDonald's: *Quality, Service, Cleanliness (QSC)*
- Poway Unified School District: *Excellence in Learning...Our Only Business*
- GM's A.B.S. plant: *Quality through Teamwork*

Tip: At first glance, many people view the rallying cry as hokey and unnecessary. This is usually the case when the organization fails to clearly connect its rallying cry to its essence or, in other words, what the organization is all about. One effective way to approach this issue is to wait until the end of strategic planning to develop the rallying cry. Then, actively involve members of your organization through an organization-wide contest for the best rallying cry. To do so, you must make them aware of your strategic plan, make sure they understand its precepts, and then ask them to submit their own ideas (this helps not only in creating a sense of ownership organization-wide, but in the actual implementation as well). Then, have top management publicly announce the winning phrase, and reward all those who submitted entries.

In Summary

To effectively follow the systems thinking of the Reinvented Strategic Planning Model, you must begin with a clearly defined Ideal Future Vision. Because its multiple components—vision, mission, core values, rallying cry, and risk assessment—are all equally important, shaping this vision will require patience and persistence.

All of these components have value, but only as they exist together, *as part of an overall, cohesive whole.* If you do only some of them or if you do them all but take them no further, you will in effect be shaping a temporary, piecemeal solution to a systems problem.

RECAP OF KEY POINTS

1.   The Ideal Future Vision step is the first real action step in strategic planning and one of the recurring key elements for organizational success.

2. The first challenge in the Ideal Future Vision step is to shape an organizational vision statement.

3. The second challenge is a realistic mission statement that describes your organization's desired, unique purpose.

4. The third challenge is the development of core values that make up your organization's culture: "What we believe in."

5. The fourth challenge is designing a rallying cry, or driving force, which states the essence of your organization—its *raison d'être*. It is often better to wait until the end of strategic planning, in order to really clarify the essence of your strategic plan.

6. It will be necessary to identify and assess the levels of risk inherent in these challenges.

7. There are five major areas of confusion in developing a mission statement:

   • Mistaking the "how" as being part of the mission

   • Failing to focus on the customer

   • Lack of clarity about "control" vs. "service" in departmental mission statements

   • Failing to properly define your "entity" in the public sector

   • "Going through the motions" only

8. In developing your vision and mission statements, it is critical to clearly define your customer in specific terms.

9. Every component in the Ideal Future Vision step is important, *as part of an overall, cohesive whole.*

10. The Ideal Future Vision is necessary but not sufficient for success. You must go further with the full strategic plan, annual plan, and implementation and change.

IDEAL FUTURE VISION: ACTION CHECKLIST

1. Develop a vision statement that "gets outside the nine dots" and expresses your ideal future as an organization.

2. Create a mission statement that clearly identifies the who/what/why of your organization.

3. Make sure your vision and mission statements relate closely to the day-to-day realities of your organization.

4. As you shape your vision and mission statements, be certain that you keep your customer clearly defined and in focus.

5. Develop a set of core organizational values to which you can adhere, organization-wide, through the long term.

6. Define your current organizational culture and the number of subculture levels throughout the organization.

7. Create an action plan that will enable you to shape a culture that is consistent throughout the organization.

8. Define your organization's driving force, so that you can develop an organization-wide motivational rallying cry.

9. Make sure your organization's rallying cry contains the essence of your vision, mission, and values statements.

10. Assess the level of risk involved in making these changes and take an honest inventory of your willingness to change.

CHAPTER 7

KEY SUCCESS FACTORS (STEP #3) (PHASE B: FEEDBACK LOOP)

*If you've never established quantifiable
outcome measures of success for your vision,
how will you know you've achieved it?*

Reshaping strategic management requires a new approach for managing the entire entity or organization as a system. This can only be accomplished if you continually focus on your desired outcomes. By following some surprisingly pragmatic, common-sense steps, you can create the ultimate outcome of a high-performance, customer-focused organization.

Step #2, creating your Ideal Future Vision, puts into words those ideals and beliefs that best represent your organization's desired future vision and values. Combining these ideals with your mission statement, which looks at the more pragmatic considerations of exactly what business you want to be in and who you want to serve (and profit from) in the future, creates the full definition of your Ideal Future Vision.

In order to steer your organization toward the tenets spelled out in your vision, mission, and value statements, you will need to create methods for measuring them. After all, once you have defined your vision, the only way it can be meaningful, and to know if you are reaching it, is through constant, steady measures. It is critical to keep in mind that any elements that are important, and not just those that are easy or expedient, can and should be measured. It may take some creativity, but it can—indeed, must—be done. This is where key success factors, Phase B in the Strategic Planning Model for the 21st Century, come in.

> *Measuring is the first step that leads to control*
> *and eventually to improvement.*
> *If you can't measure something, you can't understand it.*
> *If you can't understand it, you can't control it.*
> *If you can't control it, you can't improve it.*

In the visionary stage of the Strategic Planning Model, it is necessary to temporarily suspend reality—to be able to look at what your ideal future would be if you had no restraints or restrictions of any kind. Now is the time to become concrete with your vision through outcome measures of success—called key success factors.

The first step in developing your key success factors is to identify the key words and phrases from your vision, mission, and values and then determine methods by which they can be measured. As you begin the process of selecting these words and phrases which will ultimately serve as your organization's key success factors, keep in mind that they must represent ideas and action statements the organization can commit to, live with, and be accountable for.

KEY SUCCESS FACTORS: OUTCOME MEASURES OF SUCCESS

Key success factors (KSFs) track your organization's continual improvement toward achieving its Ideal Future Vision. By establishing concrete guidelines for measuring organizational progress, they assist in developing a high-performance, customer-focused organization. The best KSFs are those that meet all the criteria of the following definition:

> Key success factors are the quantifiable outcome measurements of an organization's vision, mission, and values on a year-by-year basis, ensuring continual improvement towards achieving your Ideal Future Vision.

The real value of establishing KSFs for your organization is that you can then use them to determine your successes, your vulnerabilities, and, where necessary, appropriate corrective actions to get the organization back on track. Otherwise, you run the very real risk of becoming an unguided missile, with no mechanisms for feedback. If you have chosen your KSFs based on the preceding definition, you can use them to answer the following questions throughout the implementation of your strategic plan:

1. How do you know if you are successful?

2. How do you know if you are heading for trouble?

3. If you are off course (in trouble), what corrective actions do you need to take to get back on track and achieve your Ideal Future Vision?

Throughout organizational literature, KSFs are referred to by many names, including objectives, critical success indicators, corporate goals, etc. It doesn't matter what they are called, as long as everyone in your organization has the same clear idea of exactly what they are—outcome measures of success.

In order to balance long- and short-run considerations, every organization has a minimum of four key areas that must be measured and tracked in order to create an outcome-based measuring system:

1. Customer satisfaction

2. Worker performance and attitude (employee satisfaction)

3. Market/customer standing vs. competition (benchmarking)

4. Profitability and/or retained earnings (organization's financial viability)

MEASURE WHAT'S IMPORTANT, NOT WHAT'S EASY

It is imperative at this point in strategic planning to take the time up front to develop these measures. Organizations that opt for limiting their measuring categories to the most easily recognized and concrete areas narrow the focus of their overall, desired outcomes. This ultimately limits their ability to "grow" and shape the organization.

Many organizations measure progress strictly in terms of budgets and sales forecasts. It is easier to measure the financial side than the "people" side of an organization. What invariably happens, however, is that the financial departments then become the driving force of the company, with customers, products, and employees often become forgotten factors in the organization's success equation. Remember, however, that only through customer satisfaction, innovative product strategies, and employee satisfaction—guided by professional management and leadership practices—can you sustain a competitive business advantage over time.

FINANCIAL VIABILITY IS NECESSARY BUT NOT SUFFICIENT FOR LONG-TERM SUCCESS

A good example of measuring what is really important, instead of only what is easy, is the British Columbia Systems Corporation, in Victoria, British Columbia. As an integrated information services firm serving the public and not-for-profit sectors, it has established its KSFs in the areas of (1) service value, (2) service quality, (3) employee satisfaction, and (4) financial viability. BC Systems believes that these KSFs are crucial to achieving its organization-wide vision. Again, BC Systems recognizes that financial viability is a necessary part of that vision, but is insufficient to fulfill it.

Being financially viable prevents failure.
Success is defined by how well we serve and keep customers.

Questions to Ponder

1. What are your outcome measures of success?

2. Do you limit your KSFs to financial measures alone?

3. What else should be included?

THE FAILURE TO FOCUS ON OUTCOMES

Another consideration to keep in mind as you select your KSFs is the contrast between "activities and means" versus "results and outcomes." It is often easy to quantify and measure your various activities and ongoing efforts, such as attendance, number of widgets produced, etc. However, your organizational activities only make sense if they directly contribute to your desired outcome. The outcomes, rather than the activities, are why you exist. All too often, the activities become ends in and of themselves in bureaucracies of all types, particularly the public sector. This is why it is significantly more meaningful to stick to measuring results and outcomes.

For example: Consider the game of baseball and the San Diego Padres in particular, for which 1993 and 1994 were not very good years. The moves made in 1993 have had severe negative consequences for the team

What happened is that they failed to focus on their outcomes. For example, the outcomes on which a baseball team would typically focus would be (1) to be financially viable so as to avoid bankruptcy, (2) to win a pennant or at least be in contention for it each year, (3) to build and sustain the team toward this ongoing desirable future, (4) to provide entertainment and enjoyment for the fans, and (5) to provide the owners with a high-profile status as pillars of both the local community and the national baseball community. These would be typical outcome measures of success that the Padres could pursue with a clearer vision of their future.

However, their failure to focus on outcomes has led them to focus on only one activity—cutting costs. The predictable result of this focus on a solitary activity—not even a strategy, such as financial viability—is that they probably experienced attendance reduced to around 1.3 million fans in 1993 and even less in 1994. In contrast, they drew about 2.6 million in 1985, when the population of San Diego was approximately one-third less than it is today. Not focusing on outcomes, and focusing on only one activity (financial cost-cutting), ultimately almost guaranteed them an outcome of financial insolvency or other drastic results.

> *In the absence of clearly defined ends, i.e., outcomes or targets,*
> *we are forced to concentrate on activities and efforts,*
> *but…we ultimately become enslaved by them.*

UNDERSTANDING KEY SUCCESS FACTORS IS EASY— DEVELOPING THEM IS DIFFICULT

Although it is simple to explain this concept, it is difficult to do it well. The reason for the difficulty is, as mentioned earlier, that some of your key vision areas are not easily measurable. It is important here to be creative in translating these vision concepts into specific and quantifiable measures.

It might be helpful at this point to consider some examples of "soft" KSFs from both the private (see Figure 7.1) and public sectors.

Examples of "Soft" Private Sector Key Success Factors

1. Customer satisfaction measures. High-performance organizations dedicate a great deal of time and effort to determining customer satisfaction on a regular basis. "Regular" can mean quarterly or less often, but this must be done a minimum of once a year. The most common first step is to utilize focus

KSF Overall Coordinator for is   *Bob Brown, MIS Manager*   (Name/Title)

KSF Areas (Headers) with Specific Factors for Each	Baseline Target 1994	Intermediate Targets 1995	1996	1997	Target 1998	Ultimate Target	Specific KSF Coordinator	KSF Achievement Accountability
1. Employee Satisfaction Factor: Conduct a yearly survey (vs. our Core Values) with a valid sample of our employees (use 10 point scale)	— Develop survey — Conduct it — Revise future targets	6.0/10	7.0/10	8.0/10	8.5/10	10/10	SH	
2. Customer Satisfaction Factors: A. Conduct a quarterly survey of a valid sample of our customers	— Determine their wants for quality products/services (Focus Group) — Develop/conduct survey — Revise future targets — Benchmark vs. top 3	7.5/10	8.0/10	9.0/10	9.5/10	10/10	CH	
B. Develop a "close to the customer culture"	— Conduct assessment vs. 7 Tracks — Develop full program with milestones set	— To be determined during baseline (1993) —	Full re-assessment/ refine plan		Full re-assessment/ refine plan	Culture achieved		
C. Set up a successful "Mystery Shopper Program"	— Use customer wants to set up program with evaluation scale; milestones	— To be determined once program set (1993) —			10/10			
3. Financial Viability Factors: A. ROE B. % Profit (NIAT) C. EPS D. Revenue Growth per Year	— Measures all factors — Revise future targets	TBD 10%/year TBD 15%/year					DM	

Note: These baseline targets must go on Priority Actions List for first year's Annual Planning.

FIGURE 7.1 KSF Continuous Improvement Matrix (Backwards Thinking)—Private Sample: Task #3 (Targets) and #4 (Accountability)

groups and conduct initial surveys to gather specific information on customer wants, needs, preferences, and expectations. The next step is to conduct external surveys of the customer base and compare results with data from focus groups. Another key step would be to regularly benchmark against top competitors.

2. Set up a "mystery shopper" program. Many organizations establish "mystery shopper" programs, as well as "mystery diners" and "mystery fliers." This is an anonymous way to gather candid customer feedback.

3. Employee satisfaction. Most organizations today recognize their employees as a key resource. So many businesses are service-oriented these days that organizations are beginning to feel that employee satisfaction is directly linked with customer satisfaction. At least once a year, organizations need to survey their employees' perceptions of how closely the organization is tracking its desired core values.

Customer Reality Check: The Quality Gap

According to a recent survey conducted by the Quality Research Institute (*Training*, June 1993), customers remain disillusioned with so-called improvements in quality. Focusing on the retail, hospitality, and utility industries, the survey tried to discern degrees of success in corporate total quality campaigns, in the eyes of both the corporate executive and the customer:

- In retail, a majority of department store executives indicated a substantial rise in their service quality over the past 12 months, but only 20% of their customers agreed.

- Also in retail, over 60% of discount store executives reported visible improvements in the quality of service, whereas only 30% of their customers believed the quality of service had improved.

- Hospitality industry executives reported meeting customer expectations "almost all the time," while only 40% of their guests agreed. In all, the guests were much happier with the quality of the physical facilities than with the service.

- More than 60% of executives in the utilities industry felt that their service quality showed marked improvement over the previous year, while only 9% of their customers could agree.

These glaring discrepancies make the most compelling argument of all for clear, precise methods to measure outcomes. Only by using such methods as KSFs can organizations determine how their internal assessments compare with their customers' perceptions.

Examples of "Soft" Public Sector Key Success Factors

1. Self-funding factor. In the public sector, staying within budget is often the ultimate goal, which is why it is so critical to track and assess what percent of budget can be self-funding. Alternative sources for funding include using "in-kind" contributors, donations, and contributions, in addition to formal fund-raising.

2. Teamwork/partnership factors. This factor often employs both quantity and quality measurements. One example would be to survey the number of partnerships within or between organizations and then conduct annual evaluations (most often using ten-point scales) of their effectiveness versus their charter.

3. Decentralized, site-based management concept. Empowering organizational members is a crucial strategy for success. It is imperative here to continually monitor the organization's balance between granting the rights of empowerment along with the responsibility to support the organizational directives. Empowering people without clear understanding as to the direction does not create empowerment. It only creates chaos. Management training is essential here, as is a clear and shared future vision.

Examples of Key Success Factors for All Organizations

1. Successful implementation of a strategic management system. Every organization needs to develop a way to measure how successfully the strategic plan is being implemented. This can be accomplished through consistent meetings of the Strategic Change Steering Committee. Another measure would be to develop and track a yearly comprehensive map of implementation steps and outcomes. Also, a performance appraisal process can be developed (using strategies and values as tools) for regular evaluation of management and other employees. Organizations should also determine on an ongoing basis whether or not they are consistently implementing their vital few leverage points for strategic change.

2. Yearly strategic management system update. This is where you develop a follow-up step for your strategic management system. By committing to this critical annual review and update, you are in effect creating an automatic reminder process for regular evaluation of how the system is working. This is the point where you evaluate the success of your organization-wide implementation process; it is also an opportunity to make necessary revisions, to both the organization's strategies and budget.

It is important to focus on a small number of the most important success areas. Therefore, keep your organization's KSFs to roughly ten or less. More than this takes your eye off the ball. A good question to start with would be: "Is the KSF a key one throughout the organization?" One way to screen your KSFs for clarity and validity is to pose common-sense questions such as:

- Does it overlap or duplicate any other KSFs?
- Is it a key indicator of your organization's success?
- Is it a tangible KSF that you can easily measure?
- Is it an actual report card, measuring results vs. activities?
- Are you willing to commit to it year after year?

The most effective way to determine if your measures of success (KSFs) meet the test is if you are able to measure them by (1) quality, (2) quantity, (3) time, or (4) cost. These four categories apply to potential KSF areas for any organization.

"Quality" Satisfaction Examples

The Navy Public Works Center in San Diego, California, views every other Navy base that it serves as its customer. Periodically, it conducts surveys of all its customers by measuring levels of customer satisfaction on a ten-point scale and then coming up with an average percentage of overall satisfaction.

Another example is the Marriott Corporation, whose managers are required to become "mystery diners" at all of the company's restaurants. This provides feedback about services from the customer's perspective.

"Quantity" Example

Quantity can be determined in any number of ways, such as internally monitoring for zero product defects. Other quantity KSFs could be the numbers of products produced within a certain time frame or ratios, such as tracking plant safety (number of industrial accidents per quarter, with a target of zero).

"Time" Example

The element of time is an excellent KSF and organizational outcome. It forces you to examine and stay on top of the organizational processes involved in providing value to the customer. Chrysler has revitalized its presence in the

U.S. automotive industry by adopting the Japanese strategy of time as one of its primary measures of success (KSFs.) Chrysler management looked at its competitive market and decided that if it turned out a new car model every 18 months, it would stand head and shoulders above the other U.S. and Canadian manufacturers. (Models from other U.S. automotive manufacturers involve a considerably longer production period. The designs can become obsolete with customers before the lines hit their return on investment; witness the Saturn's seven-year design/redesign cycle.)

"Cost" Examples

Cost is another obvious one. By using cost, organizations can easily monitor budgets, the cost of product development, or staffing costs, among other factors. It is easy and it can be a valid KSF; again, it is important to note that using cost as your only KSF is not sufficient.

KSFs are critical to every organization, whether public or private. Yet the ability to write clear goals and commit to good outcomes is missing from many organizations. In the private sector, many organizations continue to commit to financial goals alone. The public sector, unfortunately, is even more vulnerable to developing misdirected measures of success. Because organizations in the public sector rarely focus on the idea of their customers as an outcome measure of success, they often become slaves to their activities. They do not even attempt to measure outcomes. The unfortunate result of using only financial considerations as a measuring stick makes it easy to see why so many organizations experience confusion and lack a clear sense of purpose.

For example: One large school system did a great job of running a parallel process to develop ownership and commitment. However, it never reached consensus on a set of KSFs to follow as outcome measures of success. As a result of internal problems with the board of education, the superintendent resigned. His replacement lasted little more than a year. The school system had a common mission, vision, and values, but no set of clear, agreed-upon goals and measures with universal commitment.

Another example is the state of Oregon. In order to assess various state agencies for budgeting purposes, it has established its own KSFs, called "Oregon Benchmarks." The state uses them to measure quality of life and economic prosperity in a variety of areas.

Oregon's core benchmark on teenage pregnancy is a classic example of how it incorporates KSFs. It conducts regular, annual surveys on the pregnancy rate of females between 10 and 17 years of age. In 1990, the pregnancy rate was 19.6 per 1000. Oregon then set a goal of reducing that figure to 9.8 by 1995 and 8.0 by 2000. In 1992, the rate had decreased to only 19.3 per 1000; therefore, the state considers this an "urgent core benchmark." Ultimately, these Oregon Benchmarks go beyond abstract theory. The state division of Budget and Management requires at least one efficiency and one effectiveness measure in every agency's budget request.

Keep in mind that the best KSFs are those that can be stated in simple, clear language. While there is no shortcut method for establishing KSFs, once you understand the process, you will save considerable time and retraced steps later on in your implementation.

HOW TO DEVELOP KEY SUCCESS FACTORS

To begin developing the measures of success (KSFs) for your organization, there are two specific tasks that will help you determine the general areas from which you will extract your KSF areas: (1) It is critical at this point to cull out the key words and phrases from your vision, mission, and core values. To shape KSFs that will be recognizable throughout the organization, it is necessary to identify those key phrases that best define your organization's success. (2) It is also important to agree on specific, key financial and operational success areas.

Now that you have crystallized the key words and phrases that constitute success, the planning team must combine the answers for both of these tasks into a consolidated list. At this point, the team completes the development of the organizational KSFs by pruning them to no more than ten areas to be measured. More than ten areas makes it difficult to focus and can be awkward to coordinate.

Questions to Ponder

1. What are the key words and phrases from your vision, mission, core values, and driving force(s) statements that are critical to achieve success?

2. What are other key important financial/operational success areas?

3. You are aiming for no more than ten KSF areas. Can your planning team prune and combine their answers to Questions 1 and 2 and come up with a consolidated list?

Once you have established your ten (or fewer) critical KSF area "headers" (such as teamwork, strategic management system effectiveness, customer satisfaction, and decentralized site-based management), the next stage of development lies in defining the specific factors by which you will measure these headers. The teamwork header, for example, could be measured specifically by the number of partnerships in existence and yearly evaluation of their effectiveness. The KSF area header of customer satisfaction can be measured by quarterly surveys, developing a "close to the customer" culture, or a "mystery shopper" program.

Once you know how you are going to measure your KSF areas, you need to set definitive target dates for reaching them. If you are strategic planning for the year 2000, for instance, you will have to establish specific targets for measuring individual KSFs each year, up to the final target year of 2000. The most direct way to do this is to contrast your current-year baseline data (i.e., the present status of the individual KSF) against where you want it to be when you hit your target year.

You will probably have to do some initial research before you can determine the current baseline data on each of your KSFs. You will gain the best results by formally appointing an individual as an overall KSF coordinator. In addition, each individual KSF needs its own KSF coordinator who will be accountable for researching and reporting on it.

In some cases, you may not be able to assign a target yet because the specific measurement (i.e., a customer satisfaction survey) is not yet in place. In this instance, you can create an action plan to develop the survey within the agreed-upon time frame. This will then serve as your measure of success for the initial baseline target year.

KEY SUCCESS FACTOR PRIORITY SETTING

Now it is time to set priorities. This is actually a two-phase process, in which the planning team needs to (1) place your KSFs in a forced ranking priority order and (2) eliminate those KSFs that rank consistently at the bottom. Completing this process will help you focus on any remaining "weak links," verify that you are measuring what is important (and not just what's easy), and establish a natural order of priority.

It is also critical that the planning team specifically defines how it will measure KSF success for those measures not already in existence. Be specific as to the length of time you estimate for each KSF. Without a concrete plan that includes dates and accountability, other priorities and crises will invariably demand time and attention that should be spent developing your organization's measures of success.

As you prepare to fill in the KSF matrix (Figure 7.1), which will be your primary tool for measuring the success of your organization's strategic plan, go through a quick mental checklist and answer the following questions:

Questions to Ponder

1. Have we clearly identified KSF key words and phrases from our vision/mission/values (i.e., what is important)?

2. Have we developed clear, quantifiable outcome measures of success (KSFs)?

3. Is there a coordinator for each KSF to be measured, as well as an overall KSF coordinator?

4. Are we willing to use these KSF measures as bonus criteria?

KEY SUCCESS FACTORS: YOUR MAIN ORGANIZATION-WIDE FEEDBACK AND COMMUNICATION TOOL

By establishing KSFs, your organization's vision starts to convert to reality. They are the culmination, on paper, of all your previous work on your organization's vision, mission, and values. As we reinvent strategic management for the 21st century, KSFs provide a unique tool for organizations to travel from planning strategies to implementing and measuring them.

Using the KSF Continuous Improvement Matrix (Figure 7.1) as a tool, your organization will be able to chart the successful outcomes of its strategic plan. The matrix serves several purposes in your organization. For the executive team, it serves as an organization-wide "report card" at regular, specific intervals, keeping attention focused on what is important. It also provides a quick, easy way to communicate updates on organizational progress to all employees. Visually tracking the progress of each KSF on the matrix acts as a motivator, reminding employees of how much they have accomplished. In addition, because it measures outcomes in the key areas of the organization, it also makes an ideal progress report on which to base executive bonuses.

It is important, however, to keep in mind that KSFs are often something new to the organization. It can normally take a year or more to become comfortable with them and understand how to get just the right measurements. Therefore, when new KSFs are established, consider them cast in sand initially, and expect to do some adjusting and tweaking along the way. Also, it would be imprudent at this stage to publicly broadcast them. Soon, however, they will begin to feel natural and turn to concrete down the line.

It is critical to your progress that this matrix be kept up to date and be continually communicated throughout the organization. When everyone is in touch with—and comprehends—the goals and measuring sticks represented by the organization's KSFs, they will be better able to remain focused on the right outcomes.

At this point in strategic planning, you know what your Ideal Future Vision is, and you have developed outcome measures of success—called key success factors—to reach this vision. It is time to begin working your way "back toward" this future vision, beginning with today. The Current State Assessment, outlined in the next chapter, will probably seem familiar. The Current State Assessment step is where planners have traditionally concentrated their time and energy, studying about today versus building toward tomorrow.

RECAP OF KEY POINTS

1. Be sure to reflect the customer's point of view, both internally and externally.

2. Measure all key elements of your Ideal Future Vision.

3. Focus on outputs and results, except for possibly some crucial benchmarking on processes/systems.

4. Benchmarking vs. the competition may or may not be an organization-wide KSF. However, at the business unit level of the organization, it definitely is a KSF and should be tracked and evaluated as such.

5. Be sure to use the parallel process for KSFs as well; ownership and buy-in are essential.

6. Cost/benefits analysis applies to KSF development also. Use readily available data when at all possible.

7. If your vision should change at any point, remember to change your KSFs accordingly.

8. KSFs are often something new; it may take a year or so to get used to working with them and to get just the right measurement. Consider them cast in sand at first and concrete later. In other words, don't publicly broadcast the exact targets too early.

9. Some KSFs—like performance improvement—are a long-term process; just tracking and measuring in the first year is a good result. Have patience.

10. Tie your executive bonus/incentive pay and rewards to KSFs. This could be a separate project, but it is vitally important to success.

11. All performance appraisal forms should be tied to your core values (behaviors), as well as to the KSFs (results).

12. Because KSFs are outcomes/results, they are often seen as goals or objectives, and the words can sometimes be used interchangeably. Be clear in your use of terms

ACTION CHECKLIST

1. Determine your KSF areas, based on vision/values/mission and driving force(s). Do it individually first, then in subgroups, and then with the total group.

2. Set specific KSF factors and measures (targets) for end-of-planning horizon (i.e., the year 2000), baseline year (current year), and even intermediate targets if possible. (If you don't have enough time, do these later—but do them. Set a deadline.)

3. Assign KSF accountability for each KSF and also an overall KSF coordinator for total accountability to collect/report the data.

4. Troubleshoot your KSFs to ensure they are outputs/results/core values vs. means to an end. (Means should only be used when ends cannot be measured effectively or the means are absolutely essential.)

5. Define/agree on priorities for the KSFs (i.e., forced ranking of ten or less).

6. Eliminate the lowest priority KSFs if they are not critical or you have too many (ten maximum).

7. If you do not currently have the measure in place, your target for the first year will be to set it up and establish it on an ongoing basis.

8. Wherever possible, be sure to benchmark your KSFs against your competitors' best practices.

9. Set up the reporting format for KSFs and use it to track ongoing progress of target vs. actual.

10. Establish a measurement to find out whether the plan and the total strategic management system has become a practical reality, similar to a yearly independent financial audit.

CHAPTER 8

CURRENT STATE ASSESSMENT (STEP #4) (PHASE C: INPUT)

*Tolerating dissent is an essential means
by which societies cope with change.*

Peter C. Newman

ARE YOU WILLING TO TOLERATE HONEST ANSWERS?

Having established a set of quantifiable outcome measures—key success factors—in the last chapter, you can successfully track the implementation of your strategic plan outcomes. Next, you must determine the energy, time, and organizational resources you will need to get from the input of "where you are today" to the output of "where you want to be by Year X," or achieving your Ideal Future Vision. This requires absolute, organization-wide clarity on "where you are today" (i.e., an assessment of your current state).

In earlier strategic planning eras, and even today, the Current State Assessment (CSA) has been where planners spent most, if not all, of their time. The problem with this is that once the assessment is complete and the findings written up, not much else happens. Other than telling us where we are today, this type of assessment fails to identify the gaps between today and tomorrow

135

(i.e., our Ideal Future Vision); it also fails to develop specific action plans throughout the organization to *close* those gaps.

The first and most basic objective of the CSA (Step #4) is to honestly assess your current organizational performance against your Ideal Future Vision in many different ways.

When starting a CSA, you must be prepared to accept *all* of the findings and not just those you want to hear. This is part of assessing your current state honestly. Unless you rigorously deal with everything that has the potential to block your path, you will not achieve your Ideal Future Vision.

Once you have identified the gaps between "where you are" and "where you want to be," you need to problem solve those gaps and develop overall core strategies with specific actions or tactics for each one in order to close or bridge them over the life of your strategic planning horizon.

The CSA has two main components: an external assessment and an internal assessment. All of the areas necessary to complete both assessments are outlined in this chapter. There may be areas unique to your organization, however, that should also be assessed. By following the approaches suggested here, you will be able to complete a CSA that reflects your particular organizational situation.

BEST PRACTICES RESEARCH

Throughout this chapter, both the internal and external assessments include a number of mini-surveys designed to provoke thoughts and ideas and point you in the right direction to conduct a full assessment. They are not meant to be all-inclusive, but rather are designed to initiate further discussion and action planning.

These surveys have been systematically culled from research on the best practices of successful organizations and the main theorists and writers in each area. This implies that today's successful organizations are not only surviving the revolutionary changes of the 1990s, but are also beginning to move into position for the new millennium.

GETTING STARTED

You will need to address a few variables prior to conducting a CSA, including:

1. How much time does the organization need to accomplish this?
2. How much expertise do we need, or already have, among the members of the planning team?

> **3.** Has some CSA work already been done by other members of the organization or elsewhere that we can use?

Example: The planning team at a health care organization in San Diego had access to a substantial number of published surveys that would pertain to their assessment, but nobody had ever taken an organized and strategic set of actions on them. Rather than start from scratch on their SWOT (Strengths, Weaknesses, Opportunities, Threats) assessment, they incorporated the presentation of these studies, and the actions that had occurred, into their CSA (Step #4).

For each area, outside experts were used to dissect and interpret the study, ultimately providing the planning team with an executive summary. The findings from these summaries were then consolidated into an overall, usable SWOT analysis that would lead into developing strategies with action plans (Step #5).

CONDUCTING AN INTERNAL CURRENT STATE ASSESSMENT

The systems view of organizations shows clearly
that a paradigm shift in one aspect (or element)
of an organization causes the need for paradigm shifts
in every aspect of that organization.

Conducting an internal CSA in your organization will not only show you what gaps need mending to get from today to tomorrow. It will also enable you to clearly examine your systems fit and alignment throughout the organization in support of your Ideal Future Vision. Keep in mind that you will need to incorporate a parallel process in your internal CSA (Step #4), as well carefully check with corresponding levels of your organization and other stakeholders for the influences and effects of each change that needs to take place.

There are a number of categories that specifically target critical internal areas, including the following.

1. Financial Analysis

This is the most obvious place to begin, and much of the data will already be available. You will need to look at your profit-and-loss statements, organization-wide budgets, and, in order to assess the capitalization within your organization, your balance sheets.

Example: As General Motors has clearly shown, getting your "financial house in order" is a vital necessity, but it is not sufficient for long-term success. For GM, that success must now come through serving its customers with the products and services they need.

2. Core Values Analysis

If your organization approaches its core values as "nice, but not necessary," you are missing the boat. Core values, after all, are the main elements that make up your entire organizational culture. (See Chapter 6 for a detailed listing of typical areas where core values should appear and be reinforced within your organization.)

Example: In today's environment, the value of teamwork has advanced from "nice to have" to a critical success factor. See the coverage of Chrysler, Ford, and General Electric in the article entitled "The Horizontal Organization" (*Business Week,* December 1993).

3. Key Success Factors Analysis

Be sure to critique each key success factor versus your baseline data, as outlined in Chapter 7.

4. Organization Design

> *Empowered, educated people armed with*
> *technology and information do not require the same*
> *organizational framework that existed 100 years ago.*
>
> James R. Houghton
> CEO/Chairman, Corning, Inc.

A growing number of organizations today are analyzing one of the basic factors in their success: the system of jobs and the dynamics of operating relationships that constitute the design of the organization. Regardless of size, a number of dimensions exist in all organizations, including:

• Administrative components	• Formalization
• Integration	• Autonomy
• Professionalization	• Centralization
• Span of control	• Complexity

- Specialization
- Delegation of authority
- Differentiation

Traditional, hierarchical organizations are finding that the old motto of "that's just the way we do it around here" does not work any longer.

Today, hierarchical organizations are moving away from the executive/staff/line structure to a more integrative and horizontal (or cross-functional) fit. They are asking such questions as:

- How many layers of management should there be? (What is the minimum needed?)
- Where is the demarcation between needed staff and a burdensome bureaucracy?
- How do we empower our employees to serve the customer better and to take more self-directed initiatives versus waiting to be told?
- How do we manage diverse organizations that are the result of mergers, acquisitions, joint ventures, etc.?
- How do we organize geographically remote units, such as sales offices, factories, and service centers?
- Can we design structures and processes to meet customer needs?
- How can we continually manage the improvement of structures and processes across boundaries?
- How is each job designed? Are we providing our employees with holistic (Plan-Do-Control) jobs?

Finally, the organizational structure should be set up so that as many interdependent, cross-functional, horizontal tasks of the business or program area as possible are grouped together close to the customer for maximum efficiency and effectiveness.

In any case, the old cliche "mission → strategy → structure" still holds true today. Any change in your organizational structure depends on its alignment with your mission and strategies.

Example: Chrysler has set up "platform teams" to streamline the time and improve the quality of new car production. By using these cross-functional teams in its new technological center in Warren, Michigan, Chrysler has been able to produce the new Neon car in a record 31 months.

Customer-focused organizations organize by customer-focused units for all organizational products and services, using the "Lone Ranger" philosophy:

one customer = one organizational representative. They concentrate on organizing by customer *markets*–customer *segments*–customer *geography*.

McDonald's, for example, does this quite naturally by geography. In fact, the company's latest strategy is to be wherever its customers are—in schools, hotels, shopping malls, office building, stores, airports, ships, etc.—even if the restaurants themselves are much smaller or less expensive than usual (i.e., McD's ExPress).

5. Business Processes

Business processes consist of looking at your organizational systems and processes from the point of view of your customer and then later going back to radically reengineer and simplify, thus removing all *non*-value-added elements. It is about collapsing cycle time (how long it takes to perform a specific function) down to the real task time. The main idea is to bring every level and operation of the organization closer to the customer, so that the customer receives the service or product more quickly and with the highest possible quality.

Example: It has become generally well known among the vendor–supplier community that General Motors' cycle time for paying invoices is usually as much as four months. This is a prime example of the real task time (30 minutes to an hour to authorize, write, and issue a check) being overtaken by a bureaucracy which requires too many signatures at too many levels.

Tip: Survey your customers to identify the processes that are most important to them, where they have the most complaints, etc. For a customer focus, most top experts (i.e., Hammer, Conway, Deming, etc.) believe that each organization has only seven to ten processes that involve three or more functional departments. These should be your focus. Keep in mind that you reengineer *processes* as opposed to *functions*.

Example: When done right, business process reengineering will make a huge difference in the success of your organization. General Electric has been highly successful with its WorkOut program, which is designed to work out the bureaucracy existent in its business systems and processes.

6. Management/Leadership

> *It is very easy for ignorant people to think that success in war*
> *may be gained by the use of some wonderful invention*
> *rather than by hard fighting and superior leadership.*
>
> General George S. Patton

Obviously, none of these innovations, changes, or restructurings can effectively take place over the long term without professional management and leadership practices. Best practices research indicates that without the basic building blocks (or foundation) of business, nothing happens.

There is much talk about how "employees are our most important asset." Employees are certainly your organization's greatest asset, *but only if you— as their leader—let them be.* Being in management and leadership, *you* are actually the most important asset and the only difference in any organization over the long term. Therefore, assessing yourself honestly and being open to continuing leadership and development is the competitive advantage any organization can possess over time.

Tip: As a profession, managers generally do not devote the time and energy to skills that are essential for effective management and communication. Do they know what those skills are? Do they even know why management is considered a profession?

Example: Giant Industries has made a strategy in this area one of its two top priorities. In the first year of implementation, the company conducted a needs assessment and developed a leadership model with workshops, along with top-down attendance from the CEO and president on down.

7. Eight Key Human Resource Areas

If you want your organization to survive and grow, you face both short- and long-term substantial change. This change includes not only your technologies, customer contact, and organizational design; it includes your people management practices as well.

As this era continues, your organization's human resource managers will be called upon more often to serve in many new and unexplored functions. Therefore, it is imperative to carefully assess the capabilities of your human resource department in the eight functional human resource areas shown in Figure 8.1.

8. Rewards for Total Performance

As the traditional hierarchical structure continues to diminish in favor of a more horizontal, cross-functional design, the traditional methods for rewarding exceptional performance also fall by the wayside. This does not mean that organizations no longer need to reward performance, however.

The first step toward choosing the reward method that is right for you is to examine a broader perspective of financial and non-financial rewards.

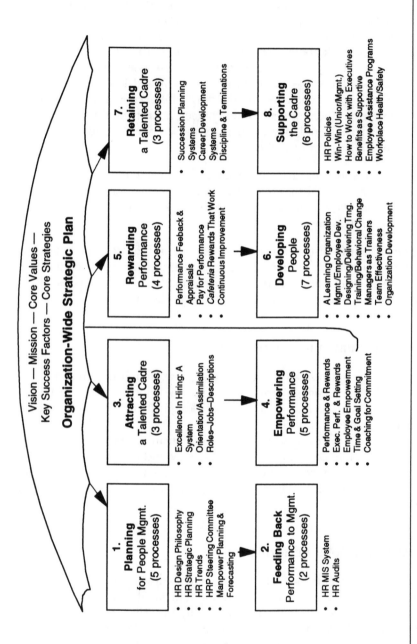

FIGURE 8.1 1990s Strategic Human Resource Management (HRM) Systems Model: 8 Areas and 33 Key HRM Processes to Creating High-Performance Organizations; Goal #3: To Ensure People Are a *Competitive Business Advantage*

Many organizations use only financial rewards for performance. However well they worked for the hierarchical organization, they alone are not right for today's organization.

Example: Human resource experts agree that pay for performance does not work, yet it is continually perpetuated by senior management. In recent years, average merit raises under pay for performance have netted the average employee an increase in take-home pay of $10 a week after twelve months of work and results. This is hardly enough to motivate anyone to do anything.

Monetary incentives are not the only acceptable way to reward performance. In today's changing marketplace, in fact, most organizations simply are unable to tie performance to money in a meaningful way, say 10 to 15% of salary. The public sector never has.

Today's high-performance organizations increasingly are turning to nonfinancial performance compensation with great success. According to best practices research on employee needs in France, Canada, and the United States, the top three motivators are:

1. Recognition for a job well done

2. Growth and development (learning and training)

3. Responsibility (opportunity for freedom of thought and action (i.e., empowerment)

On the average in each survey, the importance of money almost always comes in at fourth place. Once again, it is necessary but not sufficient for most of us.

Example: Organizations most commonly reward individuals, but the truth is that jobs are usually accomplished through teamwork. The missing link here is that rewards are based exclusively on one aspect of the job: the individual part. Although this is necessary, it is not sufficient.

Let's look at ways to gauge actual performance. Performance is about:

1. Results vs. core strategies at three levels:

    • Individual work accomplishments

    • Teamwork achievements

    • Organizational results

2. Behavior vs. core values

To determine if your reward system is effective, complete the assessment in Figure 8.2. Examine the types of performance your organization assesses

	Individual	Team	Organization
What performance is assessed in our organization?			
What rewards are given in our organization?			

What changes are needed?

Who is responsible to lead this change?

FIGURE 8.2 Internal Assessment: Performance and Rewards—Rewards for Total Performance Assessment

and rewards. If changes are needed, specify who should be responsible for leading this change.

Example: Remember that rewards must reinforce your new Ideal Future Vision, not the past. Most organizations do *not* have a reward system that supports their future vision/mission/values. Managers who do not have a reinforcing reward system are, in effect, shooting themselves in the foot. The organization is blindly pursuing its future vision despite the lack of a good analysis, change, and fit of its reward system with its vision.

9. Teamwork

> *Simple downsizing didn't produce the dramatic rises in productivity many companies hoped for. Gaining quantum leaps in performance requires rethinking the way work gets done. To do that, some companies are adopting a new [horizontal] organization model.*
>
> *Business Week* (December 1993)

As more organizations turn toward a horizontal structure, organizing around processes rather than individual, hierarchical functions, teamwork is becoming an essential ingredient for success. Without teamwork, a total focus on the customer in today's changing marketplace will not happen.

Example: A good example of the horizontal effect is Motorola's Government Electronics group. Making customer satisfaction its driving force, this group reshaped its own supply management organization. Rather than being a separate entity, it is now a successful *process,* with its external customer as the end-product.

If your organization is like most, you have probably initiated some team activities, but are searching for ways to incorporate more cross-functional teamwork effectively. Use the chart in Figure 8.3 to determine where and how teams would work best in your organization.

Example: It is becoming apparent that maximum use of self-directed work teams yields reduced costs, shorter cycle times, and greater customer responsiveness. General Electric's lighting business successfully did away with its traditional organization design in favor of a structure where a senior team (made up of 9 to 12 individuals) supervises close to 100 processes worldwide. (This includes anything from maximizing production machinery to designing new products.) A multidisciplinary team oversees and is responsible for meeting each goal of each process.

Caution: Make sure the skills training and motivation are available to all workers. However, don't forget to train the supervisors and senior managers

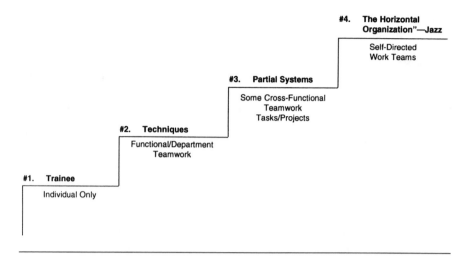

FIGURE 8.3   Level of Teamwork in Any Organization: Cross-Functional Team-work and Horizontal Organizations

first, so they really *can* walk the talk. Remember, leaders are your most important asset!

10. Core Competencies

The last element of your internal assessment should be a study of your organization's core competencies. This is about gaining a realistic sense of what your organization is particularly good at, in order to continually build on its strengths as well as eliminate your weaknesses.

Exercise: There are three primary steps to follow or questions to ask when identifying core competencies:

1. **First**, ask yourself, "What are our existing core competencies?" Are they the same across the organization or not?

2. **Next**, define how these core competencies compare to your de-sired future ideal for your driving forces. "What core competencies do we need across the organization to achieve our future vision?"

3. **Finally**, look at possible alternatives for your organization if it cannot fulfill its existing core competencies.

Summary

Now that you have thoroughly assessed the current state of your organization internally, you should have a pretty good idea of what is working. You should also have a clear grasp of what needs to be changed in order to get from where you are today to where you want to be tomorrow. Now, it is time to turn to the external environment.

Questions to Ponder

- Are you honestly willing to accept all of your Current State Assessment findings and not just the ones you feel good about?

- Do you already have previous assessment work that could be used now?

CONDUCTING AN EXTERNAL CURRENT STATE ASSESSMENT

It's simple—those with the latest and most comprehensive market information have a clear advantage over those who don't.

American Demographics, 1992

There is no shortage of potential areas you may choose to focus on during your external Current State Assessment. The following discussion is centered around a partial list of external areas frequently used; you may want to add some of your own as well.

1. Organizational Life Cycle

Obviously, all organizations go through similar life cycles: (1) research and development, (2) start-up and growth, (3) the mature business, (4) decline, and, hopefully, (5) renewal.

It is important to differentiate the mature phase (#3) from the decline phase (#4). If you fail to recognize the difference, it could prove too late for possible renewal (#5).

Example: Ten years ago, AT&T and IBM were both involved in anti-trust lawsuits with the government. While IBM won its suit, which was dropped, AT&T did not and was forced to break up into the seven "Baby Bells."

There was an interesting outcome from this. While AT&T was forced to change, it ultimately underwent a successful renewal along with the Baby Bells, whereas IBM continued on from its mature phase into a decline phase and is now struggling to renew its old marketplace dominance. This is a great case to prove that winning in the short term does not mean long-term success.

A number of factors go into studying your organization's life cycle: industry maturity, competitive position, market share objective, and sales volume. Five questions should be considered when evaluating your organization's life cycle:

1. Where are we on the life cycle matrix today?

2. Where do we want to be in the future?

3. Where are we likely to be in the future (given no proactive changes)?

4. What are the implications for today (i.e., competitors, customers, growth rate, market share, profitability, liquidity, substitutes, technology)?

5. What are the implications for the future?

2. Competitor Analysis

Your external assessment will not be complete without a thorough, in-depth analysis of your competition. You need to look at not only how they sell their product or service, but what has and has not worked for them, market share, and future projections and strategies.

Conducting an in-depth competitive analysis is of great value to your own planning; it gives you a clear picture of how crowded your market is and initiates ideas on how to capture more of it. Use the following list as a framework to conduct an analysis of your top three competitors. What is their:

- Vision, mission, values, and driving force(s)?
- Core strategies, outcome measures, or goals?
- Current state assessment (SWOT)?
- Market share and customer reputation/position?
- Pricing strategy?
- Background of key executives?
- Technology perspective?
- Core competencies and capabilities?

Conducting this type of competitive benchmark will help to accomplish two things: (1) you gain a greater understanding of exactly what you are up against and (2) you get a better overall sense of your industry.

3. Customer Focus

Organizations that do not have a clear focus on who their customers are (and what they want) have fewer customers—and considerably less profit. Just saying that you are already customer focused, or want to be, is not enough; the customer *always* knows the difference.

To determine if your organization really is customer focused, use the survey in Figure 8.4 to get to the heart of the matter. Honestly assess your organization's adherence to the Ten Commandments of a Customer-Focused Organization mentioned earlier.

If you are already following these commandments in your organization, you truly are a visionary. If not, this is a perfect time to examine your weaknesses, as well as your strengths, and create a series of actions toward improvement.

Being truly customer focused also means incorporating ongoing Customer Recovery Strategies. When you do make a mistake with a current customer, develop effective Customer Recovery Strategies by examining a number of elements, including:

- Focus on the 5- to 10-year ROI of the customer as opposed to the cost savings today.

- Examine your long-term image and reputation. (Remember, unhappy customers tell 11 others; happy customers tell only 4 others.)

- Empower the employee at the "moment of truth" to be innovative in surpassing the customer's expectations in solving a problem (i.e., solve the problem, then do something else above and beyond).

- Provide expenditure authority to do the above.

- Ensure that accountability at the moment of truth equals responsibility.

- Think about how to tie the recovery into future business opportunities (i.e., 50% off next time for the unhappy customer).

- Develop a customer guarantee and live up to or surpass it.

- Ensure that your Customer Recovery Strategies include fast response, knowledgeability, and empathy, as well as both tangibles and intangibles.

The Ten Commandments Mastery Skill Level →	A. Trainee *Going Out of Business*	B. Techniques *Dogged Pursuit of Mediocrity*	C. Systems Orientation *Customer- Focused*	D. Jazz Player *Art Form*	Comments
1. "Close to the Customer" — Sr. Executives/ Customer Involvement?	1 2	3 4 5 6 7	8 9	10	1.
2. Know customer's needs — surpassing them is Driving Force?	1 2	3 4 5 6 7	8 9	10	2.
3. Survey customer's satisfaction — regularly? (on products and services)	1 2	3 4 5 6 7	8 9	10	3.
4. Focus on "value-added" — QECD?	1 2	3 4 5 6 7	8 9	10	4.
5. Measurable service standards/expectations set — all units?	1 2	3 4 5 6 7	8 9	10	5.
6. "Moments of Truth" — all staff/1 day/year+?	1 2	3 4 5 6 7	8 9	10	6.
7. Cross-functional business processes reengineered — customer-focused?	1 2	3 4 5 6 7	8 9	10	7.
8. Structure based on marketplace?	1 2	3 4 5 6 7	8 9	10	8.
9. "Recovery" strategies — clear/rewarded? (to surpass customer expectations)	1 2	3 4 5 6 7	8 9	10	9.
10. Customer-friendly people? (hired and promoted)	1 2	3 4 5 6 7	8 9	10	10.

Total Score = _____ (100 possible)

FIGURE 8.4 Survey: Are You a Customer-Focused Organization?

Getting customers is difficult and expensive. *Keeping* them, by meeting their expectations and then doing something more that they don't expect, will pay off over and over again in the long term.

4. Market Orientation and Segmentation

This is where you evaluate how market oriented your organization really is by assessing a number of organizational characteristics, such as:

- Are we easy to do business with?
- Do we keep our promises?
- Do we meet the standards we set?
- Are we responsive?
- Do we work together inside the organization to provide coordinated and quality service?

Although many organizations protest that they already know and are close to their customers, unfortunately, few really are. In conducting this portion of your external assessment, it is imperative that you carefully scrutinize your customer base. After gathering this data, bring it back to the group of planning team members for discussion, feedback, and action.

To get a better sense of whether your organization is concentrating its energies on the most profitable customer base, examine the cost/value ratio of your customers. Ask planning team members and key participants to fill out the chart in Figure 8.5.

Identifying your customers according to who they are, how they do business with you, and how much it costs your organization to retain them will quickly help you to pinpoint where the most profitable customers are.

By focusing on your customer, you will gain a clear, sharp image of just exactly who your present and future customers should be. The more you concentrate on this criterion, the more quickly you will truly become a high-performance, customer-focused organization.

5. Value Mapping Your Products and Services (Positioning)

You will need to create an actual "map" of your products and services, which assesses where the value of each (its position) stands in the marketplace. This is an attempt to determine how you stack up against your competitors' lines and how the quality of your product or service is perceived.

Instructions:
1. Fill out Columns 1, 2, 3, and 4 individually; then as a Core Planning Team
2. Next, decide from this analysis the relative ratings in Column 5.

THE COST/VALUE OF CUSTOMERS

1. Customer Segments/Account Names	2. Relative cost to service this segment (High-Med-Low)	3. Current relative value (High-Med-Low)	4. Future Potential (High-Med-Low)	5. Final Priority (Force Rank all segments)

3. Now, remembering the 80/20 rule, who are your top 20% customers to be
    served? Circle their names above.

FIGURE 8.5 Market Segmentation

Organizations often make the mistake of thinking that just getting the product out in the marketplace is enough, but that's just not so. The fact is that product "mapping" and positioning has a great deal to do with your customer's perception of your product and the organization behind it.

As illustrated in Figure 8.6, a value map poses two questions for each of your products or services: (1) Where do we stand in terms of price, quality, and perceived value? (2) What actions we need to take if we want to increase or change this line in the future?

Perhaps most importantly, creating a map from your customer's perspec-

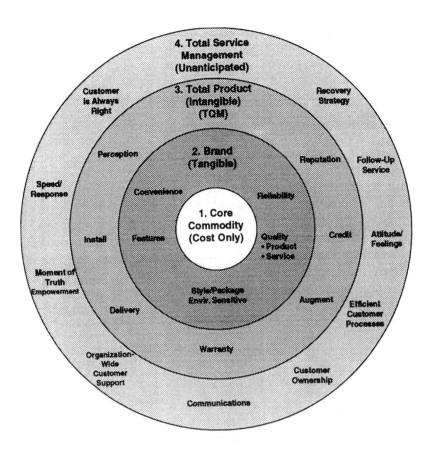

Where do you compete (Core Product or outer features)?
1. Commodity
2. Brand
3. Total Product/Intangibles
4. Total Product and Services Package/Unanticipated

FIGURE 8.6 Value Map: Total "Package" Perspective (Products and Services Combined)

---

tive will give you a total, overall perspective of in which areas (such as cost, quality, features, delivery, and customer responsiveness) your products and services are the most (or least) competitive.

Example: Many organizations compete only on a commodity (or price) basis, such as today's airlines (ring #1 on the map in Figure 8.6). It is usually better to compete on a brand basis, such as Proctor & Gamble's retail products, Tide, etc. (ring #2). The best way, however, is to focus on rings #3 and #4, the overall product *and* service package (i.e., Marriott, Nordstrom's, and Disney).

6. Market Share and Growth Rate

Once you have sized up the competition, it is time to take a serious look at how much of the market you already have and how much of it you want to have. As the familiar General Electric and Boston Consulting Group matrix in Figure 8.7 indicates, you will need to analyze your market share and your

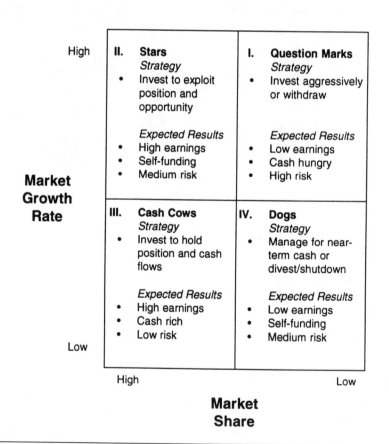

FIGURE 8.7 Growth Share Matrix: Strategic Analysis (Adapted from Boston Consulting Group and General Electric Portfolio Matrix)

market growth rate. Then you can decide what actions you should take for consistent growth and profitability over the next few years. You will need to analyze which of your products or services are strong and which ones you might consider letting go in order to free up your resources.

Once you have carefully evaluated your market share strengths and weaknesses, use the matrix in Figure 8.7 to develop the strategies to succeed in your market. You will end up with a complete portfolio management set of strategies for all of your strategic business units and products.

Use this data to consider and shape different strategies that can position your organization in its marketplace. Be sure to match the results you expect with each strategy as well.

7. Product/Market Certainty Matrix

Now that you have studied your products and business units, it is time to break your evaluation down further still by looking at your specific product (or service) lines. Use the same criteria for each end-product that you used to judge your business units, asking:

1. Are we changing this product or service?

2. What are the implications or risk of this change?

3. What actions should we take and at what point?

Develop a growth share matrix to show each product's profitability on gross margin. In addition, judge each product by its market and customer segment by developing a matrix similar to Figure 8.8, which identifies projected success rate.

Whether you are taking an existing product to a new market or evolving it into a new but related product which will sell to a different market, always analyze it carefully against the backdrop of a matrix similar to Figure 8.8. Otherwise, you are entering an uncharted course on not much more than a whim or a guess—and we all know where that got IBM when it wanted to sell its PC Junior (a new but related product) to a consumer market (a new but unrelated market). IBM only had a 20% probability of success on the matrix—and the PC Junior no longer exists.

Example: A good example of this kind of foreplanning in the auto industry is the success that Toyota and Nissan experienced when they wanted to bring new products (the Lexus and Infiniti) to a new but related upscale market.

A different type of example is provided by Sears, when it tried to introduce financial services (a new but unrelated product/service) to what it

Products (or Product Lines)

Markets (Customer Segments)		Existing	New, but Related	New and Unrelated
	Existing	90% *Very High Certainty*	60%	30%
	New, but Related	60%	40%	20%
	New and Unrelated	30%	20%	10% *Very Low Certainty*

Adapted from Hayden and A.T. Kearney (1987 FIMA tape)

1. New products/same customers = 60% success rate.
2. New products/new customers = serious problems with any success.

FIGURE 8.8   Product/Market Certainty Matrix

gambled on being a new but related customer (its in-store customers). In fact, however, Sears was trying to reach a new customer (financial services buyers in general) and failed to achieve the success it wanted. This strategy is presently being revised at a high cost.

The benefit of going through this exercise is that it forces you to concentrate on the probability of success for each product and identifies up front those products that could be problematic.

SUMMARY

8. Conducting a Strengths, Weaknesses, Opportunities, Threats Analysis

Once you have completed your assessment, both internal and external, the final step is to create a Strengths, Weaknesses, Opportunities, Threats (SWOT) analysis. The basic concept is as follows:

Internally: Build on your **S**trengths
Eliminate or cope with your **W**eaknesses

Externally: Exploit your **O**pportunities
Ease and lower your **T**hreats

A SWOT analysis allows your planning team and key stakeholders to tie up any loose ends uncovered in your Current State Assessment and answers any previously unresolved organizational issues. It is one of the most critical steps of your entire assessment, because *it incorporates both your external and internal assessments into one summary that is usable and practical.*

When identifying your SWOT, your planning team and key stakeholders should be looking for any element or characteristic that will either help or hinder your organization in its attempt to achieve its Ideal Future Vision. There will more than likely be many entries on both sides of the coin; you should therefore be sure to include all of the internal and external assessments outlined in this chapter.

Once you have drawn up a draft of internal weaknesses and strengths, ask planning team members to list corresponding action implications next to each entry. See the summary analysis in Figure 8.9 for a sample of the format to use to ensure that your SWOT is action oriented. Many are not.

Once you have completed the SWOT analysis, you will have a realistic, comprehensive list of potential actions that can be used to jump-start your brainstorming for the next step of planning: creating core strategies.

Based on the assessment tasks #1-7, which are the most important factors to consider in the strategic planning?

Which Factors Are Most Important? List Answers	Action Implication Over the Planning Horizon
1.	
2.	
3.	
4.	
5.	
6.	
7.	
8.	
9.	
10.	

FIGURE 8.9 Summary Analysis: Internal Assessment

RECAP OF KEY POINTS

1. When conducting your internal and external assessments, be willing to honestly accept all findings, not just the positive ones.

2. In your internal Current State Assessment, be sure to include thorough evaluation of the following ten points:

1. Financial analysis

2. Core values analysis

3. Key success factor analysis

4. Organization design

5. Business processes

6. Management/leadership

7. Eight key human resource areas

8. Reward for total performance

9. Teamwork

10. Core competencies

3. In your external Current State Assessment, be sure to include evaluation of the following ten areas:

1. Stakeholder analysis

2. Organizational life cycle

3. Industry structure analysis

4. Competitor analysis

5. Strategic business unit information

6. Customer focus

7. Market orientation and segmentation

8. Value map of products and services (positioning)

9. Market share and growth rate

10. Product/market certainty

4. Be sure to conduct a SWOT analysis (with action implications) as a summary, to digest all your analysis into a usable form.

ACTION CHECKLIST

1. Analyze your organizational finances and core values. Evaluate them based on their capacity to support your Ideal Future Vision.

2. Study your organization's design to determine if it will "get you where you want to go."

3. Evaluate your organizational processes from your customer's point of view.

4. Make sure you have the management and leadership skills you will need.

5. Look at organizational reward systems, both financial and non-financial.

6. Scrutinize organizational core competencies.

7. Analyze what phases your organizational and industry life cycles are currently in.

8. Conduct an in-depth analysis of your competition.

9. In your market orientation analysis, make sure that you are concentrating on your most profitable customer base. (Also, determine whether your organization is structured around customer-focused units.)

10. Develop a value map of your products or services, and define their market position.

11. Do an in-depth analysis of your current market share, and define how much your future market share should be.

12. Look closely at each product line; determine the implications or risks inherent in any changes you may make.

CHAPTER 9

STRATEGY DEVELOPMENT
(STEP #5)
(PHASE C: INPUT)

If you always do what you've always done,
you'll always get what you've always gotten.

STRATEGIES: DEFINITIONS AND DIFFERENCES

Step #5, strategy development, works on creating the core strategies and action items that will help you bridge the gaps between your Ideal Future Vision and the Current State Assessment just completed.

The result of this step will be three to seven core strategies to be implemented organization-wide. When put into practice, these strategies become the primary means to your desired end—your Ideal Future Vision. In essence, these core strategies, along with your key success factors, will become the "glue" that keeps your organization focused in a consistent, customer-focused fashion year after year.

NEW MANAGEMENT STRATEGIES FOR NEW TIMES

The 1990s have seen a proliferation of new strategies as organizations try to cope with the revolutionary change of these times. It is not as if organizations are just dealing with one change; rather, they are facing multiple levels of change, with more certainly to come. Thus, don't reform—*transform*.

This virtual revolution will require more than simple "tuck-and-cut" solutions. Organizations need new visions, new strategies, new programs, and, most importantly, new actions. In short, "micro smart" (incremental thinking) yet "macro dumb" (lack of systems-level thinking) will not work anymore.

TWELVE STRATEGIES FOR THE 21ST CENTURY

As mentioned in earlier chapters, there is good news in the proliferation of new strategies that arose in response to the tremendous changes of the 1990s, particularly the following.

1. Flexibility

Customer-focused organizations that envision success must be able to develop strategies with built-in flexibility. For example, in formulating their core strategies, Giant Industries (a major oil company based in Phoenix) and Poway Unified School District in southern California have both determined to be opportunistic and flexible in how they run their businesses.

2. Speed

Both Toyota and Chrysler have incorporated speed as a core strategy. If done well, shorter cycle times can lower cost, improve product quality, and produce better customer response time. Neither General Motors nor most European automakers have successfully implemented this core strategy yet.

3. Horizontally Integrated Products (Related Products/By-Products)

Ethanol plants are catching on in a big way; in Canada, communities are now being developed around them. Ethanol is an alcohol-based additive to gasoline, which creates less need in the United States and Canada for importing oil. As the centerpiece for horizontal, community-wide integration, it also creates (1) steam for generators and electricity, (2) a mash which is used to feed cattle, and, on the front end, (3) grain as the primary ingredient.

4. Networks and Alliances

This innovative strategy is rapidly becoming a favorite. Organizations all over the world are finding that they can't do it alone. Who would have thought that IBM and Apple would have joined forces? In Canada, MCI has recently formed productive alliances with Bell Canada and Stentor. However, the Japanese have been successfully forging alliances for some time, with their *keiretsu* interlocking companies.

Caution: Whether or not this strategy really works is a complex matter. Too many organizations seem to be rushing pell-mell into this strategy. It requires careful crafting and constant communication.

5. Value-Added

"More value for the same money" is becoming a hot strategy in manufacturing and retail industries of all kinds. Organizations are looking at products and services from a total package perspective, trying to determine where they are most competitive. Is it in their core product or in its more intangible features? An example is the Maxima, which Nissan is promoting as a luxury sedan, stressing that the buyer gets better quality and more value for the same price. Retail brand products look at value add-ons, as more and more generic products beat them in larger size and lower cost.

6. Environmentally Improved/Based Products

Environmental protection and its "3 R's"—reduce, reuse, recycle—is good business these days. No longer are we hearing as much about the "business vs. the environment" debate (except in British Columbia and the Pacific Northwest). Now, many things that are good for the environment are good for many businesses as well. Also, marketing "environment-friendly" products (i.e., products that can be recycled) is dramatically on the rise.

7. Mass Customization

Toyota is aggressively taking advantage of improved manufacturing capabilities that link with the latest in telecommunications, by allowing customers to select a base model with individual specifications and receive delivery in Japan a very short time later.

8. Commonization/Simplification

Honda does a "Value Analysis" on every one of its products and components by researching those elements of the product its customers really do not need. By trimming these elements out of the product, production costs go down, and Honda can offer its customers the same value for a lesser price.

9. Business Process Reengineering

In a management-supported, organization-wide rethinking of employee roles, General Electric created a culture without boundaries through something called WorkOut. WorkOut is a two-day training program GE runs regularly, with great success.

"You have to have...input from people who know the work best," says GE's CEO Jack Welch. "The more involved the workforce is in your decisions, the more they own them, and you make far better decisions..."

10. Organizational Learning

Numerous business writers (Senge, Peters, etc.) are reintroducing a common-sense notion to business as it moves toward the 21st century. It emphasizes that, with change being a given, we are going to need to learn how to cope with change on an individual and organization-wide basis. To do this, we must begin to create "learning organizations," in which learning is an ongoing, normal part of the organizational structure.

11. Employee Morale/Benefits: Focus on Work

Corporations have begun to recognize that, in addition to salary, employees are concerned with providing for their families in the modern sense of that diverse term. Therefore, many corporations today are introducing increased family support programs as a part of their employee benefits package. This can include anything from family leave, child care resource centers, community and volunteer time, and wellness centers to the more conventional elements such as employee stock purchase plans, life insurance, tuition assistance, and retirement and capital accumulation plans (401K plans). For example, Stride Rite Corporation offers its employees all these benefits, as well as an employee volunteer program and child/elder care services.

12. Management and Leadership Practices

Keep in mind that of all the research on the four Vital Few Leverage Points for Change, management and leadership practices has been singled out as the foundation for everything else an organization does. In actual fact, the phrase "employees are our best asset" can only be true when the organization's leadership and management create an environment conducive to motivated employees. Thus, when all is said and done, strong management skills and leadership practices are really your greatest asset.

This is not to say that dealing with ongoing, revolutionary change will be easy, but there exists a wealth of potential success through new strategies that incorporate more teamwork, greater empowerment, and faster, smarter leadership.

PUBLIC SECTOR STRATEGIES OF THE 1990s

In the public and not-for-profit sectors, widespread disappointment in the general quality or lack of services, plus high taxes, is creating the same need for new strategies that the private sector is experiencing. Many public sector organizations are now aggressively seeking and implementing strategies that are more like those used by the private sector, including:

1. Steer rather than row (facilitate vs. do it yourself)

2. Empower communities and customers to solve their own problems rather than simply deliver services

3. Encourage competition rather than monopolies

4. Be driven by missions rather than rules

5. Be results oriented by funding outcomes rather than inputs

6. Meet the needs of the customer rather than the bureaucracy

7. Concentrate on earning and making money rather than spending it

8. Stop subsidizing everyone; let the user pay by charging user fees

9. Invest in preventing problems rather than curing crises

10. Decentralize authority

11. Solve problems by market influences rather than public programs

12. Reduce regulations; cut out bureaucracy and low risk-taking

13. Privatization (except for essentials not provided elsewhere)

These thirteen strategies (some adapted from Osborne and Gaebler's book *Reinventing Government*) are being employed in the restructuring of the public and not-for-profit sectors.

Example: These strategies have been used extensively in New Zealand over the past ten years. Also, beginning in 1993, Premier Ralph Klein of Alberta, Canada, has been called "a dog with a bone" by strenuously adhering to these strategies as well. Phoenix, Arizona is often called "the best-managed city in the world."

Regardless of what strategies you and your organization choose, however, there are two types (discussed in the next section) that *every* organization needs.

CUTTING AND BUILDING STRATEGIES BOTH NEEDED

Are you "planning not to lose" or "playing to win?"

In developing your core strategies, one thing to avoid is the fallacy of thinking in terms of financial strategies, such as cost cutting, alone. By their very nature, many financial strategies are really cost-cutting strategies; they cannot stand on their own and produce long-range solutions. Strategies such as retrenchment, turnarounds, cost reductions, divestitures, reorganizing, business process reengineering, and layoffs may all be necessary to reduce overhead costs and sustain financial viability. Keep in mind, however, that they are mostly *cutting* strategies that keep you from failing (i.e., "playing not to lose").

You will need other core strategies that are *building* you toward your ideal future (i.e., "playing to win"), such as TQM, service quality, capacity building (leadership), product innovations, etc. In order for any strategy that involves cutting to be successful, it must be consciously followed by a strategy of building toward your customer-focused vision. One without the other will not work in the long term.

Caution: In addition to striking this balance between cutting and building, keep in mind that you will need a good supply of patience, because results are not usually instantaneous. It is important to recognize that you will need to be patient during the transition from cutting strategies to building strategies.

Example: In other words, if your organization chooses to defray expenses by cutting down on employee training or production costs, it also needs to consider the future-building strategy of customer satisfaction. In this way, you can ensure that you are not mistakenly reducing your employees' skills in implementing any customer recovery strategy or eliminating a feature of the product that has perceived value to your customer.

Questions to Ponder

- In developing your strategies, have you taken into consideration the twelve new strategies for the 21st century?

- In the public or not-for-profit sector, have you used some of the thirteen entrepreneurial principles of government to address your public's disappointment in the quality and lack of services available to them?

- Are you integrating building strategies as well as cutting (i.e., financial only) strategies?

- Finally, do you have a small number of focused core strategies? (Remember, the fewer the better.)

DEVELOPING CORE STRATEGIES: PUBLIC AND PRIVATE

Corporations are successful not because of
the hundred and one good little actions they take
to save money on paper clips and telephone calls,
but because of one or two major strategies that are brilliant.

Dr. Michael J. Kami

If you have been doing a good job of building your vision, mission, values, and key success factors, you have actually been focusing on strategy all along. Whenever you talk about ends or desired outcomes, you are really talking about strategy. Now you need to draw from all those conversations the elements you will use to develop core strategies.

When developing your organization's core strategies, keep in mind that they should serve you in the following ways:

1. Core strategies should define your competitive business advantages, leading to long-term sustainable organizational viability.

2. They should help you select how you define, organize, and grow the elements or strategic business unit parts of your business.

3. They should help you determine your overall organization design and structure, along with individual job design/employee initiative characteristics, and philosophy.

4. Core strategies must next lead to a list of action items for each core strategy over the life of the planning horizon. These action items are long-term, unifying directions for the lower levels of the organization.

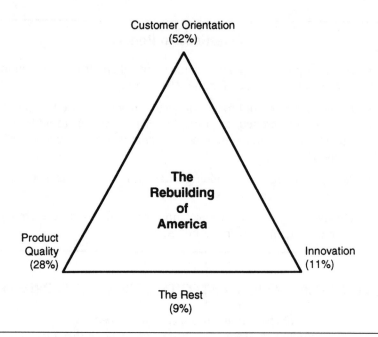

FIGURE 9.1 Triangle of Strategic Competitive Business Advantages (Source: B. Gale (speaker), "Linking Shareholder Value to Competitive Advantage," PIMS Data Base, June 8, 1987)

5. Core strategies will become the "glue," or yearly goals and objectives, around which to organize your annual planning process.

In developing your external marketplace strategies, use the formula **Q**uality, **E**nvironmentally responsible, **C**ost, **D**elivery, **S**ervice (QECDS), illustrated in Figure 9.1, to shape strategies, for both products and services, that will be based on a value-added premise from the customer's perspective. You can also use the PIMS database of over 15,000 companies to examine which financial strategies led to success (very few).

Finally, one way to assess your own strategies (and make sense out of all this discussion) is to categorize them in the following five generic strategic areas.

FIVE GENERIC CORE STRATEGY AREAS

Five strategic areas, each with different elements, are included when considering core strategies for the private and public sectors. In the private sector, they are known as:

1. Product-driven strategies
2. Market-driven strategies
3. Financial-driven strategies
4. Uniquely-driven strategies
5. Employee-driven strategies

Exercise: Use the questionnaire in Table 9.1 to begin identifying and assessing your private sector organizational core strategies (*Note:* While the list is labeled "private" and "future" core strategy profile, you can also use it to assess your current strategies or for a public sector assessment as well).

Once your planning team members have completed these questionnaires, begin group discussions and initial drafts of core strategies for your organization. As in the development of key success factors, take time to meet, draw up rough drafts, prioritize, and reach mutual consensus.

Focus, Focus, Focus

You will need to develop a maximum of three to five core strategies to successfully achieve your outcome of focusing on the customer. If your organization is like most, you will probably end up selecting too many strategies, as there are a wealth of opportunities in today's global changes. It is important to keep core strategies to a small number. Implementing and coordinating more than three or four usually becomes unmanageable, as you try to be all things to all people.

Research on U.S. savings and loans (prior to their demise) found that among the most profitable savings and loans, the average number of core strategies was three. Among the top 200 U.S. savings and loans, the worst performers had five or more core strategies. This 60% increase in the number of strategies the worst savings and loans chose consistently weakened their concentration and attention to their real issues. The overall conclusion is that carefully selected core strategies are essential to achieving a customer-focused, high-performance organization.

For example: In the 1980s, Imperial Corporation of America (a $13 billion nationwide savings and loan holding company based in San Diego) decided on diversification as the best avenue for growth. The CEO and CFO developed a matrix of 231 business niches that they could conceivably enter. Of these 231 areas, they settled on 114 different products and delivery niches, which they saw as the best areas because they had the highest profit margins.

The problem with this rationale was that high profit margins usually

TABLE 9.1 Private Sector: Future Core Strategy Profile

Instructions: Circle the number below that best characterizes your organization's overall business strategies on the following potential strategies as **you want them to be in the future**.

	Never	Seldom	Often	Always
I. Product-Driven Strategies				
1. Product/service applications (i.e., Hewlett-Packard's "What If...?")	(1)	(2)	(3)	(4)
2. Horizontal integration/related products (i.e., Arco's gas stations as convenience stores)	(1)	(2)	(3)	(4)
3. Product uniqueness (i.e., Space Shuttle)	(1)	(2)	(3)	(4)
4. Technology (i.e., Cray Super Computers)	(1)	(2)	(3)	(4)
5. Patents, legal protection) (i.e., drug companies)	(1)	(2)	(3)	(4)
6. Value added (i.e., GM's credit card; frequent flyer miles)	(1)	(2)	(3)	(4)
II. Market-Driven Strategies				
7. Geographic niche (i.e., SW Airlines; global expansion)	(1)	(2)	(3)	(4)
8. Customer segment (i.e., Cadillac/Mercedes)	(1)	(2)	(3)	(4)
9. Marketing effectiveness (i.e., Miller Lite's "Tastes great, less filling")	(1)	(2)	(3)	(4)
10. Large market share (i.e., AT&T long-distance tele-communications)	(1)	(2)	(3)	(4)
11. High growth (i.e., Marriott 20% per year)	(1)	(2)	(3)	(4)
III. Financial-Driven Strategies				
12. Low-cost price leadership (i.e., Price Club)	(1)	(2)	(3)	(4)
13. Economies of scale overall (i.e., General Motors)	(1)	(2)	(3)	(4)
14. Capital structure (i.e., Drexel Burnham's junk bond market)	(1)	(2)	(3)	(4)
15. Diversification (i.e., ITT)	(1)	(2)	(3)	(4)
16. Retrenchment, turnaround, cost reductions (i.e., IBM, GM)	(1)	(2)	(3)	(4)

TABLE 9.1   Private Sector: Future Core Strategy Profile (continued)

	Never	Seldom	Often	Always
17. Divestiture, liquidation, LBOs (i.e., Sunoco)	(1)	(2)	(3)	(4)
IV. Special-Driven Strategies				
18. Unique distribution channels (i.e., Federal Express' Memphis, Tennessee nightly hub)	(1)	(2)	(3)	(4)
19. Vertical integration (i.e., Exxon)	(1)	(2)	(3)	(4)
20. Natural resources (i.e., Weyerhauser—"The Tree Growing Co.")	(1)	(2)	(3)	(4)
21. Production capacity (i.e., IBM PC, large capital projects)	(1)	(2)	(3)	(4)
22. Environmentally friendly (i.e., solar heating)	(1)	(2)	(3)	(4)
V. Employee-Driven Strategies				
23. Unsurpassed customer service (i.e., Nordstrom's)	(1)	(2)	(3)	(4)
24. Employee productivity (i.e., Toyota's California NUMMI plant)	(1)	(2)	(3)	(4)
25. High quality reputation (i.e., Ford—"Quality Is Job One")	(1)	(2)	(3)	(4)
26. Unique selling channels (i.e., Tupperware, direct mail)	(1)	(2)	(3)	(4)
27. Creativity, innovation (i.e., Disney, car design companies)	(1)	(2)	(3)	(4)
28. Business process reengineering, culture change (i.e., GE's WorkOut)	(1)	(2)	(3)	(4)
29. Networks, alliances (i.e., Japan's *keiretsus*, IBM/Apple)	(1)	(2)	(3)	(4)
30. Speed (i.e., Toyota)	(1)	(2)	(3)	(4)
31. Flexibility (i.e., Giant Industries—market responsive, flexible systems, meet individual needs)	(1)	(2)	(3)	(4)
32. What else: _____	(1)	(2)	(3)	(4)

TOTALS FOR EACH COLUMN: ___   ___   ___   ___

indicate high risk. In addition, Imperial experienced great difficulty in managing such a large number of disparate businesses, each requiring different
strategies and professional management.. The Resolution Trust Corporation
ended up taking them over and liquidating them, at a cost of over $1.3 billion
to taxpayers.

In any case, every organization should tailor its core strategies to its own
unique situation and risk level. This will involve developing and implementing
many of the strategies outlined here. However, the driving force of any
organization as a system should always be based on the outcome of being a
customer-focused, high-performance organization.

FACING CHANGE AND DEALING WITH IT

In order to survive the changes that have already taken place, as well as those
yet to come, organizations today must examine the way they respond to
change. Change is not going away anytime soon; if anything, it will knock at
our door more and more frequently. Change is inevitable, but how it affects
us is often determined by how we react to it. If we look at change as an
expected visitor rather than an unwanted guest, we can condition ourselves
to accept it as a natural part of organizational life.

This entails looking for the right answers and reinventing the strategic
planning and implementation process so that it can be flexible enough to
accommodate change. Although this sounds simple enough, implementing
strategic planning and setting a strategic management system structure in
place actually creates change, which is why it is referred to here as "the roller
coaster of change" (see Figure 9.2, adapted from numerous disciplines, including *Death & Dying*).

Although this may seem surprising, it makes sense in a twofold manner:
(1) the *reason* you are planning is because you need things to change and
(2) the *outcome* of setting all that planning in motion is literally a "roller
coaster of change." While this can ultimately result in the desired organization-
wide outcomes, it also requires enormous skill and leadership to successfully
manage through the rough times of change.

The concept of the roller coaster of change originated in the late 1970s,
when it became apparent that this was often where the strategic change and
implementation process got bogged down. Too often, organizations would
do all their planning, conduct a parallel process, and begin the implementation stage with high hopes. If change was not realized quickly, however,
or was met with resistance, organizations would have a tendency to scrap
the whole process, thus negating all the good, hard work they had done
originally.

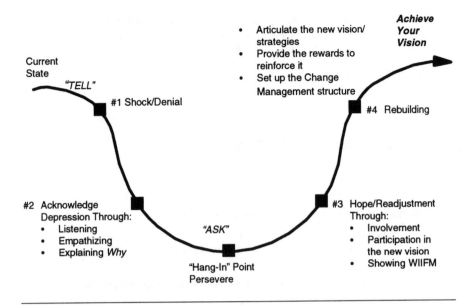

FIGURE 9.2   Roller Coaster of Change

The reality, however, is that most major change, whether an organization is conducting strategic planning, a turnaround, or a competitive business renewal, happens over a period of three to five years. Organizations must learn to bridge the gap between planning and its implementation with disciplined persistence. Organizations that successfully ride the roller coaster of change and expect resistance as a natural part of the process experience vastly higher rates of successful implementation.

Cost cutting as a strategy is a good example of what takes place on the roller coaster of change. As previously mentioned, it is almost always the first inevitable step in any change effort. Because cost cutting is such an obvious and pervasive step, it is important to understand that initiating this process causes a natural reaction of shock, anger, and depression. Organizational leaders must prepare themselves and their employees for this and find ways to manage and weather it successfully.

WHAT IS GOING TO CHANGE?

Another way to make change less intimidating is to clearly demonstrate, organization-wide, what specific paradigm shifts and changes to expect from

Core strategies are those courses of action that will guide us toward our vision. Successful implementation will require paradigm shifts from old ways of thinking to new ways of thinking to achieve strategic change.

1. **Make TQL Happen**

From	*To*
Buzzword	Culture

2. **Create a Customer-Focused Organization**

From	*To*
Inward Focus	Customer Focus

3. **Modernize Management Information System**

From	*To*
Piecemeal	Systems Solution

4. **Manage the Implementation and Executive of the Strategic Plan**

From	*To*
Strategic Planning	Change Management

5. **Enhance Our Development and Effectiveness as Members of the PWC Team**

From	*To*
People as Cost	People as Assets

FIGURE 9.3   Core Strategies

the core strategies. For example, let's say that one of your organization's core strategies is to make TQM/TQL happen. Spell it out, in simple terms, that will take you *from* TQM being just another buzzword *to* making it an integral part of your culture. The Navy Public Works Center in San Diego, California, provides a good example of some typical paradigm shifts to expect from strategies, as illustrated in Figure 9.3

You can survive change by articulating and using the "*from–to*" changes as you not only make the required *cuts* but also *build* your core strategies for the future in a participative manner. This will generate involvement, hope, readjustment, and renewed commitment, which will enable the organization to start *building* (or rebuilding) its competitive advantage and customer-focused vision. (Figure 9.4 illustrates how all this fits together.)

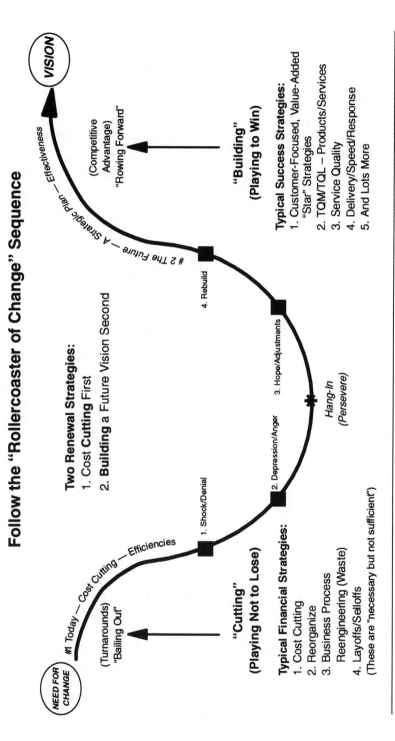

FIGURE 9.4 Turnarounds, Renewals, and Strategic Planning

CREATING STRATEGIC ACTION ITEMS

For each core strategy, every organization needs a set of strategic action items (SAIs) to achieve that strategy over the planning horizon. Thus, there are four steps to consider when creating really excellent core strategies:

1. Ensure that you have a crystal clear strategy statement for each core strategy to guide the action items.

2. Be clear about any paradigm shifts (i.e., "from–to") that are indicated.

3. Develop 10 to 15 major action items for each strategy to clarify the changes.

4. For every strategy you want to begin in the next year, set/list three top action priorities.

SETTING ACTION PRIORITIES OVER TWELVE MONTHS

Once you have reached consensus on your strategic action items, you will need to set the top three to five action priorities for each strategy over the next twelve months. These will provide direction for everyone in setting their annual, departmental, and individual goals. In effect, if you have six core strategies and three top priorities for each strategy, you have eighteen top priority actions to accomplish as an organization over the next year.

Example:　The strategy development step led the Community Care Network of San Diego to develop six core strategies for redefining itself from a regional into a nationwide firm in the growing health care field of managed care. This was a major departure, which called for a new CEO and culture change, as well as the six core strategies and eighteen annual action priorities mentioned earlier.

DEVELOP STRATEGY SPONSORSHIP TEAMS

Never tell people how to do things. Tell them what you want them to achieve and they will surprise you with their ingenuity.

General George S. Patton

The next step in strategy development is to form cross-functional teams composed of senior management change agents. Forming cross-functional teams is about creating organization-wide, enthusiastic commitment to your core strategies.

Asking the hierarchical organization to change is difficult because it was built to maintain the status quo. In order to change, a critical mass of change agents is needed. The best way to accomplish this is for volunteer senior management Strategy Sponsorship Team (SST) members (and others) to choose something about which they are particularly passionate.

For each core strategy, ask for volunteers from the senior members of the core planning team to act as champions. Seek out these individuals wherever they have a passion to see the particular change occur. In this way, they will likely be proactive in fulfilling their role as champion:

1. To be kept informed of the status of the actual implementation of the core strategy—to keep the strategy alive

2. To actively support and perform a leadership role in advocating the core strategy across the organization

3. To cajole, agitate, and otherwise push and influence the people organizationally responsible for implementing the core strategy in order to move it forward (i.e., reverse the entropy that usually occurs when achieving change within a day-to-day context)

4. To advise and recommend actions needed to achieve the strategy

5. To actively track and monitor the success of the core strategy and report on it at quarterly Strategic Change Steering Committee meetings

In any business, the toughest things to succeed at, with the highest failure rates, are the newer things, the less certain things...it should be a very high priority to put the best darn senior relevant person you have full-time on a new product in order to make that acorn become an oak tree...

Josh Weston
Chairman & CEO
Automatic Data Processing, Inc.

Once you have gotten the first champion to volunteer for his or her "passion," ask all other planning team members to volunteer to champion one or two of the core strategies. This will comprise the core of your SSTs. Use the chart provided in Figure 9.5 to list all team members. Remember to clarify the roles of SSTs versus the line organization.

When developing your teams, be sure to spread out the planning team members so that each strategy team has roughly the same number of partici-

STRATEGY SPONSORSHIP TEAMS (SSTs)

Roles of these SST champions — to "keep the strategy alive"
1.   To be kept informed of the status of the core strategy's actual implementation.
2.   To actively support and perform a leadership role in advocating this core strategy across the organization.
3.   To cajole/agitate and otherwise push and influence the people organizationally responsible to implement this core strategy to keep it moving forward. (i.e., Reverse the "entropy" that usually occurs with achieving change within a day-to-day context.)
4.   To advise and recommend actions needed to achieve this core strategy.
5.   To actively track and monitor the core strategy's success and report on it at quarterly SCLSC meetings.

Champions for Strategic Plan Implementation

SST For Each Core Strategy (Sponsors, Leaders, Champions)	Line Manager (Still Accountable for all Core Strategies)
1. Accountable to be "Devil's Advocate"; to cajole, push, lead, agitate for these to change/succeed.	1. Continue to be accountable/responsible for actions/results.
2. Report quarterly to the SCLSC on the status of the Core Strategy. Use the KISS method—mostly verbal reports/dialogue is desired.	2. Develop annual Department Plans for your area of responsibility around each Core Strategy in order to support/ contribute to, and help achieve each one.
3. Receive all Department Plans for this Core Strategy. Review/critique them.	3. Track, monitor, correct, and reward achievement of the actions.
4. Support and work with line managers on coordination and achievement of this Core Strategy. Do it in a way to ensure line manager has "no surprises" at the quarterly SCLSC meeting.	4. Work with and keep SST informed of actions/priorities of the Annual Plan company-wide.
5. Can increase in size beyond the Strategic Planning Committee membership if needed	5. Can be a member of SST as well.
	6. Participates in the quarterly SCLSC meeting discussions/future actions.

Possible Secondary Role for SST

6.   Can grow beyond SST concept into becoming a proactive coordinator or task force (half way to becoming accountable).

SST Non Role (Absolutely)

7.   Do not take over the line managers' direct accountability and allow them to assume a passive role. **This is wrong!**

FIGURE 9.5   Accountability and Responsibility of Each Core Strategy for Strategic Plan Implementation

pants. *Each person should choose a SST based on his or her passion and energy in seeing that the core strategy is actually achieved.* The end goal is to have a balanced mix of cross-functional team members instead of just people with direct line responsibility to implement the core strategy.

Tip: SSTs can also be supplemented by key stakeholders. However, keep each team to six to eight people (maximum) for ease of group dynamics/ actions. Also, keep SSTs verbal, fluid, and dynamic. Whatever you do, do not bog them down with reports and paperwork.

SUMMARY

Again and again, organizations in the United States are still struggling to learn the same three lessons. First, we have used up all our strategic reserves, or slack. The only slack still remaining is the boundless energy, creativity, and self-confidence of the American people, if only we can harness those resources to our advantage once again.

Second, the age of unrefined mass production and mass consumption is over. This is the age of highly refined, specialized, niche markets.

Third, every strategy that created success in times of stability and plenty now produces failure in these times of worldwide competition and dynamic change (the "failure" of success is thinking that things will be good because they always have been).

By implementing solid, future-based, growth-oriented core strategies— and carrying them out consistently and persistently over the life of the planning horizon—organizations will not only find that they have learned these lessons but will also find themselves thriving into the third millennium.

RECAP OF KEY POINTS

1. Your organization will need to develop a small number (three to five) of core strategies to bridge the gaps between your Ideal Future Vision and your Current State Assessment.

2. When developing your strategies, consider the following twelve newer strategies for the 21st century:

1. Flexibility

2. Speed

3. Horizontally integrated products

4. Networks and alliances

5. Value-added

6. Environmentally improved products

7. Mass customization

8. Commonization/simplification

9. Business process reengineering

10. Organizational learning

11. Employee morale/benefits

12. Management and leadership practices

3. In order to successfully reinvent your strategic planning and implementation process, you must make accommodation for "the roller coaster of change."

4. Be sure to integrate building as well as cutting (i.e., financial only) strategies. Remember to "play to win!"

5. Prioritize corresponding strategic action items over the next twelve months for each of your core strategies.

6. Create Strategy Sponsorship Teams to champion each core strategy.

ACTION CHECKLIST

1. Ascertain that your vision/mission/core values and Current State Assessment (including SWOT) are final, and then develop your new core strategies.

2. Develop a small number (three to five) of core strategies for implementing your organization's strategic plan. Make sure they serve you in the following ways:

- They should define your competitive business advantages, leading to long-term, sustainable organizational viability.

- They should help you select how you define, organize, and grow your strategic business units, including which ones your organization should create, retain, or eliminate.

- They should help you determine your overall organization design and structure, along with individual job design, employee initiative characteristics, and philosophy.

- They should act as the "glue"—or yearly objectives—around which you organize your annual planning process.

3. Develop core strategies that accommodate change, including both cutting and building strategies. Don't be afraid to be very specific.

Indicate exactly what you are changing to and exactly what you are changing from.

4. Ensure that your organization clearly understands any "from–to" paradigm shifts that will result from your new core strategies.

5. Develop cross-functional teams of change agents (called Strategy Sponsorship Teams) led by senior management. Also, assign a volunteer senior member of the core planning team as a champion for each core strategy.

6. Each strategy should have its own strategic action items, carried out over the life of the planning horizon. Once strategic action items have been agreed upon, set the three to five top action priorities for each strategy over the next twelve months. If you have six core strategies with three top priorities each, you will have a total of eighteen top priority actions.

7. Remember to take each stage of your strategy development through a parallel process in order to give all levels of your work force the opportunity to buy into their strategic plan.

CHAPTER 10

BUSINESS UNIT PLANNING (STEP #6) (PHASE C: INPUT)

A multi-division company without an overall strategy is not even as good as the sum of its parts. It is merely a portfolio of non-liquid, not-tradeable investments which has added overhead and constraints. Such closed-end investments properly sell at a discount from the sum of their parts.

Adapted from Bruce Henderson
Founder, Boston Consulting Group

STRATEGIC BUSINESS UNITS: THE BUSINESSES YOU ARE IN

To make optimum use of the core strategies that will take your organization to its Ideal Future Vision, you will need to carefully define what businesses you are in by identifying your strategic business units (SBUs).

SBUs are the business or line elements (or parts of the organization) that make up your total corporate or organizational entity. Generally speaking, SBUs can be identified if they meet the following three criteria:

- They produce and market a well-defined set of related products and/ or services.

- They serve a clearly defined set of customers in a reasonably self-contained geographic area.

- They compete with a well-defined set of competitors.

In many of today's organizations, particularly those that are of a multi-business structure, it is not always a simple matter to clearly identify and define SBUs. More detailed SBU criteria would include:

- They exist as separate and distinct units, generally more self-contained with their own mission and strategic plans (under the organization-wide plan and strategies).

- They are usually about "what we do" as opposed to "how we do it."

- They can be the business transactions you perform for a customer (but not the values or support functions).

- They are usually based on your driving force(s) or core strategies.

- They are often representative of specific skills and expertise (i.e., core competencies).

- They could be specific areas focused on specific, desired results or outcomes (but not just activities).

- They should exist where the preponderance of your business is with outside customers (as opposed to sister departments or divisions).

- They should be units that have the authority to implement and adjust plans once approval is granted.

In determining exactly in what businesses you want to be in the future and what it will take to get there, clarifying your SBUs is extremely important. It forces you to evaluate your overall portfolio of businesses to be sure you know why you are in each of these businesses and to properly allocate your resources accordingly.

Example: What businesses is General Motors presently in? In effect, GM currently has four main business units (SBUs): (1) Hughes Aircraft (defense industry), (2) Electronic Data Systems (data processing), (3) GMAC (finance), and (4) vehicle (cars and trucks) production.

In the 1980s, when GM bought Hughes and EDS, it was because GM's chairman, Roger Smith, championed these two companies. Smith believed that by acquiring these two companies, he would be adding immediate expertise (technology and data processing) to the GM vehicle business. Whether or not this has proven to be true is what GM needs to examine during its present downsizing mode. GM needs to ask two questions: (1) are either or both of these SBUs still a good fit with our other businesses and, if not, (2) should they be sold so we can "stick to our knitting," as Tom Peters puts it.

SBUs need to fit within an overall corporate strategy of relatedness (such as GMAC) to an organization's driving forces or core strategies or to its core expertise or competency. Any other reason should be honestly and clearly articulated (even if it is not a good reason). This underlying honestly should incorporate reasons such as profitability, a champion's interest (i.e., Roger Smith), or the building of a powerful conglomerate (such as ITT).

In the public sector, unfortunately, there is no such equivalent to a clearly identifiable SBU. This results in much of the confusion encountered when running or dealing with public or not-for-profit organizations.

This is a recurring problem in the public sector. For the sake of clarity, the term "major program areas" (MPAs) will be used here when referring to SBUs in public and not-for-profit organizations. See Figure 10.1 for a chart of this SBU/MPA concept.

Example: British Columbia's Ministry of the Environment includes (1) the fish and wildlife program, (2) the water management program, (3) the lands and parks program, and (4) the environmental protection program (including water, air, and some lands). Additionally, six geographic regions maintain responsibility for all these programs across the province.

This is a confusing structure, because there is no clear, identifiable construct by category (such as natural resources, inhabitants, or activities) upon which to define the businesses. For example, how would you organize your thinking about these business units? Are they (1) a construct built around inhabitants, such as fish and wildlife? If so, then what about birds? Or are they a construct built around (2) natural resources, such as water and land? If so, then why is air not included? Even more confusing, there is a further construct (3) of responsibility for *all* of these programs by the six different regions mentioned above.

This is a perfect example of why each organization needs to clearly define its business units, using either the SBU or MPA terminology. This will allow them to determine whether or not what they presently have will take them toward their desired future outcomes. With three different constructs all in use concurrently, no wonder the Ministry of the Environment has a difficult time trying to run its separate programs and regions. Not only are they all separate from one another, none of the units interlock in any way. This is an obvious example of why it is important to pick one construct and follow it.

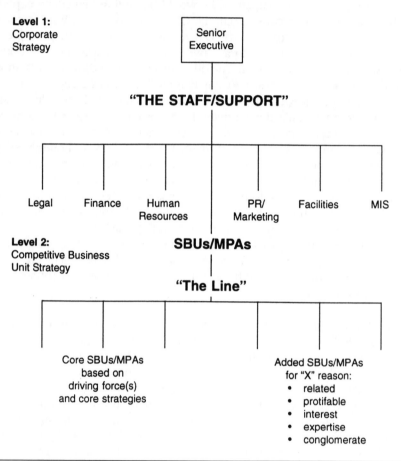

SBUs, MPAs, DIVISIONS, UNITS, etc.

Level 1:
Corporate
Strategy

Senior
Executive

"THE STAFF/SUPPORT"

Legal   Finance   Human   PR/   Facilities   MIS
                      Resources   Marketing

Level 2:   **SBUs/MPAs**
Competitive Business
Unit Strategy

"The Line"

Core SBUs/MPAs   Added SBUs/MPAs
based on   for "X" reason:
driving force(s)   • related
and core strategies   • protifable
                                   • interest
                                   • expertise
                                   • conglomerate

FIGURE 10.1   SBUs/MPAs

MATCHING YOUR STRATEGIC BUSINESS UNITS TO YOUR MISSION STATEMENT

> *Everyone talks about sticking to the knitting,*
> *but a lot of companies don't know what their knitting is.*
>
>   Benjamin Tregoe
>   Chairman, Kepner-Tregoe

Your organization's mission statement is all about who, what, and why you are in business. SBUs and MPAs represent the various "whats" within the mission statement and therefore must be grounded in it. As illustrated by the earlier example of General Motors, it is imperative that your SBUs support that statement. If they do not, you must either change the statement or change the SBUs—or settle for running a confusing operation.

Once you have clearly defined your SBUs, you are ready to determine (1) *which* SBUs need enhancement, growth, or change; (2) whether you will need to *add* any SBUs; and (3) exactly *how* (including how *much*) they need to change and grow over the life of your strategic plan.

The reasoning behind this is that your SBUs represent the smallest subdivision for which you can develop a distinct, separate business strategy. They also represent the level at which you actually compete with other organizations in your industry, especially within conglomerates.

In order to implement your organization's overall strategic plan as fully as possible, it is essential that these subdivisions create business plans of their own. Failure to do so will leave your organization with an overall "blueprint" (the strategic plan), but no specific, concrete actions for implementing the plan through your separate business units or program areas.

The goal here is not to invest in isolated projects that produce separate or incremental benefits, but to develop well-positioned business clusters whose synergy creates advantages that beat the cost of capital, increase return on investment, and build lasting shareholder value. To achieve this goal, an organization's management needs to develop overall core strategies that generally hold true for related business clusters instead of for just one business at a time.

PRIORITIZING YOUR SBUs/MPAs

Once you have identified the existing, new, or altered SBUs you will need to fulfill your overall mission, it is time to start prioritizing them. As the matrix in Figure 10.2 shows, this is done by defining the size and percent of each SBU/MPA as it will appear at the end of your planning horizon, (i.e., year X) and then contrasting its status today in terms of its desired growth rate.

As you develop this future-oriented proforma matrix for your organization's SBUs, consider the following possible uses and implications of the matrix:

1. Plan the direction of the business/product/service at a concrete level for the next two to three years.

2. Analyze expected profit performance in specific ways.

3. Define in which SBU/MPA businesses, products, or services your organization should or should not take part.

4. Decide on the amount of focus you desire within your overall vision/mission.

Instructions: Once you've identified your future SBUs/MPAs at the target future year, now fill in the intervening years and growth rates.

SBU/MPA List ⬇ Revenue ➡	Baseline 1994	1995	1996	1997	1998	Target 1999	Key Comments	Growth Rates
1.								
2.								
3.								
4.								
5.								
6.								
7.								
Total								
Minus Expenses (Budget)								
Profits/Reserves								

FIGURE 10.2   SBU/MPA Proforma Matrix: Create Your Own Future

5. Prioritize and allocate resources, energy, and time.

6. Enhance image/marketing and employee efforts.

7. Conduct an environmental scanning and competitor analysis.

8. Ensure functional plans for all departments to support the business units.

9. Determine the degree of risk you are willing to take and are taking.

10. Determine if you are going outside your core competencies and competitive edge.

It is crucial to closely analyze the factors of risk, driving force(s), organizational focus, and competitive approach. Without this careful analysis, you may be seduced further away from your mission/vision rather than closer to it. This "X" test in Figure 10.3 can help you determine the risk and the validity of a new SBU or MPA.

Developing this careful evaluation of each SBU will help you in discov-

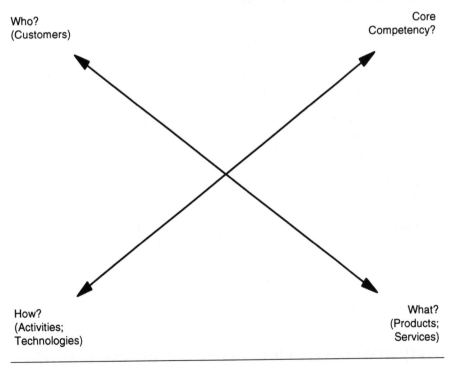

FIGURE 10.3 New Strategic Business Unit Test: X Test (If a new SBU or product/service produces a change in more than one axis, the probability of failure is very high. If the change is in the driving force(s), it is especially risky.) (Adapted from Haines, 1979)

ering and prioritizing viable business units that will take your organization to its chosen mission. In addition to analyzing risk and all the other corresponding factors, keep the following common-sense basics in mind:

- Grow where the business is; do not try to create a market where none exists.
- Keep close to the customer's needs.
- Do not assume that a good manager can run anything.
- Do not load productive people down with non-productive chores like administrative reports.
- Debt is not your friend.

MICRO-SMART VS. MACRO-DUMB: THE PORTFOLIO QUESTION

If you don't stand for something,
you'll fall for anything.

Failing to focus on and prioritize your SBUs/MPAs can drastically reduce their results down the line. You run the risk of thinking at the *micro level* (analyzing projects, products, services, and programs at the business level and making decisions on the merits of an individual case) rather than the more holistic *macro level* (analyzing a complete portfolio of business areas, lines, projects, programs, and elements and making decisions as a totality).

In other words, this is being "micro-smart" but "macro-dumb." In making strategic decisions, you need to consider your entire portfolio of business units (and potential ones as well).

Example: A firm in the high-tech field is considering a basic question: does it stay with its current technology, go to new technology, expand geographically across the United States, go into peripheral business areas—or something else? This is a true portfolio question, because each possibility makes some sense in and of itself. However, if the firm tries to do all of them at once, it will probably fail.

OVERVIEW: DEVELOPING THREE-YEAR BUSINESS PLANS FOR SBUs/MPAs

Now that you have clearly defined and prioritized your business units, the next step is to create a mini strategic or three-year business plan for each one.

This must be done for each SBU or MPA so that it can compete successfully. Of course, it is important that each of these business plans is derived from your organization's overall strategic plan, in order to exploit any synergistic possibilities.

Caution: Unfortunately, business planning is an area that is commonly overlooked by organizations. Passing it by can be a serious misstep. Organizations that fail to bring the overall strategic planning down to the business unit level (in a "waterfall effect" fashion) waste most of the hard work that has gone into their overall strategic plan for change.

In addition, you will need to develop three-year business plans for all major support units, such as finance, MIS, human resources, legal, etc. Because these departments serve internal customers, however, they are by their very nature ideally required to wait until each SBU/MPA has completed its own business plan. It will be difficult for them to properly plan prior to that, because they will not know what each business unit (their customer) is going to need from them in the way of support.

Practical tip on sequencing and timing: Once they have built their strategic plans, most organizations are close to or getting close to beginning their yearly budget cycles, which makes it difficult to focus on and devote the time necessary for this three-year business planning. To offset this potential dilemma, you will have to skip this business planning for now and go directly to building your annual plan and strategic budget (see Chapter 11 for additional detail). Once that is done, you can then come back and build your three-year business unit and major support plans. While this is not the ideal sequence, it is generally the reality of the planning and budgeting cycle.

Step #1 in Three-Year Business Planning

Just as in organization-wide strategic planning, there are specific guidelines for the business and program planning processes. Although there will be some areas in which there are variances between a business unit plan and the organization-wide strategic plan, there are many more that are exactly parallel.

Building a three-year business plan follows exactly the same systems thinking, A,B,C,D phase process as overall strategic planning. However, it is actually much faster and easier, because the organization-wide strategic plan already exists and can be used as a guide and context within which to build your business plan.

The first step in three-year business planning is Plan-to-Plan, followed by developing a three-year business plan and document (such as the one provided in Figure 10.4).

Outputs for the SBU/MPA/Major Support Departments:

1. Ideal Future Vision
2. Mission Statement/Driving Force(s)

3. Additional Core Values for the SBU/MPA

4. Definition of target markets and products/services (4 P's)
    — customer segments, demographics
    — competitors, niches, industry, trends
    — product line, areas of service
    — promotion and marketing
    — prices and places of sales (geography)

5. KSFs — Financial, Operations, Human Resources
    — SBU or product line, services proforma P/L matrix (on growth over 3 years)

6. Current State Assessment
    — SWOT for SBU/department
    — environmental scanning (STEPIC)
    — competitor analysis
    — customers/market analysis
    — product/product line analysis

7. Strategy Development
    — core strategies
    — strategic action plans for each core strategy
    — specific products, services, expansion
    — specific customers, markets, expansion
    — other major projects over next 3 years

8. Next 12 months implementation/change management process

Question: Are these the Business Planning outputs you want? If not, modify this list.

FIGURE 10.4   Standard Business Planning Document: Three-Year Time Horizon

In total, the processes involved in business/support unit planning generally require about five days to complete and can be accomplished competently by following the steps shown in the business planning flowchart provided in Figure 10.5.

Caution: The question of how to hold the SBU/MPA accountable for its profit can be a little tricky. There are different options for how to do this (see Figure 10.6).

The proper answer to the question of accountability is #4 in Figure 10.6, gross margin. However, organizations frequently hold the SBU/MPA account-

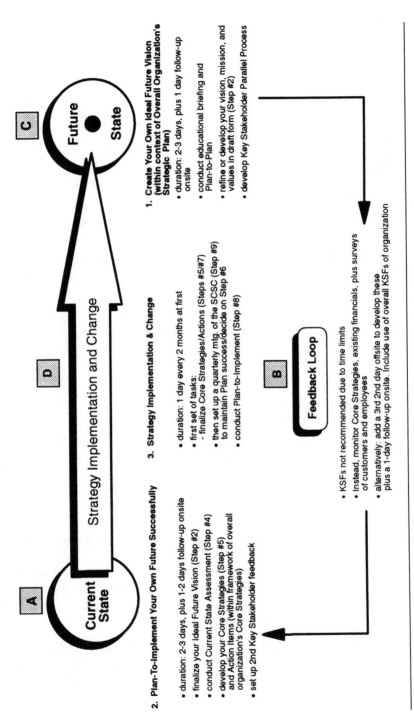

C Future State

1. Create Your Own Ideal Future Vision (within context of Overall Organization's Strategic Plan)

- duration: 2-3 days, plus 1 day follow-up onsite
- conduct educational briefing and Plan-to-Plan
- refine or develop your vision, mission, and values in draft form (Step #2)
- develop Key Stakeholder Parallel Process

B Strategy Implementation and Change

3. Strategy Implementation & Change

- duration: 1 day every 2 months at first
- first set of tasks:
  - finalize Core Strategies/Actions (Steps #5/#7)
- then set up a quarterly mtg. of the SCSC (Step #9) to maintain Plan success/decide on Step #6
- conduct Plan-to-Implement (Step #8)

B Feedback Loop

- KSFs not recommended due to time limits
- Instead, monitor Core Strategies, existing financials, plus surveys of customers and employees
- alternatively: add a 3rd 2nd day offsite to develop these plus a 1-day follow-up onsite. Include use of overall KSFs of organization

A Current State

2. Plan-To-Implement Your Own Future Successfully

- duration: 2-3 days, plus 1-2 days follow-up onsite
- finalize your Ideal Future Vision (Step #2)
- conduct Current State Assessment (Step #4)
- develop your Core Strategies (Step #5) and Action Items (within framework of overall organization's Core Strategies)
- set up 2nd Key Stakeholder feedback

FIGURE 10.5   Three-Year Business Planning: Mini Strategic Planning

1. Where to hold the SBU/MPA accountable (at levels #4, #6, #8)?

Standard Income Statement (P/L):

1.	Sales Revenue		_____
2.	C.O.G.S. (direct cost)	−	_____
3.	SBU operating costs (G/A)	−	_____
4.	Gross Profit/Margin	=	_____
5.	Organization-Wide Headquarters Operating Expenses (G/A) (Indirect Expenses/Overhead Allocated to the SBU)	−	_____
6.	SBU Profit Before Taxes	=	_____
7.	Taxes	−	_____
8.	NIAT	=	_____

---

2. Discuss/agree on this as a key to accountability/responsibility.

3. If #5 is not the responsibility of the SBU/MPA, who/how do you get accountability/responsibility there?

FIGURE 10.6 Key Success Factors for SBUs/MPAs

---

able for its profit level *before* taxes (#6) but *after* allocation of overhead expenses (#5). Because overhead expenses are usually allocated by the finance department, however, this is not something over which the SBU has much control.

The result of this "accountability" is often destructive infighting among SBUs and overhead support functions over allocated expenses. Because this is a win–lose situation, the worst part is that this allocation squabble adds nothing to the bottom line or to customer satisfaction.

Example #1: A good example of this was the method Sunoco adopted in the 1970s. A vertically integrated oil company, Sunoco broke itself into many different business units and told each unit to compete and sell on the outside.

Instead of developing into strong externally oriented companies, the business units ended up vying for profits by trying to manipulate the allocated corporate overhead expenses. Needless to say, this decentralization was a huge mistake and made serious inroads into Sunoco's overall long-term financial viability. It resulted in an ongoing, relentless demise that continues even today.

Example #2: On the other hand, for many years the Marriott Corporation has held its SBUs and properties accountable for gross profit/margin only. Marriott has seen good results, with SBUs matching their responsibility with their accountability.

A Marriott restaurant or hotel, for instance, may have 40% gross margin accountability, but no accountability for corporate overhead expenses. This has created an environment in which each SBU and property exercises active daily control over its own gross margin to ensure success. If 40% is the target, then it follows that 41% is better, but 39% is not as good. This matches accountability with responsibility and makes for a much more black-and-white, manageable scenario. Whatever formula your organization comes up with, its own best interest lies in finding ways—other than through turf battles—to control corporate overhead.

SUPPORT NEEDS FOR BUSINESS UNIT PLANNING

It is important to keep in mind that this type of planning is comprehensive enough to create its own support needs. For example, if your organization develops five business plans for its SBUs/MPAs and four three-year plans for its major support units (all in addition to the overall organization-wide strategic plan), you could be looking at nine or ten different business plans.

Because of this, you must be sure that your organization has the internal support resources it needs to facilitate the development of these plans and their corresponding change management processes. If you determine that there is a need for additional support not already in place, you may need to assign and train appropriate individuals.

Example: At Sask Energy, there was a shortfall of internal support personnel needed to carry strategic planning through to the business unit level. Following a short, intensive training session, Sask ultimately created a cadre of nine skilled individuals to facilitate the process, as well as nine others who act as SBU support personnel.

Questions to Ponder

- Have you brought your overall strategic planning down to the business unit level, with three-year business plans for your SBUs/MPAs/major support units?

- Do these plans follow exactly the same systems thinking, A,B,C,D phase process as your overall strategic planning?

SUMMARY

As you evaluate and build business units that will pay off on the bottom line, keep in mind that they all must reflect your organization's core strategies. Without clearly defined ties to the strategies that will help you achieve your Ideal Future Vision, poorly planned business units can quickly drain your organizational resources and knock you off your desired path before you even realize it.

On the other hand, well thought-out business units, with clearly designated and prioritized plans and strategies, can be your organization's greatest asset. No matter what needs arise in assessing your SBUs or MPAs, make sure they are taken care of. Once you have a crystal-clear understanding of what each business unit is all about and have made certain that the resources they need will be provided, these organizational "pieces" will reward your organization with a healthy, profitable, business "whole."

RECAP OF KEY POINTS

1. Evaluate your SBUs/MPAs to determine if any are outside your driving force(s) and core strategies/competencies.

2. Ascertain which SBUs/MPAs will need to change or be added in order to fulfill your organizational mission statement.

3. Make sure you know the risk involved and have specific plans to deal with it.

4. Bring every step of your SBU/MPA planning back to your organization-wide core strategies.

5. Limit your new SBU searches to no more than 15 to 20% of your total effort and resources.

6. In your three-year business unit planning, be sure to follow the same systems thinking, A,B,C,D phase process as in your overall strategic planning.

7. Incorporate new product development in your business unit planning.

8. Identify the market segmentation of each business unit product or service and develop support strategies.

9. Be sure to accommodate the support needs of each SBU/MPA business plan.

ACTION CHECKLIST

1. Define the SBUs/MPAs that currently exist in your organization.

2. Define the present revenue/profitability expectations of each SBU/MPA.

3. Delineate the desired future of each SBU/MPA, along with its future revenue/profits at the end of your planning horizon (year X).

4. Develop criteria for SBU or MPA selection/exclusion/elimination, especially customer/market research.

5. Analyze each SBU/MPA based on those criteria; incorporate some traditional analysis tools as well (i.e., risk/focus/etc.).

6. Force-rank a set of priorities for the remaining SBU/MPAs.

7. Analyze these decisions from a holistic perspective. Make sure that you have not lost any core competencies by selective individual decisions.

8. For those SBUs/MPAs dropped or excluded, make a choice to either say no to the customer or develop strategic alliances/partnerships with others to provide for them.

9. Establish goals/targets for overall organization growth rates of volume and profitability.

10. Establish an ongoing system to manage the changes resulting from your prioritization.

11. Develop product/market plans, organization structure, teams, and budgets to achieve your SBU/MPA targets. Then adjust or reiterate this cycle where necessary to match resources with targets.

CHAPTER 11

ANNUAL PLANS AND STRATEGIC BUDGETING (STEP #7) (PHASE C: INPUT)

Making the tough choices...
includes choosing where to start
and where not to start.

PRIORITIZED CORE STRATEGIES: THE ORGANIZING PRINCIPLES OF ANNUAL PLANS

The art and skill of prioritizing was referred to frequently in the past two chapters. However, this is where you must make it real and turn prioritizing into a viable, ever-present planning tool. In Chapter 9, we put in all the hard work to develop core strategies and set priority actions to accompany each strategy. In Chapter 10, we defined and planned for strategic business units. It would be difficult, even demoralizing, to see all that work go down the drain at this point, but without setting annual plans under each core strategy, that is exactly what can happen.

To help focus on this point, remember that the strategic plan is your blueprint—the overall design of your "house"—but it is not, and never will be, the "house" itself (i.e., implementable in and of itself). Developing annual departmental plans and budgets, based on your core strategies and annual priorities, provides the details that are necessary to make that "house" livable.

The sad truth is that this is where many organizations fall under the weight of their carefully designed strategic plans. Simply circulating a copy of the strategies, with no corresponding, visible actions or expectations, sends organizational members a clear message: "Okay, we've (the planning team) done our part. Now you're on your own to do yours. Do whatever you want because there aren't any priorities or focus!"

This is what leads to the SPOTS (Strategic Plan On the Top Shelf...gathering dust) syndrome. It is also abdication by senior management at its very worst. At the very best, it is naive. In either case, it is unacceptable behavior for senior management.

Senior management must persevere at this point and give guidance on how employees and their corresponding strategic business units are expected to "do their part." In order to avoid the very real possibility of the plan getting lost in the "I don't know what they expect me to do!" shuffle, each manager must now develop a realistic annual plan, with the clear priorities of your organization's core strategies, and detailed task expectations (remember the strategic action items in Chapter 9). These plans must be backed up with the resources necessary to implement your core strategies.

This annual planning and budgeting (Step #7) is the beginning of strategic consistency and operational flexibility and is crucial, because empowerment without direction is chaos.

Example: A good example of prioritizing is the city of Saskatoon, in Saskatchewan, Canada. In its 1993 annual plans, it chose seven core strategies as its theme. It then came up with three priorities per strategy, for a total of 21 specific, clear priorities for change within the calendar year. These were then used as guides for each department's annual plan, as well as the city's budgeting decisions.

CRAFTING AN EFFECTIVE ANNUAL PLAN

Once you have chosen your core strategies/priorities, you will need to create blank annual planning forms for each core strategy, with only the strategy shown at the top of each page. Use the format in Figure 11.1 as a guide for all departments to use in developing their annual plans.

Having everyone use the same format and the same organizing frameworks (i.e., core strategies) accomplishes two things:

#1 Strategies/Themes/Goals: (What) _____

Yearly Pri #	Strategic Action Items (Actions/Objectives/How?)	Support/Resources Needed	Who Responsible?	Who Else to Involve?	When Done?	Optional How to Measure?	Status

FIGURE 11.1 Annual Plan Format (and Functional/Divisional/Department Plans)

1. It establishes the same key ways to communicate and work together.

2. It focus everyone on organization-wide core strategies instead of separate departmental goals or turf issues. (There really should be no such thing as a departmental goal or objective; there should only be the department's contribution to the organization's overall core strategies).

Note: If you *must* have departmental goals or strategies, then slot them under the core strategies for consistency (i.e., under Core Strategy #3, list Goal 3.1, Goal 3.2, etc.).

In any case, when completing each planning form, each department head should give consideration to such things as:

- What should our actions be in order for our department objectives to support this strategy?

- How do our actions under each core strategy support the top priority strategic action items identified by management for this year?

- What resources or special support will we need?

- Who, specifically, will be responsible for seeing this through?

- What is a realistic target date for accomplishing this?

- How will we measure our progress?

Finally, it is critical to fill out the "who else to involve" column in the annual plan, especially in a functional organization, where horizontal or cross-functional teamwork is key to success.

Your annual plan, then, should present your organizational core strategies as the organizing principles. Each one should have a list of actions that must be completed in the coming year to support each strategy.

LARGE GROUP ANNUAL PLAN REVIEW AND APPROVAL

Even with the most thorough plan, it is not enough for each department to simply develop its own annual plan. In order to be a true system, the entire organization must be aware of each department's annual plans.

To fully commit to achieving your Ideal Future Vision, which serves as the focus for your strategic plan, your entire collective leadership (i.e., your top 30 to 50 people) must actively participate in a large group annual plan review and problem-solving meeting. Understanding and ownership by everyone is the key to successful implementation.

This step is rarely done in organizations once departmental annual plans have been created. The message seems to be: "I'll do my job and you do yours." Neither side looks at or discusses the other's plans. (This is analytical thinking at its worst.)

Note: At this point, you may be thinking, "Just what I hate—large group 'dog and pony' shows. How boring!" However, nothing could be further from the truth. What has proven to be successful is lots of small group interactive reviews going on at the same time.

Following the Off-Site Review Meetings

Following the off-site large group review, departments should make any necessary revisions to their plans. A planning coordinator is then assigned to collect all the plans together in one place. This person resplits the department plans out by core strategies and sends them to the appropriate Strategy Sponsorship Teams for future use. The Strategy Sponsorship Teams can use the plans to monitor, track, follow-up, and report on the status of core strategies across all departments to the Strategic Change Steering Committee that will be set up.

STRATEGIC BUDGETING: THE DIFFERENCE BETWEEN ADEQUACY AND EXCELLENCE

At this point, it is assumed that future revenue projections have been set through your key success factors, business planning, and core strategies. Your task now is to show profit and return on investment to your board of directors (or show a zero profit in the public sector).

The annual budgeting and resource allocation process done at the completion of strategic planning is referred to as *strategic budgeting*. This is because the emphasis here has everything to do with strategy, focus, and priorities but very little to do with money *alone*. For most organizations, intelligent budgeting and careful resource allocation can mean the difference in successful implementation.

In strategic budgeting, the allocation of funds is determined by priorities that are crucial to the achievement of your organizational vision, rather than by department or division power struggles. To be truly strategic, budgeting and resource allocation must meet the following criteria:

> **1.** It should reinforce and focus on your Ideal Future Vision and key success factors.

2. It must support the top priorities in your strategic plan.

3. It must result in your being able to fund and run your day-to-day business and being able to fund needed future changes.

These changing times are tough on budgets; the challenge is to find new and innovative ways—not only for cost savings, but for increasing revenues and income as well.

The key is not to cut or increase budgets evenly across the board, but rather to make budget cuts and additions that are based on your strategic plan criteria. Instead of a fixed budget driving your strategic plan, *your plan should always drive your budget.* Not viewing it in this way will almost surely prevent the successful implementation of your plan. Fortunately, it is a negative result that can be avoided.

The budget must be integrated with and linked to your strategic plan and annual plans. This can take up to two years to do properly, with around 40 to 70% incremental implementation in the first year, followed by full implementation in the second year.

NEW WAYS TO ESTABLISH YOUR BUDGET AND RESOURCE ALLOCATION APPROACH

*If money was what it took to be a success,
then how did Japan and Germany rise from the ashes?*

Looking at today's global economy shouts contention with traditional biases as to the roots of economic success. According to Anthony Carnevale in his book entitled *America and the Economy*, as well as many others, economic success is no longer based on natural resources, financial investments, saving rates, scarcity, free markets, or a military presence but rather is based on the ability to intelligently prioritize a loosely connected set of economic and social processes. How else can the Japanese and German successes since World War II be explained?

Because of a rapidly changing environment—and because no organization has all the funds it needs to explore every single revenue-generating possibility—it is more important than ever to re-examine our methods for focusing and allocating resources that will support our strategic planning and direction.

With today's drastic budgetary shortfalls, the real trick is to stay away from the rather simplistic cutting methods of the 1980s: across-the-board cuts on departmental budgets or employee compensation. It has been proven over and over that they simply do not work.

Also, these tight budget restrictions require more drastic budget cuts in order to become globally competitive. The result is that the economic structure of many industries is being altered (read "lowered") today, although this fact has gone unrecognized by many.

When weighing the priorities based on your strategies, use the following ideas to cut and/or reallocate your organization's funds in a more focused (i.e., strategic) way.

Approach #1. Macro Allocations Only (Let Managers Allocate to Their Departments)

Consider macro allocation by top management for each SBU/MPA/major support department (i.e., a pie chart). Require reallocation within existing department resources to respond to new priorities (but be sure to allow more flexibility to switch funding and priorities).

Another variation would be to have all departments create bottom-up budgets once the needs/cuts have been decided on by top management.

Approach #2. Activity-Level Budgeting (Zero-Based Budgeting)

Re-examine your organizational priorities at the activity level, focusing all the way through the organization. Have everyone force-rank their activities/ projects, along with budget and people cost implications.

Once this is done, reorganize the list from the highest priority ranking to the lowest priority. Then, fill in whatever resources you will need to support each activity. Draw a line where your resources are "used up." Finally, reach consensus through discussion and ranking as to what activities will now be included in your budget and what to delete that is below the "used up" line just mentioned.

In carrying through in this manner, you will more clearly tie your budget to specific actions, and it will be easy to spot and troubleshoot any activities that do not have enough resources to support them.

Approach #3. Require 5–10–15% Budget Cut Projections and Plans (and Cut Each Differently, Based on Its Plans)

Make more drastic budget cuts. For example, identify X% (i.e., 2 to 3%) of non-salaried "people-associated" costs that could be cut (things such as travel, office, equipment, etc.).

Another possibility would be to have everyone recommend cuts of X% (i.e., 10%) in their area, even if your goal is Y% of, say, 5% overall. This gives you flexibility to cut more or less in other areas. Then, reallocate some or all of the savings toward the core strategies.

Yet another possibility is to ask for projected cuts of 5%, 10%, and 15% from each department, along with what plans or projects would be affected. Then, cut departments individually and in different amounts, based on your strategic priorities.

Example: The government of Alberta, Canada, did this as a part of its radical, successful restructuring in 1993–95.

Approach #4. Budget Holdbacks for Requests for Proposals

Set aside X% (i.e., 2 to 5%) of your budget for a Request for Proposal process to further new pilot programs/experiments that will take you toward your vision of the future.

Example: This was an ongoing part of Imperial Corporation of America's successful budgeting process.

Approach #5. New Initiative Programs for All New Funding

Have your employees recommend new initiative programs/projects (NIPs) that tie directly to the criteria in your strategic plan. Make sure that budget and people costs/rationale are associated with each one.

If your organization is testing specific NIPs in an attempt to increase profits and you find that it cannot be done with existing staff, you will need to make a business case for each project. When seeking NIPs staffing approval, you should be able to show improved or maintained productivity ratios, increased profits, and/or reduced costs.

To make the best possible case for your NIPs, be sure to incorporate the return-on-investment principles in Table 11.1

Example: The Environmental Protection Agency in British Columbia goes after NIPs on a yearly basis; in fact, it is the new way in which it allocates resources to run its day-to-day operations.

Approach #6. Fund-Raising (Public Sector)

Start fund-raising as one of your more important organizational functions. Acquire endowments/annuities for long-term funding. Recommend new ways to increase revenue, such as fund drives, alternative sources for funds, or in-kind donations and grants.

TABLE 11.1   Return-on-Investment Principles

1. Expenditures are an investment of capital resources at the present time for a return in the future that is *more valuable* than the present expense.

2. Management, however, always has a *variety of opinions* for investing capital. Your proposal must compete with the return from a variety of potential projects that could be funded.

3. *Hurdle rates are key.* Treasury notes might be 7% ROI with no risk. The minimum acceptable return for any project might be 12% with some risk. Net present value (NPV) is also a consideration.

4. You must show that your project compares favorably with all other projects; clear superiority is key.

5. Underlying assumptions and past documentation; existing case stories must be conservative to be credible.

6. The period of return of the project's investment is key; the earlier the better; definitely within three years.

7. The opportunity costs lost elsewhere to fund your project are key—management only has so much capital.

Example: Not-for-profit organizations need to become experts in this type of activity. As an example, some public school systems now have full-time fund-raisers and complete fund-raising pyramids.

Summary: Use a combination of any or all of the preceding strategic budgeting approaches. The most important thing is to select those approaches that will work the best for you.

A WORD ABOUT PUBLIC SECTOR BUDGETS

Budgeting in the public sector can be especially frustrating, especially with having to wait for funding pronouncements. Increasingly, however, organizations in this sector are refusing to wait and instead are choosing to find ways to be more proactive, raise money themselves, and/or make their own budget reallocations, using many of the approaches listed here.

Through fund-raising, grant research, user/polluter pay, and other new sources of funds, not-for-profit organizations are making substantial inroads into bringing in financial resources that are not based on taxes or state and federal allocations.

Tip: The need for strategic budgeting is becoming more prominent in the public sector, as evidenced in the following excerpt from the September 1991 issue of *Shipmate,* the alumni magazine of the U.S. Naval Academy:

> *Many would argue, and convincingly, that it is the responsibility of the Congress to provide all the resources needed by the Superin-tendent [to run the Naval Academy]. The simple truth, however, is that the Congress does not, never has, and probably never will do so. The government provides what might be termed the absolute necessities;* ***it is others who bridge the gap between adequacy and excellence.***

INDIVIDUAL PERFORMANCE MANAGEMENT SYSTEMS

*People do what you **in**spect...not what you **ex**pect.*

Once your annual plan and accompanying strategic budgets are in place, two other crucial management systems must be installed:

1. A performance management system

2. A reward and recognition system

Both the performance management system and the reward/recognition system should be formulated and viewed as two separate—but closely re-lated—change projects.

SUMMARY: STRATEGIC CONSISTENCY AND OPERATIONAL FLEXIBILITY

No matter what you have done in the past, if you do not start to develop your annual plans and budgets around your core strategies, you will not be competitive in today's marketplace. It is not simply a case of top-down or bottom-up strategic planning, which is an outdated either–or concept. It is now a matter of *strategic consistency* at the strategic planning level, with *operational flexibility* at the annual and individual planning levels.

There are many more creative and proactive ways to approach planning, budgeting, and resource allocation these days than ever before. Some of the most results-oriented strategic budgeting approaches were presented in this chapter. Be creative in identifying other approaches of your own.

RECAP OF KEY POINTS

1. To develop an effective annual plan, you need to ensure that everyone focuses on organization-wide core strategies instead of separate department or turf issues.

2. Make sure that your actions for each core strategy support the top-priority strategic action items identified by senior management.

3. In the large group review, your collective leadership should compare all annual plans against your vision/mission/values/strategies/key success factors.

4. In strategic budgeting, allocation of funds is determined by priorities that are crucial to the achievement of your organizational vision rather than by department or division power struggles.

5. It is important to study many different proactive approaches to cutting/reallocating your organization's funds in a more focused way.

6. To cut costs in order to eliminate waste, you need to first define it. Waste is anything other than the minimum amount of equipment, people, materials, parts, space, overhead, and work time essential for added value in your products or services.

7. When seeking structural changes to do business at a lower cost, don't look only in the "now." Project into the future and consider possibilities from all angles.

8. Organizations in the public sector are finding more ways to be more proactive and raise money themselves rather than waiting for funding.

9. To ensure employee motivation and commitment to your plan, it is essential that you have both a performance management system and a reward and recognition system in place.

10. In moving from planning to implementation, create a sense of ownership among employees through a "rallying cry" contest.

ACTION CHECKLIST

1. Prioritize strategic action items under each strategy; use your core strategies as the organizing principles of your annual plans.

2. Develop departmental annual plans, including all senior department heads.

3. Have your collective leadership (your top 30 to 50 people) actively participate in a large group annual plan review and problem-solving meeting.

4. Your top executives (i.e., CEO, president, COO, superintendent, executive director, etc.) should present their Personal Leadership Plans for which tasks they will personally take on to help guide implementation of the plan.

5. At the close of your large group review, be sure that each participant prepares and presents one or two quick, easy actions he or she will take under each strategy over the next two weeks.

6. Review and adopt some of the six ways to establish your approach to budgeting and resource allocation.

7. Design a performance management system that enables individuals to set goals based on the strategic plan, as well as to take accountability and responsibility for their part in the overall plan.

8. Create a reward and recognition system that reinforces employee commitment and rewards contribution while encouraging individual success with specific, tangible rewards and/or recognition.

9. Bridge the gap from planning to implementation by holding an organization-wide "rallying cry" contest.

PART III

MASTERING STRATEGIC CHANGE: "WHERE THE RUBBER MEETS THE ROAD"

Chapter 12
  *Successfully Implementing and Sustaining Your Strategic Plan
  (Steps #8–10) (Phase D: Throughput)*

CHAPTER 12

SUCCESSFULLY IMPLEMENTING AND SUSTAINING YOUR STRATEGIC PLAN (STEPS #8–10) (PHASE D: THROUGHPUT)

Overvaluing "strategy" [by which many companies mean
big ideas and big decisions] and undervaluing execution
lead not only to implementation shortfalls...
but also to misinterpreting the reasons for success or failure.

Rosabeth Moss Kanter

STEP #8. FROM PLANNING TO IMPLEMENTATION: *CONTENT, PROCESS, STRUCTURE*

The implementation of your strategic plan is "where the rubber meets the road." You have put enormous energy, time, and care into defining the *content* of your strategic plan and its Ideal Future Vision. Now it is time to put these thoughts and visions into action through the *process* and *structure* of change in ways that will carry you successfully into the future.

The *process* of change is the series of actions you set in motion to implement your plan (i.e., how change will occur for both individuals and teams and throughout the organization as well). The *structure* is the design and mechanisms you use to manage that change. Most importantly, you must be careful to create change mechanisms that will effect the change you want but will not compromise those day-to-day activities that are crucial to the success of your organization.

Plan-to-Implement Day

Changing behaviors always requires deep feelings.

To help organizations answer questions that are raised at this point requires a one-day off-site meeting called Plan-to-Implement. It is similar to the Plan-to-Plan concept (Step #1) and consists of similar two parts: Executive Briefing and Educating on Change in the morning and Organizing Tasks for Change in the afternoon.

The key to Plan-to-Implement Day is that it must always *follow* the completion of your planning. Keeping it separate from any and all planning activities is the only way to maintain the integrity of your plan while ensuring the focus necessary for its successful implementation. This is the end of Goal #1: developing the strategic planning document. It is also the time to bridge the gap from Goal #1 to Goal #2: ensuring and sustaining successful implementation.

The fact is that most of us do not think much at all about managing change; when we do, it is in fairly simplistic terms. Even with all the current talk about the importance of managing change, there still exists today quite a preponderance of myths surrounding strategic change and implementation, such as:

"Change is easy; we just need to follow our instincts."

"The *organization* needs to change...not me personally!"

"Senior management just needs to get the *others* to change."

"If only *senior* management would change!"

"Once we get past these tight times, we'll be fine."

"Without the resources, we can't implement the strategic plan."

"Once we know what to do and change, it will get done by the normal organization...just doing our day-to-day jobs."

In the past, these myths may have provided some level of success in dealing with isolated change. However, in today's world of rapid change, we need to approach change both pragmatically and strategically in order to grow and survive.

Morning Session: Executive Briefing and Educating on Change

The purpose of the first, or morning, segment of Plan-to-Implement Day is to debrief, demystify, and educate executives on the change issues facing your organization as a result of your new strategic plan. This segment concentrates on three primary categories:

1. The skill levels necessary for mastering strategic change (i.e., "the iceberg theory of change")

2. The "roller coaster of change" as a key framework for managing change

3. Understanding organizations as systems in order to change them

Mastering Strategic Change (The Iceberg)

Mastering strategic change includes defining your *process* of change and creating a *structure* for change. We refer to this as the "iceberg theory of change" because the structure and process are "below the surface" of your awareness and yet will sink you surely as an iceberg.

To start, it is a good idea to take an inventory of what change skills you may (or may not) already possess. At one time or another, most of us make the mistake of thinking that we already have high-level, change-related survival skills. After all, we have all lived through change and survived it. Chances are, however, that we have not really used successful change skills at all; rather, we have used learned, reflex compensating techniques in isolated changes or crises.

Simply put, there is a world of difference between *surviving* change and *mastering* change. *Surviving* change is reactive. It places you in the role of a victim of change. You do not develop the skills that can assist you in implementing future change. *Mastering* strategic change, on the other hand, is about developing viable change mechanisms that you control over the long term.

Most people have probably reached the "mastery" level in some area of their professional lives, areas such as operations, accounting, legal, finance, engineering, human resources, etc. Change is no different from any of these areas, in that is a profession with scientific data on what does (and does not) work—and it can be mastered.

The first cardinal rule of change that managers should know is that *organizations* do not change; *people* change. Instead of approaching change in terms of changing the way our organization does business, you must first change and model your own appropriate behavior. Only then can you hope to assist in the behavior changes of the people who make up your organization. Although people resist change, the real stumbling block for leaders is that they do not realize that their behavior patterns are at odds with their goals in the first place. It is vital for a leader to get regular, honest feedback in order to change his or her behavior.

The second cardinal rule of change is that existing organizational structures cannot be the same as the ones you will use for change. Contrast the characteristics of change activities versus the day-to-day activities of running your organization. You will quickly see that people and their current structures have too much of an investment in the status quo to be able to readily change their ways, despite their good intentions. This brings to mind the old adage, "The road to hell is paved with good intentions." Asking the current organization to change itself is simply unrealistic because it is designed to perpetuate the status quo.

The third cardinal rule of change is that change, by its very nature, almost always loses out to day-to-day operational demands. Therefore, it is imperative that you create change mechanisms that are separate and distinct from your day-to-day activities. Managers, tasks, and processes are involved in day-to-day activities. Managers, tasks, and processes also need to be set up to manage the change.

> *If any of your new paradigms, ideas, or changes*
> *were rationally, politically, or culturally easy,*
> *you would have done them already...*
> *so don't underestimate the difficulty you're going to have*
> *in successfully implementing your strategic plan.*

In initiating your change effort, it is also important to expect that the desired changes resulting from your new strategic plan will be fragile. You should assume that they will need to be nurtured, protected, encouraged, and rewarded. Doing so in an ongoing, consistent manner can result in permanent and healthy strategic change.

No matter how beautifully you have constructed your organization's change effort, however, if your top management does not set aside the time to manage and lead the process personally, it will not go far. The only way to make change efforts work over the long term is to continually focus on the organizational vision and mission, which is an inherent part of top management's role. If your senior management delegates its accountability in this, it sends a loud and clear message throughout the organization: your change effort is not an organizational priority. This is a simple concept, yet executives often miss the point. Because your behavior sends a message, it is clearly important.

Managing the Roller Coaster of Change

Major change takes three to five years...
even with concentrated, continuous, and effective actions.

In managing large-scale organizational change, looking at how people naturally react to change is crucial. Every field that addresses change has its own theory on how people experience change. The interesting thing is that a similar pattern emerges throughout all the theories. As mentioned in previous chapters, this series of behaviors is referred to as the "roller coaster of change." It consists of four primary phases:

1. Shock and denial
2. Depression
3. Hope and readjustment
4. Rebuilding

Although these four phases illustrate a rather simplistic version of change, there is nothing simple about analyzing and redirecting people's behavior patterns. It is a complex topic that must address many serious questions, such as:

1. *When* (not *if*) will we start to go through shock and depression?
2. How deep will that trough be?
3. How long will it last?
4. Will we get up on the right side and rebuild?
5. At what level will we rebuild?
6. How many different roller coasters will we experience in this change?
7. Will we persevere at the bottom? How?
8. How will we deal with normal resistance?

> **9.** How will we create a critical mass to support and achieve the change?

This is why we use the phrase "roller coaster of change." If you look at a roller coaster from afar, you can see how complex it is, with all its turns and loops. So, too, is change complex. Thus, it is natural and normal that both management and employees will experience anger, depression, and frustration (i.e., Step #2) during a change effort. All of us tend to view change, at least initially, as a loss of some kind. Once we have experienced these emotions and reached bottom, however, we can actually *see* the changes take hold. That is when a feeling of hope returns.

Because major change takes three to five years, being persistent in guiding and riding this roller coaster through the span of your planning horizon is critical. Senior management needs to plan ahead for this roller coaster, investing as much time and energy as it takes for everyone to get through it. Management should continually articulate the Ideal Future Vision, so employees understand why they are going through change. In addition, you will need to set up a change structure system to build employee confidence in your ability to manage the change.

> *A basic truth of management—if not of life—*
> *is that nearly everything looks like a failure in the middle...*
> *persistent, consistent execution is unglamorous,*
> *time-consuming, and sometimes boring.*
>
> Rosabeth Moss Kanter

In some ways, management is called on to play the role of guidance counselor, to listen to, understand, involve, and coach people in order to move them forward. Motivation, hope, and involvement can grow and take hold if managers help employees (see "What's In It For Me?"—WIIFM). Concurrently, employees need to be apprised of the role they must play as well. They should be discouraged from overreacting and encouraged to ask questions, get involved, and be committed.

If all of this sounds like a lot of hard work—it is. However, only one thing is even more difficult—trying to evade or ignore this roller coaster. The left side of the curve of the roller coaster is a given, but the right side is optional; it depends on the ability of management to lead and manage it effectively.

This is why change, especially major change, does not come cheaply. One of the costs is the emotional roller coaster that people experience when reacting to change. If you persist, however, the payoff will be a high-performance, customer-focused organization that will continue to grow into the new millennium.

Organizations as Systems

> *Every organization is perfectly designed to get the results it is getting. Thus, if results are less than desired, the design should be changed. That includes adjusting structure, work processes, linkages, and information flows to meet new needs.*
>
> Keeping Current
> Quetico Centre, 1994

In the morning session of Plan-to-Implement Day, the last part of the executive briefing segment examines all of the pieces of the organization: its structure, budget, people, processes, technology, teams, boundaries, vision, customers, suppliers, leaders, jobs, services, quality, and more. It then proceeds to evaluate how to find a framework or model that can make sense out all of these pieces, put them together, and assist you in better understanding how to change all the parts for a better fit as an integrated system that can support your desired outcome (i.e., your vision/achievement).

The Seven-Track Organizational Systems Model (Figure 12.1) includes the

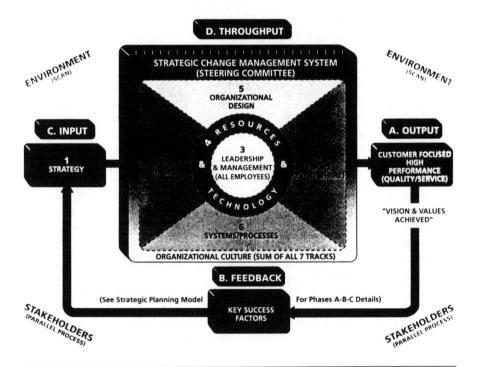

FIGURE 12.1 The Seven-Track Organizational Systems Model: A Customer-Focused Systems Solution to Creating High Performance

same A,B,C,D phases as the Reinvented Strategic Planning Model, as both are based on systems thinking. The most fundamental characteristic of the model is that it is a way to look at and assess each organization as a system (i.e., if you change one piece of the system/organization, you will need to adjust all the other pieces to a greater or lesser extent, in order to make the organization run effectively as a whole).

In other words, changing the organizational parts for a good fit leads to synergy (i.e., 2 + 2 = 5). Conversely, when the organizational parts are in conflict or simply not working (or fitting) together, suboptimization is the inevitable organization-wide result (i.e., 2 + 2 = 3). Recall the analogy about trying to make the world's greatest car, using different makes and models for each piece. The result was a car that did not fit together and, therefore, could not run.

In developing a strategic change and organizational systems model for the best way to manage radical, long-term change, thirteen different popular organizational models were compared. None of them treated the organization as a system. Only two of the thirteen models included values or technology issues, only four even mentioned the customer, and only one incorporated a strategic change management system for guiding the necessary change that has become the norm of the 1990s.

Thus, the Seven-Track Organizational Systems Model (Figure 12.1) was developed to describe any organization, whether large or small, as a system. It focuses on a systems thinking approach, as opposed to the analytic and (still the most common) traditional static or hierarchical organizational model that is incomplete. This hierarchical/analytical model largely ignores the organization's customer, technology, environment, and dynamic nature in today's world. Instead, it focuses on the more superficial, hierarchical structure with its separate workings of the internal pieces. The systems approach, on the other hand, provides an expanded, structural design of organizations as systems that more accurately reflects reality. To wit:

> *Peter Senge of MIT writes about asking business leaders who they think is the leader of a ship crossing the ocean. The answer he receives is usually the captain, the navigator, or the helmsman, but he answers that it's the designer of the ship, because everyone on the ship is influenced by the effect of its design.*
>
> *Inc.* (November 1993)

The high-performance organization that is flexible enough to grow through change into the 21st century will need each part of its overall system to be healthy. Once a working systems model exists within your organization, you will not only be able to more easily pinpoint specific problem areas, but it will also become easier to evaluate the fit of how all the parts of your system work together, leading to greater effectiveness.

Along with this model, the best practices of high-performance organizations were researched. The result is the Seven-Track Summary illustrated in Figure 12.2. Its ten parts seem to fit, complement, and even overlap with one another.

	Type Organization / Seven Tracks	A. Reactive Organization	B. Industrial Age Responsible Organization (Traditional)	C. Systems Age 1990s High Performance Organization (Proactive)
A. Output	10. Achievement of Results	Survival Level & Conflict Only	Profitability OK or Within Budget	Employee/Customer/ Supplier—QECD
B. Feedback	9. Feedback Loop	Rarely Used (Closed System)	Financial/Operational Measures Only	KSFs/Customer Value
C. Strategic Planning	1. Strategic Planning	Survival/Confusion (Near Term) Day-to-Day	3-Year Forecasts/ Business Units Operational Planning	Shared Vision/ Integrated Org'n
	2. Operational Tasks (Quality/ Service)	Firefighting/Fix It (Low Quality)	Maintain Only/ Obsolete Tasks	Organization-wide Reputation for High Quality/Service
	3A. Leadership and Management / 3B. Employees	A. Enforcing Blaming (Incompetence) / B. Avoid Blame/Wait	A. Directing/ Controlling / B. Obedient Doers	A. Mgmt/Leadership (Facilitate/ Supportive) / B. Empowered
	4A. Resources and / 4B. Technology	A. Squeaky Wheel / B. Out of Date	A. Incrementalism / B. Piecemeal Tech	A. Resources Clearly Focused / B. Tech. Fit/Org'n
	5. Organizational Design	Fragmented	Hierarchy & Bureaucracy	Networks/ Partnerships/Alliance (Flat Organization)
	6A. Human Resources / 6B. Business Processes	A. Poor People Management / B. Personal Control	A. Low Risk / B. Bureaucratic/Dept. Controls	A. Empower Emplys to Serve Cust. / B. Customer-Focused Efficient
	7. Team Development	Adversarial/ Individual Focus	Functional Teams Only	Cross-Functional Self-Managed
D. Process	8. Strategic Change Management	Avoid Pain Only (No Follow-Through)	Isolated Change Projects	Systemic Change System (plus Cont. Improvement)

(Paradigm Shift →)

FIGURE 12.2 A High-Performance Organization: Seven-Track Summary of Best Practices Research (a diagnostic tool for understanding and managing accelerated change)

Following the Seven-Track Organizational Systems Model has tremendous advantages. Not only is it practical as a fundamental template or model, but it also provides a superb diagnostic tool for analyzing your organization and all its subunits, as well as checking the fit, alignment, and integrity to your overall vision. It is also extremely useful as a common, interactive structure for communicating and working together in order to change parts of your organization so as to be better able to achieve your vision.

Workshops on Mastering Strategic Change and Leadership

It is important to note here that while the morning session of Plan-to-Implement Day provides a good overview for understanding the afternoon segment on organizing tasks, this half-day executive briefing will not provide enough detail or skills to help you achieve your own mastery, or systems, level of change.

At this point, all management levels should attend a two- to four-day in-depth, experiential, and emotionally stimulating training simulation on mastering strategic change. In this type of program, management truly begins to develop a deeper awareness and understanding of many of the previously discussed concepts and how to make implementation happen.

Knowledge about change is not what is critical; *skills* and *attitude* make the real difference. In addition, a workshop on visionary leadership skills is also essential. The practical skills of a trainer/coach/facilitator are the leadership skills of the 1990s, as mentioned earlier.

This is critical to every organization's change effort; after all, before your managers can effectively change behavior, including their own, they must first understand existing behaviors and develop new skills. It is also critical because of the span of time involved: major change usually takes three to five years to achieve lasting results.

Afternoon Session: Organizing Change Tasks

In the second, or afternoon, segment of Plan-to-Implement Day, all of the tasks that are necessary to organize your change effort should be decided, including the following.

1. Strategic Plan Rollout:
Communicate, Communicate, Communicate

Once your strategic planning document is finalized, you will need a communication rollout. Josh Weston, chairman and CEO of ADP, Inc., explains it best:

Most people think they've communicated when they've sent out a memo that describes something, or in today's age you might send out an audiocassette or a videocassette that says what you want to say. That's not communication; that's a one-way street. Nothing is communicated unless it's been read or heard, also understood, then believed, and furthermore, remembered. I have found in our business, among other things, you must be multi-media...We take advantage of audiocassettes, of videocassettes, the written word, and lots of informal meetings in order to say and say yet again that which has been said, in order to reinforce important communication.

In order to ensure that your strategic plan is indeed being understood, you need to ask, "What are we going to do as a communication rollout, both organization-wide and with key stakeholders, to create a critical mass of understanding, and how will we do it?"

2. Strategic Change Leadership Steering Committee

A Strategic Change Leadership Steering Committee, led by top management, must be set up to guide and control the overall implementation of any large-scale, organization-wide strategic planning and change effort. Failure to do so guarantees failure in implementation.

Example: At BC Systems Corporation, in British Columbia, Canada, the ongoing Strategic Change Steering Committee includes 35 top executives. Needless to say, with such a large number of top management participants, there is an unusually strong sense of ownership and involvement in implementation of the strategic plan.

Without a steering committee, there is no check-and-balance system to ensure that the change effort does not lose out to the demands of your organization's day-to-day business activities.

3. Internal Support Cadre

Although top management needs to actively lead and conduct regular follow-up status checks with the steering committee, your organization will also usually require a support staff to manage the change effort between meetings. Individuals who make up this cadre would normally include:

- An internal overall change management coordinator and facilitator (who should have access to his or her own support person as well)

- An internal communications coordinator
- A key success factor coordinator
- Strategy Sponsorship Team leaders
- An external consultant who specializes in corporate strategy, change, and this process

These are general guidelines for structuring your internal support cadre; the size and requirements of your particular organization will determine the number of individuals you need. Keep in mind, however, that these will probably become permanent tasks in your organization (because change is so constant). Therefore, it is wise to view them as such and build these positions into your regular structure.

4. Allocating Resources for Change

Resources will be needed to effectively manage any transition. Identify those resources necessary for each change action. Then, specify who will be responsible for supplying them.

5. Comprehensive Yearly Map of the Change Process

The yearly map displayed in Figure 12.3 is the focal point around which the success or failure of the process of implementing your strategic plan revolves. Its purpose is to create a specific, "by the numbers" implementation process and plan that is visible, easy to track, and easy to follow. Creating this map and tailoring it to your organization is the primary task of the afternoon session.

By putting down on paper those specific actions that will take place in the twelve months immediately following your planning, organizational members go beyond compliance and begin to build active commitment to your vision. Management of this map should then be turned over to your overall change coordinator.

Examples: One of the primary reasons Giant Industries is currently enjoying high profits and growth is due to its persistence and patience with internal mapping.

By following its own strategic management implementation process, the San Diego County Regional Occupational Program (ROP), composed of 26 school districts, has become the model ROP district in the state of California.

Instructions: Fill in all blocks completely for the next year.

Yearly Tasks	Quarterly Meetings			
	#1	#2	#3	#4
1. Date of SCSC Meeting				
2. Indepth Review & Problem Solving of Core Strategies (Do only some each quarter)	yes	yes	yes	yes
3. KSF Matrix Report of Actual vs. Target Status—Problem Solve Gaps	yes	yes	yes	yes
4. Follow Up Written Communications	yes	yes	yes	yes
5. Any Changes to Strategic Plan (Dynamic Environment)	yes	yes	yes	yes
6. Next Year's Core Strategies or Themes			yes	
7. Annual Plans and Budgets	Annual Mgmt. Mtg. (large group review)		Typical here is *Kick-Off* of process	Follow-up/ Approval Plan
8. Key Stakeholder Face-to-Face Meetings? Especially Qtrly Middle Mgmt. Mtgs.	yes	yes	yes	Yes
9. Business Plan (Cascade): A. Development, and B. Reviews			Large group review meeting	
10. Annual Plan Review Meetings (large group)				
11. Reward/Celebrate Successes	yes	yes	yes	yes
12. Organization Diagnosis/Alignment of 7 Tracks (Culture Audit)		Do yearly—Current State Assessment		

FIGURE 12.3 Strategic Change Steering Committee Yearly Comprehensive Map (Part 1)

Yearly Tasks	Quarterly Meetings			
	#1	#2	#3	#4
13. Conduct Yearly Follow-Up "Strategic Management System Review"		Leads into next year's priorities/plans		
14. Modify Rewards System to Reinforce the Strategic Plan	yes	yes	yes	yes
15. Alternative Funding/Resources Acquistion				
16. Conduct Needs Analysis/Skills Inventory & Development Plan to Support Vision				
17. Contingency Planning Needed?				
18. Develop/Review Personal Leadership Plans (PLPs)				
19. Environmental Scanning System Review				
20. Strategic Change Projects Set Up				
21. Focus Implementing on the Four Vital Few Leverage Points for Strategic Change				
A. Total Quality and Service				
B. Organization Redesign and Restructure				
C. Business Process Reengineering				
D1. Professional Management and Leadership Practices				
D2. Revise Strategic HR Programs				

FIGURE 12.3 Strategic Change Steering Committee Yearly Comprehensive Map (Part 2)

6. Personal Leadership Plans for CEOs and Senior Executives

Another organizing task is for senior management to develop individual Personal Leadership Plans (PLPs) that define the personal tasks they will do as their value-added contribution to the change effort. Because most senior executives do not present annual plans, the question becomes: What do they "bring to the table" as it concerns your core values, the change effort, and core strategies?

PLPs are vital to building senior leadership's commitment to your change effort. Unless top management is willing, as leaders, to personally change, your organization will not change. Employees look at management and think, "Why should I change...*they're* not going to change!" Leaders must "walk the talk" as well as model openness in their own behaviors through presenting their PLPs.

In this task, which is accomplished and presented at the first Strategic Change Steering Committee meeting, each manager develops his or her own PLP, stating clearly what he or she will do to further the change effort.

If you truly want to strategically change your organization so that it achieves your vision, then your top managers must be willing to personally model, mentor, and coach others as a regular part of their job descriptions.

7. Create a Critical Mass for Change

In order for true, lasting change to occur, you must build a critical mass for change. This means building an organization-wide mass of commitment to achieving the implementation of your strategic plan. To gain this ongoing commitment to your plan, you will need to rely heavily on the second "seemingly simple element": people support what they help create.

It can take one to two years to fully build your critical mass. The strategies for creating a critical mass for change can be summarized as follows:

- Modify strategic plan drafts; using the parallel process, listen and review.

- Develop and share annual plans each year for all departments/divisions.

- Implement simple changes and actions quickly, right after annual plans.

- Develop three-year business plans, involving both key stakeholders and staff.

- Create trust in your leadership by being open, via the Strategic Change Leadership Steering Committee and on a daily basis. Involve skeptics—and listen to them.

- Use Strategy Sponsorship Teams as change agents for tracking and reporting.

- Continue to hold parallel process meetings with key stakeholders throughout.

- Issue updates after each Strategic Change Steering Committee meeting.

- Answer "What's In It For Me" (WIIFM) for employees on a regular basis.

- Review and revise the reward systems and the performance appraisal form.

The "Lily Pond" Example

A good analogy is to imagine a lily pond. The premise is that it takes 30 days to fully populate the pond with lily pads and that each lily pad creates a second one (i.e., the number doubles) each day. How many days does it take to fill half the pond with lily pads? How many days does it take to fill 25% of the pond?

Answer: 29 days for half of the pond, 28 days for 25% of the pond.

Although building a critical mass takes time, it is worth the effort. Every step, no matter how small, takes you closer to your future vision, further cements employee commitment, and virtually guarantees the successful implementation of your plan.

Summary

Each task—from your strategic plan rollout, through developing personal leadership plans, to creating a critical mass for change—is covered in the afternoon segment on organizing tasks as part of Plan-to-Implement Day. It may not be necessary to give each task equal emphasis. However, each organizing task must be present and accounted for in your Plan-to-Implement Day. After all, these are the "10,000 little things" that make the difference between ongoing implementation and sustaining your plan and the SPOTS syndrome.

STEP #9. STRATEGY IMPLEMENTATION AND CHANGE (CONTINUALLY CHECK THE FIT, ALIGNMENT, AND INTEGRITY OF THE SYSTEM TO YOUR VISION)

*Changing people's habits and ways of thinking
is like writing your instructions in the snow during a snowstorm.
Every 20 minutes you must rewrite your instructions.
Only with constant repetition will you create change.*

Donald Dewar

Many times, managers read long-range plans, nod in agreement—and then wait for something to happen. A good example of this is when organizations begin a quality improvement process, which is a complete strategy for changing the culture.

If nothing visible happens right away, management tends to panic. Management expects the process itself to somehow magically do all the work—that having educated their employees, formed teams, and told them to start holding meetings will automatically start some sort of mystic plasma flowing. Managers often do not realize that they have to lead—and in some cases drag—people along. Failure to do so shows a lack of integrity on management's part, and it is a serious failing.

It is a good idea at this time to check the overall alignment and integrity of your system. This deals with each part of the organization and its relationships to the others. Each part of your organization's system must be aligned with every other part in support of the vision. This is the real task of strategic change by senior management.

To accomplish true system fit, alignment, and integrity, you must develop *commitment to*, as opposed to compliance with, your new vision. You will need constant, repetitive follow-up tactics and techniques for ensuring success, dealing with resistance, maximizing commitment, and minimizing disruptions. Because the level of change you are dealing with tends to generate disruptive fallout in the organization, it is important to create situations as needed in which there can be quick visible successes—with all the attendant ceremony and hoopla.

Example: The Navy Public Works Center in San Diego has an excellent weekly executive board meeting and review, created specifically to engineer successful implementation.

As you begin the implementation of your strategic plan, be sure to pay ongoing attention to the cultural changes that will need to take place. That attention cannot be limited to top or bottom levels only. It is also important to be aware of the various levels of possible difficulties in any organization.

In particular, pay attention to middle management, so named because managers at this level are "caught in the middle" and are frequently the ones who block change. Often, they have worked hard to get where they are, only to have the newly empowered culture undermine the authority it took them so long to acquire. Employees are your greatest asset—*but only if you allow them to be!* It is important to focus here on middle and first-line supervisors instead of just the worker level.

Strategic Change Leadership Steering Committee in Operation

*The transition from the current state to the future state
has traditionally been underestimated,
understaffed, and inadequately addressed.*

Bill Veltrop
Exxon Corporation

The essential step in ensuring that implementation of your strategic plan is underway is to establish a Strategic Change Leadership Steering Committee (SCLSC) with regular meetings. The mission of this committee is to regularly check, adjust, and report on the progress of overall implementation. It needs to meet at least quarterly, and in each meeting it should address the three purposes previously mentioned.

The SCLSC is the organization's primary instrument in advancing implementation. As such, it should use its meetings as more than a casual check or status report. The SCLSC should act as a motivator, communicator, coordinator, problem solver, and, when necessary, mediator.

A typical day-long SCLSC meeting should not only ask in-depth questions about key success factors, core strategies, and annual plans. It should also problem-solve performance issues, evaluate and make suggestions on priority and environmental changes, coordinate major performance improvement projects, and communicate progress on all of the above to key stakeholders throughout your organization.

Finally, and most importantly, an all-management meeting should be held following each SCLSC meeting, as well as an all-employee meeting whenever possible. This will serve to cascade the direction, results, and discussions of the SCLSC in face-to-face settings throughout the organization.

STEP #10. ANNUAL STRATEGIC REVIEW (AND UPDATE)

*Thinking is easy. Acting is difficult.
To put one's thoughts into action is the most difficult thing in the world.*

Goethe

To persist in sustaining your implementation up and running year to year as a strategic management system—even after the newness has worn off—you will need to conduct a yearly follow-up to diagnose the overall success of your implementation. Also, be sure to recycle your strategic plan and its annual priorities.

Each year, every organization has a yearly independent financial audit, but a yearly independent strategic audit is usually nowhere to be found in the literature or in practice. Instead, similar to SCLSC meetings, this annual strategic review and update should include a review, assessment, and feedback report, with recommendations from an external, unbiased perspective on the status of your organization's strategy implementation. Unlike the SCLSC meetings, however, this one will address two overall purposes:

1. Management attention to the strategic management system and implementation process itself

2. Management attention to actual results and achievements accomplished under the strategic plan

Once your assessment is completed, a yearly strategic update of your plan needs to be done. You don't need to spend time on a brand-new strategic plan each year, but you *do* need a refresher or annual update of the plan. This is much quicker than the actual planning process, but it is a must. The yearly update should consist of a two-day off-site meeting that achieves the two goals above.

The next steps in your yearly update should include:

1. Require all your key department managers to again develop their annual plans within the context of your core strategies as the organizing principles.

2. After this, hold a one- to two-day large group annual plan review meeting to ensure that all department plans are correct and in alignment with each other.

Finally, it's time to:

1. Develop strategic budgets

2. Reenergize the SCLSC, Strategy Sponsorship Teams, etc.

How often should organizations completely redo their strategic plans? Realistically, in today's changing world, a plan can last two to four years before it needs to be done again. On the other hand, you should expect to do a new plan, or revise your existing one, if your organization experiences major change in its direction (new or changed goals), its environment (marketplace), or its leadership (if the CEO leaves, for instance).

Tip: The annual strategic review and update is key to learning to be and sustaining a high-performance organization. Without strict adherence to this part of the process, you won't need to worry about how long your change effort is taking—you simply won't have one.

Questions to Ponder

- Does your organization have a SCLSC, led by the top, to guide and control the implementation of your strategic plan?

- Do you have an internal support staff to manage your change effort between meetings?

- Have you created a yearly map, showing a specific, "by the numbers" implementation plan, and have you allocated the proper resources for it?

- Are Strategic Sponsorship Teams in place to champion your core strategies?

- Do you continually track progress on your key success factors?

- Has your organization's senior management developed individual Personal Leadership Plans?

- Are you building individual and team commitment to your plan with an effective performance and reward system?

- Is your organization firmly committed to an annual strategic review and update (similar to its yearly independent financial audit)?

SUMMARY

The ongoing key tasks for effective change management that you will need to cover in the last three steps of your strategic management framework have been presented in this chapter. Each task—from workshops on mastering strategic change and visionary leadership skills; to managing the "roller coaster of change" and understanding your organization as a system; to completing all your change tasks; checking the fit, alignment, and integrity of your system to your vision; and conducting an annual strategic review and update—plays a key role in the implementation of your plan.

Setting these last three strategic management steps (Steps #8 to #10) into motion as ongoing, organization-wide change management processes enables you to come full circle each year. They will provide your organization with the necessary content, process, and structure to successfully implement your strategic plan while making solid progress toward achieving your vision, year after year. After all, that is how we were able to put a man on the moon: step by step, task by task, and year by year—just like any good strategic plan.

> *What we think, or what we know, or what we believe*
> *is, in the end, of little consequence.*
> *The only consequence is what we **do**.*

RECAP OF KEY POINTS

1.   At the completion of your strategic planning, have a Plan-to-Implement Day with two segments: Executive Briefing and Educating and Organizing Change Tasks.

2.   The first cardinal rule of change is that organizations do not change; people do.

3.   The second cardinal rule of change is that you must design and develop structures for managing change that are separate from existing, day-to-day organizational structures.

4.   If top management does not set aside the time to manage and lead your change effort, it will not go far. Employees watch what you do—and what you don't do—for clues about your real priorities.

5.   You must prepare for and be ready to manage the four phases in the "roller coaster of change" on a constant basis, because people change at different rates and speeds: (1) shock and denial, (2) depression, (3) hope, and (4) rebuilding.

6.   In order for your change effort to succeed, understand that your organization is a living, breathing system. Use the Seven-Track Organizational Systems Model to ensure the fit, alignment, and integrity of your system.

7.   When initiating the implementation of your strategic plan, be sure to incorporate all of the change management tasks.

8.   A critical senior management task is to check your change management system for its fit, alignment, and integrity to your vision on a constant basis.

9.   Conduct yearly recycling of your strategic plan.

ACTION CHECKLIST

1. Develop an initial rollout and communication plan.

2. Establish an organization-wide annual plan that reflects the strategic planning priorities for the first year.

3. Align the budget to reflect the strategic planning priorities.

4. Build all department/division/unit annual plans around the organization-wide annual priorities or goals.

5. Set up an ongoing Strategic Change Leadership Steering Committee to manage the change process.

6. Establish a yearly map, or master work plan, for twelve-month implementation and follow-up. It should include three-year business plans for any strategic business units/major support departments without them.

7. Establish a key success factor monitoring, tracking, and reporting system.

8. Revise your performance and reward system to support your new vision, core strategies, and values.

9. Put an environmental scanning system in place, both yearly and in quarterly Strategic Change Steering Committee meetings.

10. Make sure top management has an ongoing, active leadership role in your change process.

11. Build an internal support cadre with the expertise and skills to coordinate implementation of the strategic plan and manage change.

12. Ensure that key Strategy Sponsorship Teams are set up to build a critical mass for change.

PART IV

GETTING STARTED: DIFFERENT OPTIONS AND CUSTOMIZED APPLICATIONS

CHAPTER 13

STRATEGIC MANAGEMENT APPLICATIONS

Nothing splendid has ever been achieved
except by those who dared to believe
that something inside them was superior to circumstances.

INTRODUCTION

Although it is easy to feel powerless and battle-weary amid the rapid-fire change of today's environment, change is a constant that we must learn to deal with and overcome. Avoiding change—and the tough choices that come with it—only enables the future health and performance of your department or organization to be determined by circumstances beyond your control.

By using a systems thinking approach, however, and "thinking backwards" to the ideal future you envision, it is possible to implement innovations that are custom-fit to your organization—innovations that raise you above those circumstances you cannot control and give you an overall approach that you can control.

THE A,B,C'S OF STRATEGIC MANAGEMENT REVISITED

In recapping the underlying concept of the Reinvented Strategic Planning Model, we have seen that the systems thinking approach to strategic management boils all planning issues down to four main questions within the four A,B,C,D phases of the systems model:

Phase A.   *Future outcomes*: Where do we want to be? (Ideal Future Vision)

Phase B.   *Feedback*: How will we know when we get there? (measures of success)

Phase C.   *Today's input*: Where are we now? What strategies should guide us?

Phase D.   *Throughput actions*: How do we get there? (successful implementation)

The beauty of approaching your planning and implementation in this way is that no matter where you are in your planning or actions, you can maintain a focused, systems perspective, make adjustments in response to change, or, if necessary, even change direction by simply stepping back, reviewing these questions, and then having the courage to act on the answers, *always* focusing on the outcome.

Although it is not necessary to religiously adhere to the ten steps for strategic management via the systems approach outlined in this book, it is critical to incorporate each of the four phases in order to successfully implement your strategic management system. The four A,B,C,D phases are the framework for each and every step in the Reinvented Strategic Planning Model. They are also unique to this systems model; no other planning process in existence today includes all four phases.

As this systems model comes from the scientific discipline of the General Systems Theory, its characteristics were set up to be a generic application to all open systems. It is these characteristics that make this approach timeless and universal. The four-phase systems approach to strategic planning can be applied to any situation. Whether you are planning for an organization, a department, a project, or even yourself or your own family, this systems thinking approach works for any and every kind of system.

SIX USES OF THE FOUR PHASES OF SYSTEMS THINKING

This chapter illustrates how to use this generic, four-phase systems thinking approach in the following six specific applications.

Use #1. Comprehensive Strategic Planning

Comprehensive strategic planning, of course, is what this book is all about: developing in-depth strategic plans and implementing change efforts that will enable any organization to successfully install a new strategic management system to achieve its Ideal Future Vision. The complete ten-step model is most applicable to larger organizations that need to galvanize, in one direction, an entire organization made up of hundreds (if not thousands) of people.

Even with the full ten steps, however, rather than following the same rigid application, the key is to tailor it each time you conduct strategic planning. The application should fit the unique requirements of your organization at a particular time. In general, this comprehensive strategic planning will require approximately eight to twelve days over a period of four to six months (but less if tailored differently).

While four to six months may seem like a long time, consider that you are really setting up the annual/yearly cycle for managing the organization as a system, in a strategic fashion. If you can keep this more outcome-oriented perspective in mind, it will probably make more sense to you over the long haul.

The suggested time line generally consists of two two-day off-site planning sessions each month for the number of months required, based on your tailoring. Plan on about a month between each meeting in order to hold a series of parallel process meetings in which you will conduct a review of the strategic plan developed so far with your key stakeholders.

Example: Many examples of successful comprehensive strategic planning processes can be found throughout this book, including Giant Industries, British Columbia Systems Corporation, Sask Energy, Poway Unified School District, and the Alberta Department of Agriculture.

Use #2. Strategic Planning Quick: Five Days

The reality in the fast-paced modern world is that we sometimes just don't have the time available for as in-depth planning as comprehensive strategic planning suggests. Time and speed in particular are key competitive advantages today. Also, there may be any number of other reasons why you may not be in a position to enter into comprehensive strategic planning at this time, including:

- Crisis (have to act quickly)
- Need to rapidly refocus on a new direction
- Limited time available, limited resources

- Smaller organization

- Awaiting new CEO/major board changes, but want to get started

Typical businesses that have used Strategic Planning Quick successfully range from small to mid-sized organizations. The Reinvented Strategic Planning Model can be tailored to conduct still-viable strategic planning from start to finish in only five days of off-site meetings over a period of two to three months. As illustrated in Figure 13.1, the steps and step numbers designated in the comprehensive strategic planning are the same in the Strategic Planning Quick model but are condensed.

Although Strategic Planning Quick can be done off-site in five days, you should plan on conducting an informal Plan-to-Plan session beforehand, as prework. In all, there will be two two-day off-site sessions, with time between them for two parallel processes, finishing up with a one-day off-site meeting. If you are considering this framework, keep in mind that it, too, should be tailored to fit your specific needs. For instance, instead of five days, four, six, or seven days may be better for you.

Example: Throughout this book, many examples of such entrepreneurial organizations as Allenbach Industries, Community Care Network, and British

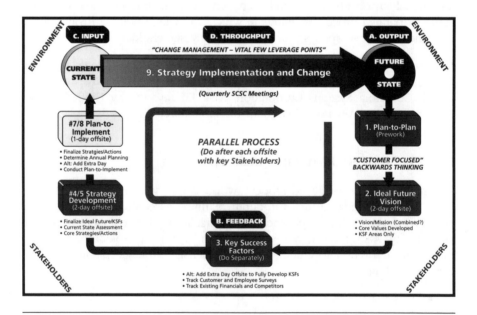

FIGURE 13.1 Strategic Planning Quick—Five Days: A Customer-Focused Systems Solution to Creating High Performance

Columbia's Mineral Titles branch, all of which have used Strategic Planning Quick with good results, are provided

Use #3. Micro Strategic Planning: Three Days

Micro Strategic Planning often represents an organization's first foray into authentic strategic planning. It is also sometimes used by very small (50 or fewer employees) organizations or by small departments within an organization. It is modeled on Strategic Planning Quick, but instead of two two-day off-site meetings, it is condensed to only two one-day off-site meetings (Phases A,B,C). Following these two days of meetings, you immediately need to establish and begin quarterly Strategic Change Steering Committee meetings (Phase D).

Because the tightness of Micro Strategic Planning lends itself to a certain rigidity, and because most work must be done off-line, you must ensure that the entity for which you are planning has a strong feedback loop. Also, because you won't have time to concentrate on key success factors, you should instead focus on and monitor core strategies, and existing financials, along with surveys of both customers and employees. As you complete this key success factor off-line, you can gain approval later.

Caution: Micro Strategic Planning requires quicker decisions, with time for only one parallel process. Be sure to do all preliminary work off-line as prework and save the meeting time for any key consensus discussions that are needed to address crucial issues.

Example: It *is* possible to get results using Micro Strategic Planning. It has been used successfully in such firms as Central Credit Union, Wheeler Frost Associates (a small financial services firm), and the Health Care Alliance, a strong community foundation.

Use #4. Three-Year Business Planning

Strategic planning in large corporations is typically done on the basis of five or more years. Below the corporate level, however, are many different line departments or business units. In addition, there are major support functions such as public relations, human relations, finance, legal, etc. Each of these line and support units needs its own strategic plan, usually called a three-year business plan. To review business unit planning, see Chapter 10 for full details.

Example: Some excellent examples of three-year business planning for departments or units within organizations that conduct the larger, comprehensive strategic planning process (Use #1) include Giant Industries, Sask Energy, Poway Unified School District, and British Columbia Systems Corporation.

Use #5. Strategic Change Projects

Most change efforts falter because they pursue only a "partial" systems solution. In fact, when strategic planning is allowed to lead the way, major tasks and change efforts (such as TQM, business process reengineering, empowerment, self-directed work teams, etc.) are often among the most immediate, visible beneficiaries. This is because the four phases of a true systems thinking model can be applied to any change project or program as a whole system within itself.

In other words, it is possible to initiate a successful major change project even if it exists within an imperfect, partial systems environment. Focusing on the entity you want to change and then applying the A,B,C,D phases can accelerate your desired changes and ultimately tie them into other major changes that should potentially be core strategies as well. The outcome is actually solid strategic quality planning, strategic business reengineering planning, etc.

Example: Many of the Navy's Total Quality Leadership change projects are currently floundering because they are treated as separate issues, unconnected to the system as a whole. Instead, they should be tailored to and integrated with the Total Quality Leadership program as an overall strategic plan for the command. The same is true for a number of firms that are focusing exclusively on business process reengineering, which is an analytic approach to a systems problem. (Most change projects are systems problems, which is why they often fail to succeed as advertised.)

Note: Project management experts may say (and justifiably so), "What's new here? We've been using systems/outcome thinking for decades." They are right. Project managers seem to be the only people in Western society who use systems thinking as the norm.

Use #6. Strategic Life Planning

Adapting the systems thinking approach to planning your personal life is remarkably simple and just as effective. Strategic Life Planning returns to the basic four questions that accompany each phase:

  A. Where do I want to be (i.e., my ends, outcomes, purposes, goals, holistic vision)?

B. How will I know when I get there?

C. Where am I now? What are the issues and problems in my life today?

D. How do I get there (i.e., close the gap from Phase C to Phase A in a complete, holistic way)?

The four-phase systems concept is exactly the same, except that the focus of your outcomes and desired future will vary. Also, it is easier than other strategic planning, because fewer people are generally involved. However, you still need to identify and involve key stakeholders (i.e., family/others) to ensure that someone plays devil's advocate with your plans.

To start Strategic Life Planning, find a relaxed time and space in which you can focus solely on the personal visioning exercise in Figure 13.2 Once you have begun your personal visioning, to free up your mind to focus on the future, you can proceed with the phases of the Reinvented Strategic Planning Model.

Doing strategic planning as a couple raises fundamental points as to how each can see their desired future. Therefore, couples should be aware of the risk that strategic planning poses. If both parties have different visions of the future in mind, substantial problems can arise unless both are willing to be flexible.

Example: I can speak personally to the rewards of doing Strategic Life Planning. Three years ago, my wife, Jayne, and I created our five-year life plan, and we have been seen concrete results and a very positive influence on our life together. Writing this book was one of our goals, and we are ahead of schedule. Another goal was to work and travel extensively throughout the world, and we are well on our way to achieving that goal.

Finally, it has been very gratifying to see members of the Centre for Strategic Management (and lots of others) successfully develop and implement their own personal life plans, reaping fuller, more holistically balanced lives than they had previously experienced.

PUBLIC VS. PRIVATE SECTOR PLANNING DISTINCTIONS

Although the private sector still has a long way to go in its approach to strategic planning and change management, it has at least begun the battle. The public sector, where it has taken any steps at all, has viewed strategic planning as a project instead of a way of life. However, many organizations are now beginning to recognize that it is a serious undertaking that fundamentally changes how a business is run on a day-to-day basis.

More and more frequently, government leaders are pursuing such con-

My Future Vision For Myself at Year _____ is:

Note: Brainstorm this and then share it with the planning team.

1.	Roles	Vision
I.	**Personal**	
	1. Physical/Health	
	2. Mental/Learning	
	3. Emotional/Spiritual (ethical)	
II.	**4. Lifestyle/Wealth**	
III.	**5. Job/Career**	
IV.	**Interpersonal**	
	6. Social/Friends	
	7. Community/Service	
	8. Home/Spouse (immediate family)	
	9. Extended Family (parents/siblings/cousins)	

2. How will I know if I've achieved my vision (i.e., what measures will I use?)

	Roles	Measures of Success at Year _____?
I.	**Personal**	
	1. Physical/Health	
	2. Mental/Learning	
	3. Emotional/Spiritual	
II.	**4. Lifestyle/Wealth**	
III.	**5. Job/Career**	
IV.	**Interpersonal**	
	6. Social/Friends	
	7. Community/Service	
	8. Home/Spouse	
	9. Extended Family	

3. My vision is (one sentence/paragraph):

4. My "Rallying Cry" should be (8 words or less):

FIGURE 13.2 Personal Visioning

cepts as privatization and competition as their new core strategies. (See Chapter 9 for the thirteen principles of reinvented government.) The reasons behind this movement are many, but at their foundation is a desire for improved effectiveness in the face of dwindling and limited funds.

Example: Many organizations in the public, government, and military sectors are working diligently toward a systems thinking approach to strategic management, including the city of Indianapolis, the Ministry of the Environment of British Columbia, Milwaukee, Mineral Titles, San Diego's Navy Public Works Center, Poway Unified School District, San Diego County Regional Occupational Programs, and the Alberta, Canada Department of Agriculture, to name but a few.

The following is a list of the most visible strategic issues that the public sector must resolve.

Issue #1: Mandate vs. Mission

Every government organization has a legislative mandate, but this is not the same as having a mission. A mandate is sometimes so broad that it becomes necessary to zero in on just exactly what the organization's primary focus should be; after all, no organization, whether private or public, can be everything to everyone. That is surely a blueprint for failure.

Example: British Columbia Systems Corporation had a legal mandate stating that it can serve any public sector organization in the world. What has served it better, however, has been a mission that focuses primarily on serving the public sector in British Columbia, a far more manageable aim.

Issue #2: Lack of a Profit Motive

Because there is no profit motive in the public sector, organizations frequently interpret this to mean they do not need to be business oriented. They read "business" as synonymous with "profit," when in fact they are two different concepts.

Running an organization as a business means using proven business concepts and tools with which to run any organization successfully. There is some science to running *all* organizations, and it only makes sense to use what is known to work, even in the public sector. Although an organization in the public sector definitely is not profit oriented, a business-thinking mindset can substantially increase responsibility, accountability, and, even more importantly, achievement of the mission.

Example: A good example of how a "business" mindset can change government budgeting accountability is the county of Santa Clara in northern California. In streamlining its administrative work via a customer-focused approach and establishing an aggressive computer network, Santa Clara is in such good financial shape that it was able to build a long-term fund with a $30 million budget surplus in 1994.

Issue #3: Politicians as "Board of Directors"

Public organizations do not have a board of directors; instead, politicians act as stewards for the public/voters. Therefore, in order to successfully develop and implement a strategic plan, the electoral cycle must be taken into consideration. Otherwise, a five-year comprehensive strategic plan may be completed only to be discarded for a "new and improved" version brought in by the new regime. A strategic plan should be timed to coincide with electoral cycles, but should look beyond politics to a vision that is shared by all.

Issue #4: Lack of Customer Focus

With the lack of competition per se in the public sector, government organizations are often vague as to the identity of their customers. As a result, they often end up either trying to serve everyone, which is an impossible task, or just themselves. This lack of clarity, and lack of systems thinking, as to who the customer is leads to an unclear sense of purpose, or mission, as well.

Not knowing who the customer is or what the mission is leads to concentrating on bureaucratic activities rather than working with a clear sense of mission. Public sector employees need to view themselves as true public servants instead of following a bureaucratic, hierarchical structure and system.

They also fail to distinguish between the services they provide and the staff support they need, again confusing ends with means.

Issue #5: Missing Outcome Measurements of Success

> *When you're inside Washington you see signs of that goalless condition everywhere. For instance, there's a big management-by-objective program in the Commerce Department. Every quarter it produces a document that's an inch and a half thick. I looked at one and discovered there wasn't a single defined objective or any reported progress toward an objective in the whole document. In-*

stead there was an amazing amount of information about activity.
The closest thing to an objective was that some group had held 12
meetings on some subject that quarter, compared with 10 meetings
the previous quarter—representing, as the report stated, a 20%
increase in activity. In Washington, that's what passes as progress
toward a goal.

John Rollwagen
former CEO, Cray Research
(also second-in-command to
Commerce Secretary Ron Brown in the spring of 1993)

As inferred in this quote, focusing primarily on activities makes it very difficult for government organizations to develop concrete, visible outcomes and factors that can be used to measure progress and success.

This is where the key success factors come into play for public sector organizations as a new paradigm for creating outcome performance measurements. Otherwise, these organizations continue to confuse means and ends, which results in poor direction and focus.

Issue #6: Parallel Process = Public Consultation

In the public sector, there are many more stakeholders (other agencies, politicians, public "customers," special interest groups, etc.) than exist in the private sector. This creates an even greater need for a parallel process. The public sector needs to be more open in consulting with its clients, not just to share information but to obtain and use their feedback as well.

Example: The provinces in western Canada use what they call "open government." They are very proactive with their public "customers," funneling all information through an open consultation/feedback forum.

Issue #7: Low-Risk Leadership Styles

Strong leadership in change efforts, as well as accountability, has been missing in the public sector for far too long; look at almost any government around the globe today, and you will see signs of severe distress and unrest in the public that should be the beneficiaries of these services. In all fairness, it is more difficult to take a strong stand as a public figure because it involves the risk of offending any number of constituency members.

More often, individuals at an administrative level in the public sector tend toward bureaucratic work flow. Rather than serving the public beneficiaries, they only serve "upward" to the politicians. You cannot ignore the upward pressure, but neither can you surrender the leadership of your organization in serving your clients and customers.

Examples of fine public servants: Dr. Robert Reeves, longtime superintendent of Poway Unified School District, is a public servant who is one of the finest executives, public or private. As a result of his continuous innovative and creative leadership over the years, this school district is one of the most recognized and respected in California.

Premiere Ralph Klein of Alberta, Canada; Governor Barbara Roberts of Oregon; Vice President Al Gore; Mayor Lino Callegari of Sunnyvale, California; Don Fast, executive director of Environmental Protection in British Columbia; and Commissioner Sandra J. Hale of the Minnesota Department of Administration also deserve recognition for their attempts to fundamentally change and reinvent government. All are unafraid to make change, take chances in a savvy way, and manage their governmental organizations with a business-like approach.

Hats off to these leaders and all those like them who understand the value of leadership, accountability, integrity, and business thinking.

Issue #8: Perceived Resource Constraints

This is an area in which the public sector is very different from the private sector. Private sector organizations must first gather their resources and then use them to get more (i.e., it takes money to make money, as the adage goes). Public sector organizations, however, often mentally start with a set number of resources as a given, and from there just spend them.

The very real problem with this approach is that it does not foster any real knowledge about how to get resources in the first place. Therefore, when government organizations have gone through their allotted supply, rather than move ahead and find more, they tend to stop all progress on the basis of resource constraints.

Government organizations need, and in some cases are beginning to get, administrators who have such skills as raising revenues through fund-raising and user fees and working out bureaucratic practices through business reengineering, privatizing government services, etc. They need to use resource allocation to set priorities based on their strategic plan and focus on the future instead of yesterday.

Example: Private companies now regularly provide many of the municipal services in such large U.S. cities as Dallas, Houston, Kansas City, New York, Los Angeles, Phoenix, and Philadelphia. (See the monthly magazine *Governing* for continual examples of innovation in government.)

Issue #9: Lack of Staff Support for Strategic Management

The staff support services that are routinely available for strategic management in the private sector are usually absent in the public sector. Rarely will you find (1) someone who serves in a planning department, (2) effective human resource support, or (3) someone who has organizational development/facilitator skills. Add to this the fact that you almost never find (4) someone skilled in measuring outcomes, and it is easy to see why strategic management hits so many glitches in the public sector. There usually is no infrastructure in place to provide the organization with the internal support cadre necessary.

Example: Ministries and departments in Alberta, Canada are currently struggling with their strategic management process. Although they have been successful in doing the right kind of strategic/business planning and budgeting, they do not have a strong internal support function to assist strategic change. As a result, this is currently endangering the success of the entire process of change and the major reinventing government initiative throughout Alberta.

The reverse is true in the city of San Diego, California, however, where an entire organization effectiveness department to support city planning and change has been in existence for the past decade.

Issue #10: Ineffective Change Management

> *As the co-author of* Reinventing Government, *I am often asked what I have found to be the greatest obstacle to innovation in government. I always respond with one phrase:* **the power of outdated ideas** *. It's easy to dream up new approaches to problems. People do it all the time. The hard part is selling them to those who still see the world through old lenses. Why? Because the transformation from bureaucratic to entrepreneurial government is not just a change—it is a shift in world view. It is a paradigm shift.*
>
> David Osborne

Paradigm shifts are without a doubt the greatest challenge to all strategic management and change, whether in the public or the private sector. Although the private sector has more of a pattern of acceptance and growth through strategic change management, the public sector still has a far distance to travel. Just because President Clinton and Vice President Gore are cutting 250,000 people from the federal government payroll does not mean that there will be a more effective, responsible government. Remember, *both* cutting and building strategies are necessary for future success.

SUMMARY

Six different and specific ways in which you can apply the four-phase systems thinking approach to your strategic planning and change management needs were presented in this chapter.

The most important thing to remember about the Reinvented Strategic Planning Model is that its primary elements—the A,B,C,D systems phases—are the constant in the formula. No matter what configuration your planning effort may require, as long as you maintain and integrate these phases as its foundation, you will be able to tailor a strategic planning and change process that is uniquely yours.

RECAP OF KEY POINTS

1. In the systems thinking approach, all strategic management is conducted within the four phases of the systems model.

2. In systems thinking, the focus is always on the outcomes, especially the key outcome of serving your customers and clients.

3. There are six specific ways in which you can apply the four-phase systems thinking approach to strategic management:

   1. Comprehensive strategic planning

   2. Strategic Planning Quick

   3. Business unit planning

   4. Micro strategic planning

   5. Strategic change projects

   6. Strategic life planning

4. Public sector organizations are finding that they are experiencing many of the same problems that face the private sector and are beginning to use a business orientation and a systems approach to their planning.

5. In applying a business thinking approach, public sector firms face specific, contradictory issues in the following areas:

   • Mandate vs. mission

   • Lack of a profit motive

   • Politicians as board of directors

   • Lack of a customer focus

- Missing measurements of outcome success
- Parallel process = public consultation
- Low-risk leadership styles
- Perceived resource constraints
- Lack of staff support for strategic management
- Ineffective change management

ACTION CHECKLIST: TEN ABSOLUTES FOR REINVENTING STRATEGIC MANAGEMENT (PLANNING AND CHANGE)

1. Have a clear vision/values of your ideal future, with customer-focused outcome measures.

2. Develop focused core strategies as the glue for all goal setting and action planning.

3. Develop and gain public commitments in Personal Leadership Plans prepared by all top management leaders.

4. Redo your human resource management systems to support the new vision and values.

5. Set up an internal cadre support team with overall change management coordination that reports directly to the CEO/executive director.

6. Set up Strategy Sponsorship Teams of cross-functional leaders for each core strategy.

7. Establish a Strategic Change Steering Committee to guide, lead, and manage all major changes.

8. Focus on and phase in the four Vital Few Leverage Points for Change over the next two to five years.

9. Institutionalize the parallel process with all key stakeholders as the new way to run your business day to day.

10. Create a critical mass for change that becomes self-sustaining throughout the development of three-year business plans for all major divisions/departments.

CHAPTER 14

GETTING STARTED IN SUSTAINING HIGH PERFORMANCE

Just because we cannot see clearly the end of the road,
that is no reason for not setting out on the essential journey.
On the contrary, great change dominates the world,
and unless we move with change we will become its victims.

John F. Kennedy

STARTING AT PHASE A,B,C,D

The real key to a true systems model is not its A,B,C,D phases or even its ten progressive steps. It is the circular nature of a system—and systems thinking—that is the key to its use in a very personal, practical, and flexible way.

The four-phase systems thinking approach (and Reinvented Strategic Planning Model) enables you to easily tailor your application to your own needs and current situation. With the systems approach, you can begin strategic planning and sustaining change at any of the four phases. In other words, if your organization has already developed its vision/mission/values statements (Phase A), you can begin your planning process by shaping organizational key success factors (Phase B) and proceed from there. If you have a complete Current State Assessment and have already developed your strategies, you can start your full planning process at the three-year business plan stage or during annual planning and budgeting (end of Phase C).

This systems thinking approach is not one of those processes where you have to scrap everything you have done and are doing and start from scratch. The major benefit of this systems thinking approach and model is its flexibility. Whether you are a step ahead with certain portions of the planning process, have never done any of the planning elements, or are in the midst of TQM or other large-scale change efforts, the Reinvented Strategic Planning Model, with its systems thinking approach, will adapt itself to your unique situation and help you sustain a high-performance organization.

In general, there are four different options for how to begin this curricular process.

Option #1. Plan-to-Plan

If you have never conducted a full-scale strategic planning and change process, this is the best starting point for you. The Plan-to-Plan step exists as a way to engineer success up front, before getting into the actual development of your strategic planning documents. (For detailed descriptions, refer back to Chapter 5.)

Option #2. Plan-to-Implement

If you have already completed your comprehensive strategic plan but need to bridge the gap between planning and implementation, this is the perfect starting point. It is where Goal #2, ensuring and sustaining successful implementation of your strategic plan, comes in. (For further detail on this step, refer to Chapter 12.)

Option #3. Some "Join-Up" Points

As mentioned earlier, when looking for the best place to begin building your strategic management system, it is always best to start wherever you are today. Thus, with a circular systems model, you literally just "join up" to the model right where you are and proceed from there. The options open to you include:

- Conducting an annual strategic review and update as your starting point and then proceeding based on the recommendations/decisions that result from this audit

- Conducting just the phase you need right now, such as visioning, measurements (key success factors), or core strategy development, and then creating a Strategic Change Steering Committee to guide implementation

- Conducting a pilot strategic planning process for a strategic business unit or major support department

- Conducting annual planning via your core strategies/goals. Set the top three action priorities for each core strategy as the glue and organizing principles for all annual plans

- Conducting large group reviews on annual department plans

- Beginning with a strategic budgeting process

- Finishing your budgets, and then setting up strategic change project teams on large, cross-functional issues

- Setting up a Strategic Change Steering Committee to guide and coordinate large-scale change (i.e., TQM, business process reengineering, etc.) that is already in existence

- Setting up Strategy Sponsorship Teams for each core strategy to guide and report on successful implementation

Option #4. Some Educational Ways to Begin

In order to initiate an optimal strategic management system, some initial staff training may be needed. Again, there is no set rule for the amount or type of training you will need to provide before beginning. It is up to you to tailor the training so that it fits the particular needs of your organization. There are a number of possibilities, including:

- Having internal staff trained and licensed to facilitate the systems thinking approach to the Reinvented Strategic Planning process

- Having internal staff trained in mastering strategic change

- Conducting a workshop on visionary leadership practices to kick off your strategic planning or change project

- Conducting a workshop simulation on mastering strategic change to re-energize or kick off a major change project, such as TQM, business process reengineering, etc.

- Training senior and mid-level management in these systems thinking concepts through a two- or three-day workshop in which the Reinvented Strategic Planning Model is introduced

- Holding an annual management conference, with a keynote presentation on strategic planning and/or change

CRUCIAL SUPPORT NEEDED TO SUSTAIN SUCCESS

Obviously, implementing and sustaining your strategic plan will not amount to a hill of beans if you do not plan realistically for just how much support—in terms of people, time, and money—is required. A checklist of all the elements you will need as the support necessary for success follows.

Active Commitment of Senior Management

More than half of the strategic plans that fail do so because commitment from the top is either sporadic or half-hearted. If you want your strategic planning and change process to be successful, you will need a firm consensus and active commitment from your top management. Senior executives must play an interactive, visible role, not only in initiating the strategic plan but also in persistently following it through—all the way.

Trained Internal Support Cadre

After you have initiated your strategic planning and change process is not the time to decide what kind of or how much staff support you will need. Whether or not you will need clerical or administrative support, coordinators, and liaison personnel for key success factors, strategy implementation, Strategy Sponsorship Teams, and Strategic Change Steering Committees must be determined, and assigned, beforehand.

External Facilitator

It is easy to quickly get into trouble here because the scope of knowledge needed throughout this process is great enough to require the use of an outside facilitator.

If you choose to use only internal (or no) facilitators, the training time required is often substantial enough to negatively impact the original time frame of your strategic plan. For this reason, many organizations choose to use an external strategic planning and change management expert. Although you will ultimately revert to internal facilitators, a professional consultant/facilitator can go a long way toward saving money and time.

Budgeting and Resource Allocation

In order to effectively manage any transition, you need resources, both people and money. Look at every activity required by your strategic planning and change process and resource it properly.

- Strategic Change Steering Committee meetings
- Mastering strategic change workshop
- Key success factor tracking
- Communication and rollout
- Skills training (leadership/change management)
- Training overall manager/coordinator/internal facilitator
- External facilitator/consultant
- Business unit planning
- Key stakeholder meetings
- Yearly follow-up strategic management system review
- Strategic change projects (four Vital Few Leverage Points for Change)

Identify and allocate all the resources you will need for these elements (including who is responsible for supplying them), and budget for each one.

Project Planning/Yearly Map

The best way to keep track of what activities you will need in your change process is to create a yearly map each year—a specific, "by the numbers" implementation process that is visible, easy to track, and easy to follow. Developing this tangible list of those things you will need to do in the next twelve months provides you with a quick and simple checklist.

Creating a Critical Mass for Change

Holding to the theory that people support what they help create, creating this critical mass is probably the single most effective way to guarantee the success of your change process. It does, however, require a substantial, ongoing investment of time and energy, so be prepared to commit to it and anticipate it.

Leadership Capacity Building

Another, more subtle, spin on creating a critical mass for change is capacity building. This is about building a leadership within your organization that has the capacity to lead, guide, and sustain the strategic planning and change process to the benefit of the organization. Having the range and depth of leadership that can see this type of long-term process through is crucial to your success and growth. Remember, it is the only true competitive advantage you have over the long term.

PUTTING IT ALL TOGETHER: A SYSTEMS APPROACH TO SUSTAINING HIGH PERFORMANCE

> *Strategic planning and strategic change management is really "strategic thinking." It's about clarity and simplicity, meaning and purpose, and focus and direction.*

Throughout this book, analytic thinking and true systems thinking have been compared. Until relatively recently, analytic thinking (breaking the problem or issue down into its individual parts and then problem solving each part separately) held sway as the traditional approach to strategic planning.

The problem with this approach is that starting only with today's issues and problems, breaking them down into their smallest components, and then solving each component separately has no far-reaching vision or goal. Low interaction exists between departments; therefore, no critical mass for change exists, and change quickly deteriorates as a priority.

In the systems thinking approach, the only element you focus on is the system that makes up your organization. From the General Systems Theory, we know that a system is understood not by analysis, but rather by synthesis, looking at it as a whole within its environment.

With this approach, you shape your organizational system into a customer-focused, market-driven organization, using the Seven-Track Systems Model to check every change for system fit, alignment, and integrity. To truly manage strategically, you not only need a strategic plan, but you must also install a strategic change management system to guide and sustain its implementation.

The key to succeeding is the ability to bridge the gap from Goal #1 to Goal #2. Typically, it is at this point where most plans fail. Within the Reinvented Strategic Planning Model, however, this is achieved through the very crucial Plan-to-Implement step (Step #8) and the mastering strategic change workshop simulation. This is particularly unique to the Reinvented Strategic Planning Model; no other planning model includes such detailed systemic change implementation steps to sustain a high-performance organization.

Another key to sustaining long-term success is the annual strategic review and update. Rather than limiting your organization to just a yearly independent financial audit, you also need to conduct a yearly follow-up to diagnose the overall success of your strategic plan's implementation and change process. (Also, be sure to recycle your strategic plan and its annual priorities at this time.)

In addition, a further key to sustaining long-term success is increasing the range and depth of your leadership practices, including the skills of trainer/coach/facilitator (see the visionary leadership practices workshop, among others). Remember, this the only competitive business advantage for any organization over the long term.

Lastly, systems thinking is based on the theory that a system is, in essence, circular. Using a systems approach in your strategic management, therefore, provides a circular implementation structure that can evolve, with continuously improving, self-checking, and learning capabilities. (Recall the feedback loop—the essence of the learning organization.)

FOCUS, FOCUS, FOCUS

As in any ongoing activity, the key to successfully implementing your strategic plan will lie in whether you choose to focus on the "trivial many" or the "vital few." To successfully implement and sustain your organization's version of the Reinvented Strategic Planning Model, you will especially need to focus on each step along the A,B,C,D way, including:

- What is your mission? Who do you serve?

- What are your core values? (Limit them to those most important to you.)

- Do you have ten (or fewer) *prioritized* key success factors?

- Have you developed a small number of core strategies, with three annual priority actions attached to each? (Keep the number of core strategies small, with "from–to" clarity on anticipated changes.)

- Have your annual plans been formulated under the umbrella of your core strategies/action priorities as the glue and organizing principles?

- Do you have your budget in place, based on your strategic action items (i.e., the top three priorities for each core strategy)?

- What about your three-year business plans to focus each business unit/major support department (again, under the same umbrella)?

- Are your performance appraisals focused on evaluating everyone against your core strategies (results) and core values (behaviors)?

- Have you shaped priority agendas for both (1) the regular Strategic Change Steering Committee and (2) the weekly executive staff meetings using the key success factors as well as the core strategies (with their top three action priorities) as primary agenda items?

SUSTAINING HIGH PERFORMANCE

As illustrated in Figure 14.1, with a sense of integrity and a commitment to focus, discipline, and persistence, you can design, build, and sustain a strategic management system to serve as the foundation that leads to the achievement of your customer-driven, high-performance organization. It may take three to five years or more, but it can be done—even in today's dynamic and revolutionary, globally changing environment.

Once you have checked, prodded, and poked your strategic management system, you have done everything you can. Now it is a matter of follow-through, persistence, and firm commitment to your organization's integrity in pursuing your Ideal Future Vision. While we do live in the real world, and acknowledge that we will not achieve perfection, you will come much closer to it by following this strategic management system. Remember, however, that no matter how proficient you become in the processes of strategic planning and implementation, sustaining high performance will not occur without both discipline and persistence.

> *Nothing in the world can take the place of persistence. Talent will not; nothing is more common than unsuccessful men with talent. Genius will not; unrewarded genius is almost a proverb. Education will not; the world is full of educated derelicts. Persistence and determination alone are omnipotent.*
>
> Calvin Coolidge

IT'S TIME FOR QUICK ACTIONS AND PROGRESS!

In lieu of the usual Recap of Key Points and Action Checklist, a recap of 44 fail-safe mechanisms is provided here. As you begin to create your Ideal

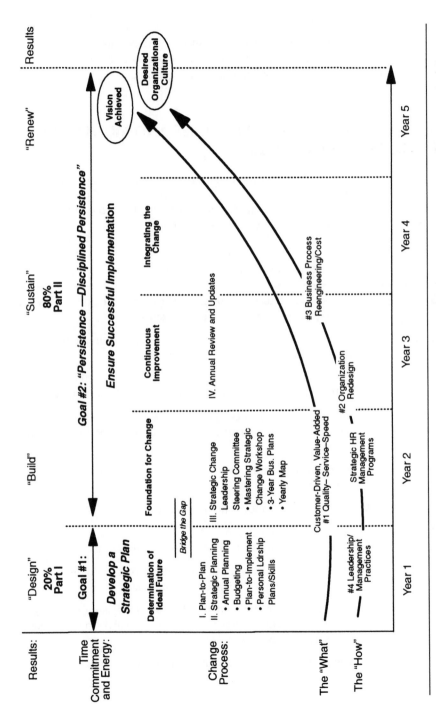

FIGURE 14.1 A High-Performance Organization through Installing a Strategic Management System: A Practical Systems Approach to Continuous Improvement

Future Vision, use this list to check your current status and progress. Better still, go over the list now to see what you should begin doing immediately.

Good luck in all your efforts toward a fully integrated strategic management system that leads you to sustaining high performance.

CHANGE MANAGEMENT STRUCTURES AND MECHANISMS: 44 CHECKS AND BALANCES

Instructions: Review the following list to make sure that you have implemented all those items that you need to do. Note: * denotes the "must do's" that are most essential to success (crucial fail-safe mechanisms. Actually, the more of these you set up, the higher your probability of successful implementation.

	Do We Have These?
	(Yes, No, or Needs improvement)

_____	*1. Plan-to-Plan/Executive Briefing (first) and Engineer Success (two goals of a strategic management system)
_____	*2. Parallel process throughout the planning and implementation process (key stakeholder involvement)
	• Buy in; stay in
	• Build critical mass for change, especially middle management
_____	*3. Two-part Strategic Management System and Systems Thinking— a *new way to run your business*; the basics; an ongoing process
_____	*4. Vision–mission–core values statements in usable formats; customer focused
_____	5. Cultural/values audit and the creation of a *culture change action plan*—strategic change project
_____	*6. Core values placed on your performance appraisal form
_____	*7. Board of directors involvement/ownership of the strategic plan; regular status/communications to the board
_____	8. A crisp and clear single driving force and associated *rallying cry* that is the essence of your vision; it is the CEO's personal task to institutionalize this ("monomaniac")
_____	*9. Key success factor coordinator/cadre and reporting system

Do We Have These?
(Yes, No, or Needs improvement)

_____ *10. Key success factor continuous improvement matrix fully filled out with targets and measurements

_____ 11. Benchmarking vs. highly successful organizations (*best practices research*)

_____ 12. Establishment of an environmental scanning system with specific accountability and feedback mechanisms

_____ 13. SWOT—staff involvement; reality checks

_____ *14. Paradigm changes to strategies (from → to) and a focused number of strategies

_____ *15. Strategy Sponsorship Teams set up for each core strategy

_____ *16. Core strategies also used as the key result areas on performance appraisals

_____ *17. Annual planning format using strategies as *organizing framework* (the "glue")

• Lines to strategies

• Lines to MBO and individual goal setting/performance

_____ 18. Use of SBU proforma matrix to develop clear financial accountability

_____ *19. Three-year business planning for all SBUs/MPAs to ensure clear competitive strategies; three-year business planning for major support units also (by strategies)—WIIFM (especially a strategic HRM plan for people management)

_____ 20. SBU definition to lead organization design philosophy and efforts, focused on the businesses we are in, the customers we serve, and the employees we empower to do their best

_____ 21. Development of a priority maintenance system to handle interruptions/new ideas and lack of focus on strategies, business, and product development

_____ *22. Large group annual planning review meeting

_____ 23. Strategic Change Project Teams on big, cross-functional ideas

_____ *24. Personal Leadership Plans/commitments developed by the CEO and top three executives of the organization ("monomaniacs with a mission")

Do We Have These?
(Yes, No, or Needs improvement)

_____   25. *War room* with all the changes and timetables on the wall

_____   26. Contingency planning; *what if* scenarios on key probable events

_____   *27. Annual planning and priority setting first to drive the budgeting process (top three actions per each core strategy); looking at alternative ways to gain funds

_____   *28. One day off-site: Plan-to-Implement/Executive Briefing on change process

_____   *29. Workshop on mastering strategic change; simulation taught to all management personnel; in-depth understanding of change management

_____   *30. Strategic Change Leadership Steering Committee to guide:
   • Strategic planning implementation
   • All change of any nature
   The goal is *alignment and integrity of the system*

_____   *31. Yearly comprehensive map on the next 12-month process of change management

_____   *32. Internal coordinator/facilitator and cadre for the change process—to support senior management

_____   33. Create a critical mass action plan to support the vision, with ongoing communications planned throughout

_____   *34. A rollout/communications strategy plan and reinforcement materials (PR/HR led)

_____   35. *Organization as a system framework* (Seven-Track Organizational Systems Model); mini-diagnosis and a way to ensure *alignment and integrity of the system* to the strategic plan

_____   *36. Individual goal setting by all exempt employees tied to the strategic plan, then a true performance management system used and modeled by top management as a way to manage individual performance

_____   *37. A *rewards diagnosis and improvement plan* to ensure your rewards support the strategic direction (both financial and nonfinancial)

Do We Have These?
(Yes, No, or Needs improvement)

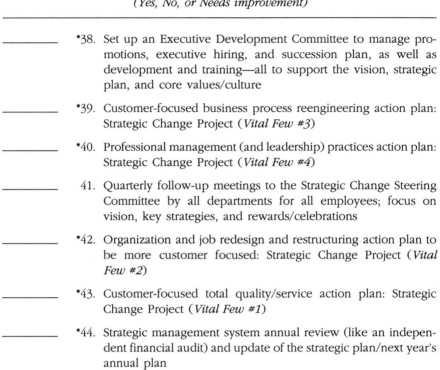

_____	*38. Set up an Executive Development Committee to manage promotions, executive hiring, and succession plan, as well as development and training—all to support the vision, strategic plan, and core values/culture
_____	*39. Customer-focused business process reengineering action plan: Strategic Change Project (*Vital Few #3*)
_____	*40. Professional management (and leadership) practices action plan: Strategic Change Project (*Vital Few #4*)
_____	41. Quarterly follow-up meetings to the Strategic Change Steering Committee by all departments for all employees; focus on vision, key strategies, and rewards/celebrations
_____	*42. Organization and job redesign and restructuring action plan to be more customer focused: Strategic Change Project (*Vital Few #2*)
_____	*43. Customer-focused total quality/service action plan: Strategic Change Project (*Vital Few #1*)
_____	*44. Strategic management system annual review (like an independent financial audit) and update of the strategic plan/next year's annual plan

BIBLIOGRAPHY

Ackoff, R. (1970). *A Concept of Corporate Planning*. NY: John Wiley & Sons.

Ackoff, R. (1981). *Creating the Corporate Future*. NY: John Wiley & Sons.

Ackoff, R. (1984). *Guide to Controlling Your Corporation's Future*. NY: John Wiley & Sons.

Ackoff, R. (1989). *Management in Small Doses*. NY: John Wiley & Sons.

Ansoff, I. (1988). *New Corporate Strategy*. NY: John Wiley & Sons.

Band (1991). *Creating Value for Customers: Designing and Implementing a Total Corporate Strategy*. NY: John Wiley & Sons.

Bean, W. C. (1993). *Strategic Planning that Makes Things Happen: Getting from Where You Are to Where You Want to Be*. Amherst, MA: HRD Press.

Bryson, J. (1988). *Strategic Planning for Public and Nonprofit Organizations A Guide to Strengthening and Sustaining Organizational Achievement*. San Francisco, CA: Jossey-Bass.

Bryson, J. (1993). *Strategic Planning for Public and Nonprofit Organizations*. Oxford: Elsevier Science.

Buzzell, R. & Gale, B. (1987). *The PIMS* Principles, Linking Strategy to Performance*. NY: The Free Press.

Clarke, C. J. (1993). *Shareholder Value: Key to Corporate Development*. Oxford: Elsevier Science.

Cope, R. G. (1989). *High Involvement Strategic Planning: When People and Their Ideas Really Matter*. Oxford, OH: Planning Forum in Association with Basil Blackwell.

Crosby, P. (1988). *The Eternally Successful Organization*. NY: McGraw-Hill.

Day, G. S. (1990). *Market Driven Strategy*. NY: The Free Press.

Doz, Y. (1986). *Strategic Management in Multinational Companies*. Oxford: Elsevier Science.

Drucker, P. (1954). *The Practice of Management*. NY: Harper & Row.

Drucker, P. (1973). *Management: Tasks, Responsibilities, Practices.* NY: Harper & Row.

Drucker, P. (1989). *The New Realities.* NY: Harper & Row.

Dunham, A. & Marcus, B. with Stevens, M. & Barwise, P. (1993). *Unique Value.* NY: MacMillan.

Freedman, N. J. (1991). *Strategic Management in Major Multinational Companies.* Oxford: Elsevier Science.

Goodstein, L. D., Nolan, T. M., & Pfeiffer, J. W. (1992). *Applied Strategic Planning: An Introduction.* San Diego, CA: Pfeiffer & Company.

Hax, A. & Majluf, N. (1984). *Strategic Management: An Integrative Perspective.* Englewood Cliffs, NJ: Prentice-Hall.

Hayden, C. (1986). *The Handbook of Strategic Expertise.* NY: The Free Press.

Hellebust, K. & Krallinger, J. (1989). *Strategic Planning Workbook.* NY: John Wiley & Sons.

Hussey, D. E. (1994). *Strategic Management: Theory and Practice* (3rd Ed.). Oxford: Elsevier Science.

Judson, A. (1990). *Making Strategy Happen: Transforming Plans into Reality.* Cambridge, MA: Basil Blackwell.

Kami, M. (1988). *Trigger Points: How to Make Decisions Three Times Faster, Innovate Smarter, and Beat Your Competition by Ten Percent (It Ain't Easy!).* NY: McGraw-Hill.

Karlof. (1994). *Benchmarking: A Signpost to Excellence in Quality and Productivity.* NY: John Wiley & Sons.

Klir, G. (1969). *An Approach to General Systems Theory.* NY: Van Nostrand.

Kono, T. (1992). *Strategic Management in Japanese Companies.* Oxford: Elsevier Science.

Mason, R. & Mitroff, I. (1981). *Challenging Strategic Planning Assumptions: Theory, Cases, and Techniques.* NY: John Wiley & Sons.

McNamee, P. (1990). *Developing Strategies for Competitive Advantage.* Oxford: Elsevier Science.

McTaggart (1994). *The Value Imperative: Managing for Superior Shareholder Returns.* NY: The Free Press.

Mesarovic, M. (Ed.) (1967). *Views on General Systems Theory.* NY: John Wiley & Sons.

Meyer (1993). *Fast Cycle Time: How to Align Purpose, Strategy, and Structure for Speed.* NY: The Free Press.

Migliore, H. (1986). *Strategic Long Range Planning.* Jenks, OK: RHM & Associates.

Mills (1992). *Rebirth of the Corporation.* NY: John Wiley & Sons.

Mintzberg, H. (1994). *The Rise and Fall of Strategic Planning.* NY: The Free Press.

Mintzberg, H. & Quinn, J. B. (1992). *The Strategy Process: Concepts and Contexts.* Englewood Cliffs, NJ: Prentice-Hall.

Mitroff, I. (1983). *Stakeholders of the Organizational Mind*. San Francisco, CA: Jossey-Bass.

Naisbitt, J. & Aburdene, P. (1990). *Megatrends 2000: Ten New Directions for the 1990's*. NY: William Morrow.

Nutt, P. C. & Backoff, R. W. (1992). *Strategic Management of Public and Third Sector Organizations*. San Francisco, CA: Jossey-Bass.

Osborne, D. & Gaebler, T. (1992). *Reinventing Government: How the Entrepreneurial Spirit Is Transforming the Public Sector*. Reading, MA: Addison-Wesley.

Pfeiffer, J. W. (Ed.) (1991). *Strategic Planning: Selected Readings* (Rev Ed.). San Diego, CA: Pfeiffer & Company.

Pfeiffer, W., Goodstein, L., & Nolan, T. (1986). *Applied Strategic Planning: A How to Do It Guide*. San Diego, CA: Pfeiffer & Company.

Porter, M. (1985). *Competitive Advantage: Creating and Sustaining Superior Performance*. NY: The Free Press.

Porter, M. (1990). *The Competitive Advantage of Nations*. NY: The Free Press.

Rappaport, A. (1986). *Creating Shareholder Value: The New Standard for Business Performance*. NY: The Free Press.

Robert, M. (1993). *Strategy Pure and Simple: How Winning CEOs Outthink Their Competition*. NY: McGraw-Hill.

Schonberger (1990). *Building a Chain of Customers: Linking Business Functions to Create the World Class Company*. NY: The Free Press.

Shanklin, W. & Ryans, J., Jr. (1985). *Thinking Strategically: Planning for Your Company's Future*. NY: Random House.

Shapiro, E. C. (1991). *How Corporate Truths Become Competitive Traps*. NY: John Wiley & Sons.

Stalk, G. Jr. & Hout, T. M. (1990). *Competing Against Time*. NY: The Free Press.

Steiner, G. (1979). *Strategic Planning: What Every Manager Must Know*. NY: The Free Press.

Tregoe, B. & Zimmerman, J. (1980). *Top Management Strategy: What It Is & How to Make It Work*. NY: Simon and Schuster.

Trotter, W. (1984). *Strategic Planning Theory and Application*. Oxford, OH: Planning Executives Institute.

Von Bertalanffy, L. (1968). *General Systems Theory*. NY: Braziller.

Waddell, W. (1986). *The Outline of Strategy*. Oxford, OH: The Planning Forum.

Watson (1993). *Strategic Benchmarking: How to Rate Your Company's Performance Against the World's Best*. NY: John Wiley & Sons.

Weil, D. (1994). *Turning the Tide: Strategic Planning for Labor Unions*. NY: Lexington Books.

INDEX